Reaching Children
Through Play Therapy

An Experiential Approach

THE PUBLISHING COOPERATIVE

DENVER, CO

Reaching Children Through Play Therapy

An Experiential Approach

by

Carol Crowell Norton, Ed.D.
and
Byron E. Norton, Ed.D.

THE PUBLISHING
COOPERATIVE
DENVER

THE PUBLISHING COOPERATIVE
1836 Blake St.
Denver, CO 80202

Excerpts from Disney's animated copyrighted feature *THE LION KING*
are used by permission from Disney Enterprises, Inc.

Publishing Cooperative books are available at special discounts
for bulk purchases, sales promotions, fund raising or educational
purchases. Contact The Publishing Cooperative,
1836 Blake Street, Denver, CO 80202.

Library of Congress Cataloging-in-Publication Data

Norton, Carol Crowell.
    Reaching children through play therapy: an experiential approach
    /by Carol Crowell Norton and Byron E. Norton
             p. cm.
    Includes bibliographical references and index.
    ISBN 0-9644849-4-3 (alk. paper)
    1. Play therapy.   I. Norton, Byron E.   II. Title.
    RJ505.P6N67   1997
    618.92'891653—dc21   97-1139
                                             CIP

First Edition: May 1997

10 9 8 7 6 5 4 3 2 1

Manufactured in the United States of America
Cover artwork by Colette B. McLaughlin

*The paper in this book meets the guidelines for permanence and
durability of the Committee on Production Guidelines for Book
Longevity of the Council on Library Resources.*

∞

Printed on Recycled Paper

Dedicated
to
Our Children,
Amy and Drew,
Who Have Always Had To Share Us
With the Others

In Loving Memory of
My Grandmother
Delma Louise Hobbs Holloway
Whose Life Was About Love and Giving

— C.C.N.

CONTENTS

Illustrations

Tables

Foreword

We are well into a new era in which children of all ages and from every socio-economic background are pushed toward television, computers, and battery operated toys instead of imaginative and creative play. This leaves many children developmentally deprived since imaginative and fantasy play allows children to explore their world and express their innermost thoughts and feelings, hopes and fears, likes and dislikes. Through play, decisions can be made without any penalty or fear of failure. Play allows children to gain control over their thoughts, feelings and actions, and helps them achieve a sense of self-confidence.

Play with imagination and fantasy as its partners is the natural medium of self-expression and one of the most revealing roads to the child's conscious and unconscious inner world. The role of imaginative and fantasy play in play therapy is somewhat more ambiguous than is commonly believed. It's striking that play therapy often is a field in which clinicians are the driving force for change, using a variety of techniques and approaches instead of giving the child permission to be self-directed within some limits. Noted play therapist Virginia Axline stated in her watershed book *Play Therapy* (1969/1947b) that, "Regardless of the type of symptomatic behavior, the individual is met by the therapist where he is ... and [the therapist] lets that individual go as far as he is able to go ... because the client is the source of the living power that directs the growth within himself." Experiential play therapy is an innovative approach in which the clinician reacts to the child instead of initiating actions of his/her own beliefs and values. This approach is also based on the belief that the child has the ability to solve his/her own problems within the context of a warm and caring therapeutic environment.

Experiential play therapy is an approach that is a contrast to other approaches. In the past, play therapy approaches have often been focused on problem behavior, and the direct application of techniques is based on this behavior. This is found across a broad variety of theoretical approaches. Experiential play therapy, in contrast, is an approach where children are given the opportunity to play out their feelings and experiences, which is the most natural and self-healing process for children to engage in. It is unfortunate that this approach has not yet filtered down to a host of practitioners and students.

Today, training programs in social work, counseling, marriage and family therapy, and psychology seldom offer play therapy courses. Instead, play therapy is often addressed in the context of other courses, such as parent/child relationships, and only a few hours are devoted to this important topic. The absense of, or limited number of play therapy courses in graduate level training programs, in conjunction with the limited play therapy-appropriate situations during clinical practica, consequently result in clinicians who feel unprepared to deal with the growing requests for play therapy. Currently there are an increasing number of appeals for clinicians to provide play therapy in both public and private sectors, such as elementary schools, where more and more school counselors are faced with this challenge. Play therapy is an effective form of child therapy for a broad variety of settings; clinicians, however, often lack training in it and therefore depend on communication skills instead of understanding the child's symbolic communication methods.

This book is unique in providing a comprehensive overview and description of experiential play therapy. It also effectively addresses the different aspects of assessment and diagnosis in the approach and provides guidelines for using it to treat specific childhood problems such as abuse, separation anxiety, traumatic stress, etc.. The book is designed to help clinicians gain therapeutic insight into the symbolic meaning of toys, which allows clinicians to "speak the child's language."

Karin B. Jordan, Ph.D
University of Colorado at Denver

Preface

In order to understand our philosophy of play therapy, it becomes necessary to first understand our view of children. Observing the young child, one will notice how the child relates to the world. He encounters something new in his world and becomes enraptured with the process of learning about it. He touches it, smells it, looks at it, moves it around to view it from all angles and manipulates it with his hands and occasionally even with his mouth. In other words, he experiences it and its potential before he assimilates it as a part of his world.

In the same manner, a child must experience events or situations in his life in order to assimilate them into his perceptual world. Parents utilize this concept when attempting to teach their values to their children. The child is requested to perform in a certain style. When he does not, the thoughtful parent describes the desired behavior while explaining the reasons why this particular behavior is appropriate. The parent then offers another opportunity to perform in the desired style. Once the desired style is obtained — often through trial and error — the parents assume the child has assimilated the value.

When the nature of the events in a child's life is emotionally disconcerting or traumatic, the child is developmentally unable to utilize cognitions, history, or his basic belief in himself to stabilize his well-being. Therefore, his perceptual world becomes distorted. In an effort to gain some comprehension of the situation and of himself and other individuals in the situation, he will recapitulate the situation in play. The scenes, of course, are a reenactment of actual events that have been screened through the child's perceptions. The scene will be replayed numerous times, each time adding to the child's experiential field. With each reenactment of the situation, the child also reexperiences the effect associated with the original situation. Before the pattern of these perceptions and the child's emotional experience can be altered, they must be experienced within a new format. Slight changes are made by the child each time the perceptions are reenacted. When the child is fortunate enough to participate in experiential play therapy, the assistance of a therapist creates changes that are health oriented and which move the child toward a new perspective of the situation.

Incorporating the above philosophy of children and play therapy into practice has, for us, resulted in the successful treatment of many children. Consequently, we believe it is important to share this philosophy with others. The fundamentals of the theory are introduced in this book along with examples of applications. This book is intended as an introduction to the theories of the experiential model of play therapy. Additionally, it lays out the process of play therapy as treatment advances.

The play of children is highly metaphorical; one of the primary objectives of this book is to aid the clinician in understanding the symbolism of the child's play. Once the metaphor is grasped by the practitioner, he is facilitated in knowing how best to respond to the child in order to promote the child's movement toward therapeutic goals. The book is practically oriented so that it can be immediately useful to the clinician.

It is our hope that, through the use of this book, knowledge will be gained by practicing clinicians that will assist them in their work with children. After all is said and done, there is no more important work in a healthy society than helping children to survive the travails of growing up.

Acknowledgments

It is with sincere appreciation that we acknowledge the contributions of two important individuals without whom this feat would have taken many more hours of work on our parts. Anyone can accomplish a task, but these two have performed in an outstanding manner and with as much devotion and commitment to its quality as we have given it ourselves. They also have shown their caring for the children for whom this work is intended to benefit.

Franci Crepeau-Hobson possesses an amazing capacity to locate any research, comment or tidbit in literature, no matter how vague we made it for her. We were fortunate to have found her and to have had her assistance. We feel confident that her career as a psychologist and play therapist will be notable.

Susan Kreitler Skinner was asked to function as a typist, and it soon became apparent to us that not only were her abilities in that realm excellent, but her editing skills were strong as well. Her questions and comments as an individual with no experience in play therapy have assisted us in viewing this information from the perspective of the novice who would be reading this book.

This has been a major undertaking for all of us, and we appreciate their commitment to its completion.

Prologue

The Sage

This story begins in a land nearby, where lies a village. The people who live in this village go about their everyday lives growing food and making clothing and shelter for their families. Also in this village lives a sage. Everyone knows where the sage lives. Many people come to visit her each day. They bring their families to visit the sage. The youngsters come to the sage and say, "Play with us." And they play. And they feel good. And they learn. The parents see their children become happy once again. And they are pleased.

And this goes on for several years. Soon, however, the sage begins to notice that fewer children are happy. There are even more unhappy children than ever before. She notices pain in the children. There is a plague in the village, and she is unable to help the children be rid of the pain caused by the plague. And she begins to feel their pain. The play is no longer enough. She begins to feel her own pain and knows that the plague is causing her, too, to wither and crumple.

One day, on a walk through the village, the sage overhears several of the town council folks speaking of a wondrous fountain. As she leans closer, the council people address her directly. She learns that the fountain has wonderful curative powers. It is told that people return from the fountain with a new life in them. However, the fountain exists at the end of a long journey. The journey is completed only by those who endure. Those who do endure, though, return with the water of new life.

The sage learns that the pathway to the fountain begins near her home. She begins her journey. She travels over land that is familiar (yet new), terrain that is smooth and jagged, and through water that is safe and treacherous. She picks up tools to help her keep walking when it would be easier to quit. Along the way, she encounters adventure, fear, pain, danger, confusion, clarity, joy, strength and renewal.

Finally she recognizes that the fountain is near. The ground around her has become more fertile. It feels like the softest of carpets under her feet, caressing her tender skin as she moves across it. The trees and grass are colored in brilliant hues, with the golden sunlight filtering in to highlight the rich shades. She hears the sounds of life; the earth is awake and vital.

While inside her lies the heaviness of the plague, she also feels herself awakening in excitement. Soon she hears the sizzling effervescence of the bubbles exploding from the ground, a small sound at first, but growing in intensity as the water plunges forth. As the streams of water grow, they glisten in the sunlight, sparkling as diamonds. The kaleidoscope of colors creates a rainbow around her.

Then, as if on cue, she begins to consume the water in every possible way. First, she cups her hands and drinks, even as trickles of the water flow through her fingers. Then, she moves into the water and feels it soaking through her protective clothing to touch her body and refresh her skin. The whole while she hears the water splash as it lands all around her. She sighs and sings as she feels new life flowing into her. She begins to glow with an intensity she has not felt within her since the plague touched her. She sees the rainbow in radiant colors around her. She becomes aware that she has been enhanced so that both the health and wisdom she already possessed are magnified.

As the flow from the fountain diminishes and then comes to an end, she realizes that she has received that which she sought. The trip home is much easier and seems shorter than the trip to the fountain, although she feels as though she has left a friend behind. As she returns to her village, she still enjoys the feeling of freshness as she remembers the sounds of the fountain and the sights of the glistening streams of water.

When the people of the village see that their sage has returned, they go to visit her once again. As the children come to her, they can see the glow and feel the serenity from the sage, and their pain is diminished as the new life flows from the sage into them. And they play. And they feel good. And they learn. And the new life in the children flows from them into their own children and to their children. The parents see that their children are happy. And they are pleased.

Now that she has made her first trip to the fountain, the sage recognizes that the fountain is much closer to her than she realized. On her first trip, she lost her way several times. Now, however, she knows the way and realizes that she can visit the fountain whenever she chooses.

CHAPTER 1

AN OVERVIEW OF THE TENETS OF EXPERIENTIAL PLAY THERAPY

Significance of Developmental Play

Children encounter their world at an experiential rather than cognitive level. Play is their medium of expressing their experiences as well as their feelings about themselves. In fact, play for a child is as water for a fish, the jungle for a monkey, or the desert for a cactus. It becomes a rehearsal for adult life for the child who has had her basic physical needs met on a consistent basis, has experienced emotional nourishment and cognitive enrichment in life, and has had opportunities for and permission to play (Lewis, 1993). Rehearsal for life play enables a child to assimilate and integrate new cognitive and social skills, values and moral judgments.

This experiential development through play lays the foundation for the cognitive styles of adults. It is interesting to note that in today's fast-paced world of technology, the tendency of adults is to view play as simply a child's way of filling her time, or as wasted, even unproductive time. Credit is not given to the experiential development that lays the foundation for future cognitive abilities. Even research is lacking in validating the significance of the contribution that play makes to the personal/emotional/intellectual functioning of the adult. It is understandably difficult to document the play of a child and correlate that to adult functioning. However, a good example of the development of a style is found in the story of a graduate student by the name of Greg.

Greg was one of six graduate students participating in a class on play therapy. After orientation, the six students were taken into the playroom and given instructions: "This is a place where you can play. Go ahead and play. These are the basic rules you need to be aware of ..."

As the students began to play, the professor walked out of the room and turned on the videotape machine which was located behind a two-way window. This was standard procedure at this particular university. Later, when the students were back in the classroom, the professor asked, "What was it like?"

They unanimously said, "Oh, it reminded me of childhood!"

At that point, the professor said to Greg, "I know how you decided to come to this university."

"You could tell that from watching me in the playroom? How?"

The professor went on to explain. "You checked out a number of universities, narrowed the choice down to five or six, visited each one of these schools, and then decided to come here."

Greg looked at the professor and said, "That's exactly what I did. How did you know from my play in the playroom that I had done that?"

At this point, the professor said, "Let's turn on the videotape and watch your play."

Of the six students who entered the playroom, five of them went over to an area in the playroom and incorporated the toys located there in their play. Greg, however, stood back and watched the other five people start their play. He then went over and joined one person for a few minutes, then another, and so on around the room. After spending some time with each of the other five students, he decided who he was going to join and then got involved in the play.

When the professor pointed this out, Greg was astounded. In effect, Greg's process was at his experiential level, and he was unaware of what he was doing on a conscious level. When shown at the cognitive level, he realized right away. As a child, this was his style of functioning on an experiential level, although he was never consciously aware of it. He utilized it consistently, however, and developed it into his cognitive style.

Effects of Missed Play Opportunities

The extensive works of Piaget (e.g., 1936/1952, 1937/1954, 1962) have shown the necessity of children's experiences for cognitive development as well as the importance of attainment of certain levels of competence and understanding in order to advance to the next developmental stage. When these experiences do not occur, the ability of the child to develop and integrate life experiences for use in adulthood is contaminated, just as if they had been denied nutritious food in order to develop physically (Delpo & Frick, 1988; Lewis, 1993).

Sadly, as a result of physical, mental, or sexual abuse or divorce or death — in fact, any kind of trauma[1] — many children lose this type of play opportunity during childhood. Rather than experience the type of play that benefits their current developmental stage, much of their time and emotional energy goes into trying to protect themselves (emotionally and/or physically) as well as in trying to resolve the trauma. In addition, the child's emotional memories remain in the developmental stage in which the traumatic event occurred and remain so without intervention. Development in and of itself then becomes associated with the traumatic event, as opposed to security, comfort, protection, etc. This will cause the child to experience difficulty at each new developmental stage thereafter.

Children cannot return to their developmental experience through confronting the stark reality of the trauma. It is this reality that caused their dignity, power, sense of control, and well-being to be stolen. Indeed, if the reality of the painful memories enters the consciousness of the child, it can flood her emotions to the point of incapacitating her. Because play is the language in which children communicate, they must confront their pain experientially through play.

Without therapeutic intervention, when these children become adults, essential parts of their character may be missing. For instance, they may find it difficult to empathize with the feelings of childhood (e.g., those feelings of inadequacy at being unable to accomplish physically what is desired, or the feelings of frustration at having very little control over

---

1. Trauma may or may not be an event that actually occurred. In order for an event to be traumatic, it has to threaten one's well-being. Just the reality that one could have been maimed, violated, or killed is enough to cause trauma.

one's life). This may lead to difficulty in relating to their own children and an inability to allow their children freedom in their play (Plaut, 1979).

Children Approach Therapy at an Experiential Level

When a person becomes an adult, she may realize the difficulties in her life and begin reading the many self-help books available or become active in psychotherapy. During her reading, or with the assistance of a therapist, she may cognitively recognize the correlation between her childhood experiences and the feelings and behaviors she exhibits today. As an adult, she is capable of associating the two cognitions to gain a new awareness of her intrapersonal dynamics and begin to move toward change. Children, however, encounter their world, including therapy, at an experiential level. They must disclose their emotions in more primitive ways than verbal communication (Bow, 1988). Consequently, formal categorizations of childhood disorders, such as the DSM-IV (American Psychiatric Association [APA], 1994) or the DRG (Health Care Financing Administration [HCFA], 1984), as well as *pop psychology* self-help books, have no meaning to them. Children must communicate through their own medium — play.

Around the age of two, children have the ability to take a symbol outside of themselves and let it represent them (Garvey, 1977). This is why they respond so eagerly to games such as "This Little Piggy Went to Market" while playing with their toes. With this ability, they are able to recreate an environment using symbols which recapitulate the same emotions experienced in the actual environment (Irwin, 1983). This is particularly important for the child in therapy because it enables that child to communicate about a traumatic event by actually recreating that experience in play by attaching metaphoric and symbolic meanings to toys.

Children want to communicate the status of their well-being. They constantly *talk* through their play (Axline, 1947b; Bromfield, 1992; Ginott, 1960). In addition, they don't waste time in idle play (communication). The purpose of this *talk* is to reveal the status of their existence or well-being at any given moment (Perry & Landreth, 1990). It is also through their play that children make repeated attempts to discuss this status. Unfortunately, in spite of the importance of this conversation, people who have not been trained in understanding the language of children do not hear it. For the most part, adults tend to focus on a child's behavior rather than on her feelings. After constant failures in the reiteration of these feelings to adults, children eventually accept an attitude of defeat.

During the first session of play therapy, however, a child will communicate to the therapist, "Here's how life is treating me. Here's my state of being." It is at this point that it is of the utmost importance that the therapist be accepting of whatever the child presents (e.g., anger, fear, caution, etc.), because what the child is presenting is how she protects herself and how she maintains a sense of safety in her world. It is important for the therapist to honor the child's need for that safety and protection. In addition, this acceptance also validates the child and communicates that the therapist believes her. By experiencing acceptance from the therapist, she begins not only to believe in herself but also to look more closely at the therapist. When the child believes, "This person understands me, and I feel good around her," a relationship begins to develop.

Importance of the Child/Therapist Relationship

Clark Moustakas, the only living founder of play therapy today, states, "The alive relationship between the therapist and the child is the *essential dimension*, perhaps the only significant reality, in the therapeutic process and in all interhuman growth" (1959/1992, p. ix, emphasis added). Although this statement was made over 30 years ago, play therapy literature continues to support it (e.g., Gil, 1991; Landreth, 1991). By providing a secure relationship for the child, the therapist lays a foundation upon which the child may build her therapeutic issues, test them, watch them crumble, then rebuild them in such a way that she can understand, tolerate, and accept them. In other words, as the therapist provides the relationship, the child begins to add content to her play. As the child does this, the therapist provides acceptance, warmth, comfort, and empowerment through the relationship, and the two of them travel together on a journey through the child's travails toward resolution (Cattanach, 1992). Children cannot face their pain without the support of this relationship.

In addition, the therapist cannot help the child face her pain without letting the child lead the way. This is an extremely important concept, because participating in play therapy with a child can be likened to taking a journey with that child, not knowing what will be encountered along the way or the detours that will be necessary. The therapist may not even have a thorough understanding of what is taking place intra-psychically in the child. Although this may be uncomfortable for the therapist, it is not necessary in terms of providing good therapy for the child. Children initially have a natural propensity to move toward the events that caused them pain in order to bring resolution. Only after experiencing multiple defeats do they move away from the openness of their search for comfort in their environment. Given the support, protection, and freedom to direct their own play, they will move directly toward their pain. Because the relationship with the therapist is providing acceptance and safety, children will play out the traumatic event and the healing process will begin.

Five Stages of Therapy

Due to the significance of this relationship between child and therapist, it is important to gain an understanding of the different stages involved in therapy and how the relationship is involved in each of these stages. Without appropriate responses on the part of the therapist, it will be impossible to reach each stage, thus hindering therapy. (See Chapter 8 for further discussion of these appropriate responses.)

Essentially, there are five stages of therapy: (1) the Exploratory Stage (honoring the child); (2) the Testing for Protection Stage; the Working Stages, including (3) the Dependency Stage and (4) the Therapeutic Growth Stage; and (5) Termination. Although briefly discussed here, a more in-depth study of these stages is contained in following chapters.

The Exploratory Stage

When a child enters play therapy, she begins to explore her role in the setting (playroom) as well as with the therapist. At this point, there are certain fundamentals necessary for a therapist to provide. First, it is necessary *to be present* with the child. This is accomplished by the therapist focusing her full attention on the child. In essence, the child is the most valuable person at that moment in time. Second, the child is entitled to acceptance no matter what she does or says (Axline, 1947b). If she wants to be angry, it is accepted. In fact, within the limits of protection, anything the child does or says is acceptable. By showing this acceptance, the therapist validates the child's experience in order for the therapeutic alliance to develop (Moustakas, 1955). This is the *honoring process*. Suddenly, the child is in the presence of someone who is communicating, "I believe you; I understand you; I accept you; I respect you; I hear you; I know what your experiences are" (Moustakas, 1953). The child begins to be drawn to this person. She likes the therapist and wants to be with this adult. By the end of the session, as the child and therapist walk out together, the child says to the parents, "I don't want to go. I want to stay here!" This is often the very child who did not want to come into the playroom at the beginning of the session. Unfortunately, this type of response on the part of the child may be threatening to her parents. (See Chapter 3, *Consultation With Parents*, for further discussion of the therapist's involvement with the parents.)

THERAPEUTIC STAGES IN PLAY THERAPY

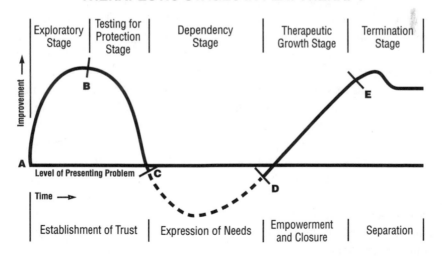

Illustration 1-1

In Illustration 1-1, the horizontal line represents the level of the present-ing problem (i.e., anxiety, bed-wetting, stealing, etc.) and the child's level of functioning when she presents for therapy. The curved line represents the child's actual functioning in relation to the presenting problem as she proceeds through therapy. While this will vary for each child, this is a general representation of the fluctuations that can be expected as children progress through treatment. Functioning (behaviorally and/or affective-ly) that is represented above the horizontal line symbolizes an improve-ment. Functioning that is represented below the horizontal line symbol-izes an increase in *inappropriate* behaviors and associated affect.

During the Exploratory Stage, the child's functioning generally shows a rapid improvement as represented between points A and B. With the honoring and acceptance that the child has received during this initial stage, the child's sense of isolation and frustration begins to dissipate while hope increases, thus the immediate (although temporary) improve-ment in level of functioning.

Testing for Protection Stage

When this child comes back for her next session, she will want to make sure this honoring process is still intact. Initially, she may be somewhat wary until she has had time to reassess the situation. Once she has deter-mined the current existence of the therapist's respect and reverence for her, she will, at that time, find it necessary to test this condition to make sure it is perseverant. At this point, she enters the Testing for Protection Stage. "Will this person accept my not-so-socially acceptable material and actions? How safe am I with this person? Will she protect me from my own emotionality?"

This Testing for Protection Stage is represented in Illustration 1-1 between points B and C. During this time, the child's *acting out* behav-ior will increase both in the playroom and at home. It is important in establishing credibility with the parents to predict this downturn in the child's behavior. The parents will benefit from the support and encour-agement given by the therapist during this time as well as the ensuing therapy time that immediately follows. Once the child has tested the rela-tionship and the therapist has passed the test, therapy begins.

Working Stages: Dependency and Therapeutic Growth

At this point, the child feels safe enough to disclose her pain and enters the Working Stages of therapy. Much like *Pandora's box*, she begins to disclose traumas, pains, struggles and fears by adding *content* to her play. This puts therapists in the position of witnessing the unbelievable acts that have been perpetrated against children. During this process, as a child's play intensifies, a typical result is that she may become frightened as her emotions begin to get out of control. When this occurs, the child will come out of her play to assess the relationship with her therapist in order to ascertain her level of safety. It is necessary, therefore, for the therapist to provide statements of safety, security, and protection for the child. Once she feels safe again, she'll go back into her play. Also, if the child encounters areas that are too difficult, she will stop playing, look at the therapist to make sure the therapist is comfortable with what is taking place, and then go back into her play again. Through these repetitions of safety determinations, the child is finally able to confront the pain and trauma of violations that have happened to her (Barlow, Strother, & Landreth, 1985).

The Dependency Stage is represented in Illustration 1-1 between points C and D. At this point, the child's play and behavior assume a confrontational stance (the downward slope). Then, upon completion of the confrontation, empowerment and level of functioning begin to improve. Now that the issue is no longer so imposing for the child, she can reclaim her identity by integrating the empowerment (which had been externalized in the play only) into an internalized sense of empowerment and self-worth. The internalized sense of empowerment and self-worth is reflected in an elevated level of functioning. This occurs during the Therapeutic Growth Stage and is represented between points D and E.

Termination Stage

As the child gains a new sense of well-being, control, dignity, and empowerment appropriate to her age and stage of development through the Working Stages of therapy, her play will turn to a rehearsal-for-adult-life style. The child's desire to be in the playroom will even diminish. It is at this point that the therapist begins to introduce termination to the therapeutic environment. Because of the trust established between the therapist and child, termination is a delicate process in which the child says goodbye to her play, the safe environment of the playroom, and the relationship with the therapist. (See Chapter 9 for further discussion of Termination.)

When termination is introduced, at point E in Illustration 1-1, the child may react by briefly returning to some of the play behaviors that precipitated the referral for therapy. As the child accepts the loss of the relationship and realizes her own empowerment, she will quickly return to her elevated level of functioning.

Children Have a Natural Propensity to Move Toward Health

Amazingly, children have the internal knowledge of the necessary direction for healing, although it is often at an unconscious level (Landreth, 1991; Nickerson & O'Laughlin, 1980). They know when their environment has been inappropriate. Whether subtly, through the lack of good nurturing skills on the part of their parents, or more dramatically, by having been perpetrated against, children possess an inner sense of impropriety in relation to these events. The authors, with over 25 years' experience in observing children in a therapeutic setting, believe that children have a natural propensity to move toward the event(s) that caused pain in order to confront that pain and resolve it. In fact, many children will communicate this direction in their very first session, as did Adam in the following example.[2]

Adam is a young boy whose father had been killed in a lumbering accident two years earlier. While the rest of the crew was getting the bottom of the tree ready, Adam's father was topping it.

___

2. When children have been sexually abused, and that abuse is still current, they may,. upon first entering the playroom, enter dramatic play before a relationship has been developed with the therapist.

Suddenly, the tree began to crack and fall. Although Adam's father was able to get down and run, the tree fell in his direction and crushed him. During Adam's first session in play therapy, he walked around the room, stopped at the sandbox, took his hand, and rubbed it across the sand. When he got to the center, he said, "There's gold buried right here!" Then, he moved his hand on across the sand. Knowing the intake information and seeing him place value in something buried in the sand, the therapist realized that this spot represented Adam's father's grave. At that point, however, it was not appropriate to verbalize this knowledge because stating it would bring it out of metaphor and into consciousness. This type of identification was not something Adam was ready to consciously acknowledge. By doing so, the therapist would have taken Adam's control and pacing away from his therapy. Consequently, the therapist said, "That's a very valuable place," giving recognition but not taking control. In time, Adam returned to this play and completed his work.

Allowing a Child to Direct
Her Own Therapy

The astute therapist who understands the language of children will be receptive to the message that the child is communicating, have faith in the child's knowledge of her own emotional needs, and allow the child to direct her own therapy. Following is a good example of the necessity for allowing children to do this.

During a play therapy workshop, a therapist attended who had been trained in behavioral therapy. Before the workshop, he had been working with a child who had been lying, stealing, and cheating in school. Although there were many other toys in the playroom, the therapist informed the boy during their first session together that they were going to play checkers. The therapist had decided to acknowledge and compliment the boy every time he did something appropriate and confront him every time he either lied, stole, or cheated, thereby attempting to make the child's behavior fall back into line by talking about right and wrong behavior.

After six weeks of playing checkers, the therapist contacted the boy's school to see whether the child's behavior had improved. They responded that there had not been any change at all! It was at this point that the therapist attended the play therapy workshop. Over the course of the next three days, the therapist shifted his entire view of children. As a result, he went back into the playroom with this little boy and said, "We don't have to play checkers anymore. Let's play what you would like to play."

The little boy looked at him as if to say, "Wait a minute. I'd better check this person out! Is this for real?" After testing this, the boy began to play the type of play indicative of a child who has been sexually abused. He found himself in the jungle fighting alligators, later climbing a mountain, finding a castle, and conquering a fire-breathing dragon. His play shifted from a boy who conformed to what the therapist asked, to someone who was allowed to direct his own play and take that play where it was necessary to go in order to face the pain and trauma in his life. All of a sudden, this therapist gained new perceptions of the child, to which he responded in a supportive rather than confrontive manner. As this occurred, the lying, stealing, and cheating began to diminish.

Although there are limits of safety placed in experiential play therapy, basically a child is allowed the freedom to use whatever medium is available in the room to act out her trauma. This type of unstructured play therapy grew out of years of observing children instinctively knowing what they needed to act out through fantasy play in order to face the pain in their lives. Children (for whom play therapy is the appropriate treatment modality) allowed to direct their own therapy are able to *reframe* the experiences of their trauma, resulting in a restored sense of well-being. (For further discussion of *reframing*, see Chapter 7.)

It also became evident that if a child is not able to return to the event that caused pain, it is necessary for the therapist to make several determinations.

1. Is the abuse still occurring? If so, therapy will not progress because the child is struggling for her daily existence. If the abuse is cur-

rent, the child cannot leave the present, with its accompanying need for protection, in order to regress to the developmental stage in which the abuse began. This regression occurs in order for the child to resolve the pain from her trauma.

2. Has the child externalized her trauma and become a perpetrator of other children? If so, her energy can be expressed through fantasy play rather than through violating other children. When expression begins in play therapy, violation of others diminishes.

3. Is the pain so repressed that the child is no longer aware of it? In this case, it may become necessary to help her through directive play (Gil, 1991).

If directive play is used as a therapy style, it is important to understand its use and misuse. If misused, the child can actually be retraumatized through the misuse of power inherent in the directive style. This may occur in the guise of returning to the trauma in order to move beyond it. Retraumatizing the child by forcing her to confront the trauma on a conscious level is unnecessary. The therapist with a basic belief in the health-seeking goals of a child will only take a power position when a child is out of control and needs protection from herself.

Each play therapy session presents new information disclosed by the child. Sadly, it is all too common for therapists to think they know what is best for the child without understanding what the child is communicating through this disclosure. Since the child is the one who knows her experiences and the direction and means of approaching her own sense of well-being, it would be presumptuous on the part of a therapist to, first, *think* she knows what the child has experienced, and second, *decide* what to do *to* the child to make the child feel better and, consequently, act better. In other words, a therapist may set a goal for a child to reach via a style of play the therapist considers appropriate without having observed what the child is communicating. In this case, the therapist assumes she knows the best way for the child to approach the world in order to resolve the child's struggles. In reality, what the therapist has done is misuse power. In many cases, it was a misuse of power in one or more of the child's relationships that brought the child in for therapy. Thus, it would be unreasonable on the part of a therapist to think that the use of power could be perceived positively by this child in order to help her gain emotional well-being. Indeed, the child will most likely feel that this use of power on the part of the therapist is similar to the misuse of power experienced at the hands of a perpetrator. In which case, the child will act on the assumption that she needs to protect herself from the therapist rather than enter into a trusting relationship enabling healing.

In addition, as seen in the example with the boy being told to play checkers, when a therapist says, "We're going to do this activity today," children may simply comply on a superficial level. This will lead children in the direction of performing more of the same behaviors they used as a form of defense. In fact, there may actually be an exacerbation of the acting out of these defenses.

Sometimes, therapists become directive as a way of pushing children away. When a child is allowed to be the director of her own play, she will create an environment in such a way as to let the therapist know what it *feels* like to be this child and live in her world. This may cause the therapist to leave the session with negative feelings inside herself (e.g., confusion, anger, frustration, dislike, or a general discomfort), even to the point of feeling frightened or overwhelmed. Naturally, when the time comes for the next session with this particular child, the therapist may find herself dreading it, anticipating the same feelings will occur.

Although this is not a pleasant experience for any therapist, it is actually an indication that the therapist is performing adequately in the helping role. This child's entire life is spent feeling the unpleasant emotions that the therapist is allowed to feel for only the small amount of time spent with the child (Bromfield, 1992). Even though it would be the tendency of any therapist to want to avoid receiving this type of message (feeling), it is, however, extremely important to stay present with the child and support her while she struggles to move beyond these feelings toward a resolution. Refusing to do so could foster feelings of betrayal in the child. When the child enters her pain, she needs a companion and protector. Without this security and strength from the therapist, the child will, once again, feel abandoned and betrayed.

During this type of non-directive, unstructured therapy, children will use a number of styles to incorporate the therapist into their play. One style is to put the therapist into a passive role. For instance, a child comes into therapy and during the first couple of minutes takes out a toy gun and shoots the therapist. Boom! The therapist lies down and plays dead. She may lie there the entire time the child plays out the trauma of perpetration, because the child does not want the therapist to interfere. Rather, the child wants to have complete control over the play — just the opposite of the out-of-control feelings she experienced when being victimized. The next opportunity the therapist has to speak may be 40 minutes later, when she says, "You have five minutes left." At this time, the child may start putting closure on her experience by including the therapist, or she may again pick up the gun and shoot the therapist once more, as if to say, "And you're going to be quiet the last five minutes, too!" The alert therapist will get the point! If this is the case, the child will continue to work on her issues, only allowing the therapist to be a witness.

Another style children will use is to incorporate the therapist into their play (Guerney, 1983). Since the therapist has become such a security object, the child will often put her into the traumatic play and let her participate. What an honor it is for the therapist when a child does this, because the child is actually communicating, "I'm willing to be in a relationship with you. I trust you to keep me safe." When invited to join a child's play, it is very important for the therapist to do so.

It is by allowing the child to direct the play that the therapist plays a vital supportive role (Barlow, et al., 1985; Guerney, 1983). In fact, because of the child's trust in the therapist, the therapist is able to provide an emotional boost for the child. This empowers the child to achieve greater accomplishments, change, and movement than could have been possible without this relationship (Axline, 1950). For instance, if the child wants the therapist to be a passive witness, she will do something to put her in that position (i.e., shoot the therapist). Then, the therapist may respond from that position, even if her response is to remain passive, because the child feels empowered just by having the therapist there as a corpse. The empowerment may come from the child's having conquered her fears or simply through having the control to keep someone incapacitated. On the other hand, if the child wants an active participant, she will draw the therapist into her play, and the two of them, for instance, will go together to fight the dragon. The area in which the child needs help is where she will put the therapist.

It is the child's choice as to whether she wants the therapist to join the play or not (Bolig, Fernie, & Klein, 1986). For the therapist to expropriate that decision from the child is presumptuous on the part of the therapist. The presumption lies in the fact that the therapist believes she might know how the child will approach work on the issues most relevant to the child. It would be more judicious on the part of the therapist to trust in the inherent ability of the child to know her own pain and struggles and how best to approach confronting them. Children have not yet become so sophisticated in their defenses that they will deny their pain and struggles to themselves.

It is important for the therapist to be watchful of supporting the child and possibly expanding the play, but not adding another dimension to the play that might take it in a direction unintended by the child. For example:

> *Marcie was a young girl struggling with the impending birth of a sibling. During play, she said to the therapist, "You play the child while I play the mommie." While playing the part of the mother, she became very preoccupied with her baby, leaving the child (played by the therapist) to her own devices. At this point, the therapist saw an opportunity to gently lead Marcie to a deeper level of play and said, "But Mommie, I want you to play with me."*
>
> *Marcie quickly said, "I can't play with you! I've got to take care of the baby!"*
>
> *The therapist responded, "But Mommie, you never play with me anymore — ever since the baby came."*
>
> *"Well, I can't because I've got to sweep the floor," Marcie replied.*
>
> *"But Mommie, I miss you!"*

Notice how the therapist gently led Marcie to a deeper level of play by role playing in such a way as to cause Marcie to think, "Boy, how do I feel about this? What is going to happen when this actually occurs?" Over several sessions, Marcie was able to work through to an ending where she realized that she could let someone else watch the baby while she spent time with the child (i.e., the therapist). The therapist just gave Marcie a little nudge. She didn't force the issue or redirect Marcie's play. While a child's pain and struggles may not be conscious, the play does access unconscious material in that it becomes the child's creation of her own metaphor to move toward healing — thus the necessity of allowing the child to lead the way.

The question of incorporating the therapist or not, is one way in which the child expresses her own individual style of play. Other ways might include, for example, the aggressive child whose behavior is out of control and hurtful toward others. This child may participate in name-calling, may be oppositional to authority, may lie, steal, and/or cheat. On the other hand, the opposite may be the case (i.e., the child may be withdrawn because her risk circle is so tightly closed). The withdrawn child is very fearful and afraid to interact with the world. When she comes into play therapy, she will exhibit the same kinds of behavior during initial contact, because these are the defenses she has developed in order to live in her world. Over time, as the therapist communicates to the child that she is valuable, honored, and respected, an observable shift will take place in the child's view of the world and, accordingly, in her behavior. Although this shift may occur slowly at first, it will gain momentum with time and empowerment from the therapist, and the child will begin to forego the defenses she has previously utilized in her other world.

When to Give Structure to a Child's Play

It is extremely important to understand what directive play therapy is because there are times when directive play therapy is appropriate. Directive play is not instructing a child in an activity. True directive play therapy is mild, soft, and non-threatening. It does not take away from children their sense of empowerment. In directive play therapy, the therapist might use statements such as, "And how were you feeling right then?" "Can you put a sound to that?" "What did the monster's face look like?" "Can you make a face like it?"

Creating structure to help a child face the pain of trauma is a delicate task. For instance, if a child experiences a traumatic event at the hospital, a therapist might direct the play by finding some toys representative of a stay in the hospital and then saying to the child, "These toys are over here too. I just wanted to make sure you were aware of them." Depending on the depth of the trauma, a child may either start playing with them right away or may take weeks to do so. Although a therapist can create a structure such as this, it may be too frightening for the child. It may take a period of time before the child experiences enough courage to play with the toys. The important concept is never to force a child, either obviously or subtly.

The following example shows a lack of use of the basic premises of play therapy. The adult perspective, rather than the child's perspective, was utilized with the result being a skewed treatment approach.   The child's needs were unheard and unmet.

The mother of a young boy made an appointment with a therapist to discuss her son [whom we shall call Jimmy].   She explained that Jimmy had been born with a pinhole in his heart. When he was two years old, the doctors operated and repaired the pinhole. Two or three times a day since the operation (which was now several years past), Jimmy would say, "I'll never let anyone ever operate on my heart again! I would rather die than let anyone operate on my heart! If anyone ever touches my heart, I'll die."

The mother went on to explain to the therapist that the doctors had found another hole in Jimmy's heart that needed to be repaired surgically. Jimmy was now five years old. Up until this point, the mother had not been particularly concerned about her son's statements. Now, however, she felt tremendous fear about what Jimmy was saying to himself.

In addition, she told the therapist that she and her husband had a very unusual marriage. He would work in Alaska for six weeks, come home for two, and then return to his job. During the first week home, she and her husband were fine. The second week, however, they would argue constantly. Then he would be gone for six weeks. At the time the mother found out that Jimmy needed surgery, her husband had just returned to Alaska. She was concerned that if she let him know about the operation, he would take a leave of absence to come back home. Because the surgery was scheduled for five weeks in the future, she was not sure their marriage could survive this time together. The mother finished the session by asking the therapist to help prepare Jimmy for the needed surgery.

About a week later, she called her husband to tell him the news. He did exactly what she predicted and came home. The first week they were fine. The second week, they started to argue. Suddenly, they remembered the boy's situation and decided to forego their arguing until their son was through his crisis. At this point, all three of them went to see the therapist, where the father explained to Jimmy that the doctors had found another pinhole in his heart which needed to be repaired by surgery.

Jimmy became hysterical. He went over to the corner of the office, put his hands over his face and body, as if to protect himself, and began screaming and crying. Seeing this, the father said, "If you had a car and the carburetor didn't work, you wouldn't throw the car away — you would fix the carburetor. Then, the car would run fine and everything would be okay." During the time the father spoke, the little boy was screaming — literally for his life.

Several weeks later, Jimmy went in for a session alone. The therapist set up a structured play therapy situation with an operating room and asked him to play out the operation. Even though the therapist had no understanding of the child's emotional perceptions and reactions to his situation, the therapist basically said, "We'll do it this (i.e., "my") way." He didn't invite Jimmy to play out the operation but misused his power by telling him to play it out. As Jimmy began to operate, he suddenly turned to the therapist and said, "He's not making it. He's not going to make it." He continued to work a little harder and then stepped back and said, "He didn't make it. He died!"

The therapist, filled with anxiety, not only because the child predicted his own death but also because of his own unresolved issues, said, "Let's make him live." At that point, a complete reversal of roles took place — Jimmy reenacted the scene so that his patient lived for the benefit of the therapist. The session then ended.

When Jimmy went in for the operation, he didn't die — the operation was a success. Then, while driving Jimmy home from the hospital, the mother and father suddenly realized that the crisis was over and began to argue. When they came to a stop light, the boy said, "Mom, Dad, I can't take your arguing anymore." That night, Jimmy died in his sleep of heart failure.

In looking at this example in light of the knowledge that children communicate through associations, metaphors, and symbols, certain points become evident. First, Jimmy communicated what he needed to convey in order for his mother to know the condition of his heart.

Basically, he said, "I can't let anyone touch my heart. It's so painful to live in my world that I can't let anyone get close to me. It's too painful!" In essence, what he had been talking about over the past three years was the way his parents related to each other.[3] "I can't let you near me. I'm in so much pain that I don't know whether I want to live or die." He clearly communicated this message, but no one heard him because no one knew his language.

Second, Jimmy was in a state of pain and needed nurturing. When they fought, his parents were oblivious to his needs. In essence, he was saying, "I don't feel secure enough to survive." Then, when the therapist brought the family together, he used the same ineffective family system to tell the boy that he was in crisis. By saying, "You are going to have an operation," they depersonalized him from being a member of their family to being singled out as the one needing an operation.

What did Jimmy hear when the father told him of the need for another operation? He heard that he was going to be annihilated, that this was the end of his being, and that there was no well-being left in him anymore. He was going to be destroyed and would die. This is why he went over to the corner of the room and tried to cover himself up, screaming as loudly as he could. He did everything he could to push that experience away.

At this crucial moment, notice what the father did. He went to a cognitive level and talked about the carburetion process of an automobile. The father was trying to communicate on a cognitive level when Jimmy was communicating on an experiential level. They never connected. Even though the father tried to do a good job, he did not know how to communicate on a level his son could grasp.

There are alternative approaches for the therapist. First, he could have requested information concerning the possibility of postponing the operation in order to teach this family how to nurture a member of their family. This would have allowed the parents time in which to learn how to give this type of information as a caring unit. For instance, the father could have taken this little boy, put him on his knee, and said, "*Our fam-*

3. Carl Whitaker states that children have a mother, a father, and the relationship between them. It is this relationship between them (i.e., how the mother and father treat each other) that provides the foundation for the child's view of herself and the world more so than anything else (Whitaker & Bumberry, 1988).

ily is going through a crisis, and we're all concerned. We are going to be together. It's focused on you, but we all are going through this together." Notice how important it is to have a sense of unity within the family. By focusing on his having the operation, the theme of abandonment surfaced again — the same feeling he experienced several years earlier. In evaluating this case clinically, Jimmy died of emotional neglect.

Second, when the therapist heard from the mother that the boy needed an operation, he only focused on the operation. Because he did not understand the language of children, he missed what Jimmy had been communicating for several years through his statements: "My state of well-being is in crisis." If Jimmy had been allowed to enter into experiential play, he would have clearly communicated this through that play. Sadly, when Jimmy operated and his patient died, the therapist abandoned him in his therapy.

Experiential play therapy involves emotional energy. This energy can go anywhere — to the future, to the past, up to the moon, anywhere. It can go as far as the imagination of the child will let it go. It can even go into death and be alive in death. This is where Jimmy wanted to go. Then, he could play out his pain through death when he couldn't do it through reality. He had to die in order to examine his pain. In other words, by playing that his patient died, he was shifting into another medium in order to work on the issues in his family. The therapist, however, cut off his fantasy, causing Jimmy to be abandoned in the midst of therapy.

Not only is this an example of the misuse of power under the guise of *directed* play therapy, but it is also a sad example of the devastating results of a therapist not understanding the language of children. It would have been more judicious on the part of this therapist had he developed faith in the inherent ability of a child to know where her pain and struggles lie and in his ability to approach them in his own way.

Because of the way Jimmy's play touched on an issue of the therapist himself, he was unable to set that aside in order to follow Jimmy's direction. This is a good example of the fact that great caution should be taken when using directive therapy.

Summary of Tenets

To summarize, therapists do not cure children. Rather, they provide a relationship and an environment in which the child can begin to heal. As children are honored and provided with a place of safety and protection, they honor therapists by allowing the therapist to go on a journey with them. At that point, children begin to play out the traumatic event through associations, symbols, and metaphors, reapproaching their painful emotional experience of the event in the developmental stage occurring at the onset of the trauma. The first time a child goes through these events, it is extremely painful.

During this traumatic type of play, a child will stop briefly in order to obtain reassurance of the security she has with her therapist. Then, she will return to her fantasy play, this time going to a deeper level. She only confronts, however, as much as she can tolerate at any given moment. Each time this pattern (playing, seeking reassurance, and then playing again) is repeated, the child gains a sense of control, dignity, and empowerment (appropriate to her age and stage in development) over that part of her play. She reaches a time when she knows she has conquered the negative emotionality surrounding those parts of her emotional experience. In essence, she is reframing her experiences with a restored sense of empowerment, dignity, and control. It is during this process that healing occurs. Although the child will never completely forget the event(s) which happened to her, the painful emotional responses associated with it do not incapacitate her. No longer does she experience a sense of being out of control with the accompanying feelings of high anxiety and loss of a sense of well-being. Now, she can return to her appropriate development with her play shifting to a rehearsal-for-life style of play.

Expectations for Successful Outcome of Treatment Utilizing Experiential Play Therapy

In order for children to benefit from play therapy, they must first be capable of symbolic play. Developmentally, this ability to symbolize usually occurs around the age of 20 months, although some children can be ready as early as 18 months or as late as two-and-a-half to three years of age.

When a very young or developmentally delayed child has been
for play therapy, it is important, before involvement with the
determine the appropriateness of this style of treatment for the child.

In order to assess the child's potential benefit from experiential play
therapy, it is necessary to establish the child's accomplishment of the following:

- Can the child reenact events that she sees in everyday life?
- Can the child build a setting and create a new dramatic presentation with her toys?

These two forms of play differ from the play of the child who simply
manipulates the toys. For experiential play therapy to be effective, it is
necessary for children to be capable of recapitulating their struggles and
projecting those issues, needs, and desires onto the toys. The toy and the
play become symbols of intrapsychic dynamics. Without this ability, it is
play for accomplishing motor development, object constancy, etc., and it
is not possible to accomplish psychotherapeutic goals.

At the upper age ranges, children begin to be interested in more structured types of activities around the age of nine — however, an eight-year-
old may come in one day wanting to play and another day wanting to just
sit and chat or play a more structured game. Between the ages of eight
and 10, it becomes necessary for therapists to be flexible in their expectations of the child's behavior on any given day, as it will fluctuate from
a child-like playfulness to a more adult-like desire for rules and structure.
Even considering this, it is prudent to allow the child to set the stage for
the type of activity for the day, keeping in mind that her choice of activity style (i.e., how she sets the scene and plays it out) provides clinical
information as well as what she chooses to do. Allowing the child the
freedom to reveal her needs through fantasy play is vital. If the child
chooses not to be involved in fantasy play for that day, it is still possible
to gain information from the child within the confines of the formalized
game she chooses to play and from the conversation that occurs during
the play.

Reactive Disorders

Breaking down the general term "disorders" according to etiology, children best suited for play therapy are those children who are experiencing a Reactive Disorder. This type of disorder is most evident in a child who has been developing normally, but something has occurred in the child's life that has created an elevated level of stress. The child is attempting to come to an understanding of this stressful situation. This understanding is one she will create in her own young mind. Although the child may be assisted by explanations from adults, ultimately, the child must experience her own creative perception of the situation. In this evolving process, however, the child's behavior has become offensive and troublesome for herself and for those around her. Therefore, she requires some assistance in arriving at an understanding and acceptance of this situation and, if possible, alleviation of the stress-inducing agent.

Constitutional Etiology

Children who will be least likely to benefit in play therapy are those whose disorder is organic, constitutional, or biological in etiology.

Client Disorders[4] Appropriate for Experiential Play Therapy

The following is a perspective of certain specific disorders that fall within the Reactive Disorders category and how each would be expected to respond to play therapy.

---

4. Unless otherwise specified, diagnostic categories from the DSM-IV (APA, 1994) are utilized.

Conduct Disorders — Childhood Onset

The aggression toward others, destructiveness, disregard for the rights of others, and deceitfulness displayed by children exhibiting the full range of symptoms for this diagnosis places them at a level of social and interpersonal sophistication where play therapy would no longer be useful. However, if onset is early — between five and six years of age — and symptoms are mild, this form of play therapy will be useful for children from a family where there is no history of related disorders. Extensive involvement with the family will also be necessary. Family therapy is desirable; however, if this is not possible, the play therapist may be involved in both a supportive role and a consultative role with the family.

Because the child shows disregard for any rules mandated by the parents, and consequences and punishments are ineffective, the parents feel defeated. They will appreciate any ideas on effective discipline. In addition, they will need the understanding and support of an outside party while their child is progressing through her treatment. Strong emotions are elicited when the child is testing for protection and confronting her own personal demons. At such times, these strong emotions will likely overflow from the playroom into the home and school. The parents must be educated about the process in order to facilitate understanding and acceptance on their part. The necessity of exhibiting love, support, and understanding, while at the same time maintaining firm boundaries for the child, must be emphasized. This requires a parent who is capable of laying aside her own personal needs in order to meet the needs of her child during this three- to four-month period of time.

If the parents and the home environment are determined to be contributing to the child's disorder, it will be necessary to assist in locating residential placement outside the home. Under these circumstances, play therapy may continue and be more effective.

Oppositional-Defiant Disorder

Considered by most therapists to be the precursor of Conduct Disorders, many of the children seen in therapy are diagnosed as Oppositional-

Defiant Disorder. This child's behavior is interfering with the normal, ongoing routine of the child's surroundings. Oppositional-Defiant Disorder in children manifests as angry, argumentative, defiant, rude, and/or vindictive, frequently involving obscene language. These children appear to be motivated by revenge toward authority figures. Teachers may add that they tend to be loud. A parent might say her child "is so temperamental that she has us all walking on eggshells at home. We never know when she is just going to fly off the handle and change from being this sweet little charmer into being a little monster."

Joey was a four-year-old who was brought to the therapist by his grandparents. He was temporarily in their custody while their daughter was in the process of moving her home. The child's mother had been battered and verbally abused by her husband, who had a tendency toward out-of-control anger. Their son had seen his dad practically destroy the home during his explosive episodes. Finally, the wife left the husband, but not before the boy had been exposed to a great deal of anger and out-of-control behavior.

One day the grandparents took their grandson with them to a doctor's appointment where they experienced a long wait before seeing the doctor. The boy played quietly for quite a while, but eventually began to get restless. Finally, the grandmother was called back to the doctor's office. Although Joey was restless, the grandfather tried very hard to keep him occupied. However, when the grandmother finally came back out, Joey stood up and said, "Oh, good, let's go!"

She said, "Well, not yet. I need to get a prescription filled first."

At that point, he said, "Nope! We're leaving!"

The grandmother, however, just walked over to the pharmacy in another part of the clinic to get her prescription filled. This was against the little boy's plan, and he began to tantrum.

Most people are not too surprised to see a three-year-old tantruming, but the child let forth with a stream of expletives such as the grandparents had never heard. They were totally humiliated. That afternoon, they called for their first appointment with the therapist. The grandparents reported that the child was exhausting them with his continual demands and uncontrollable behavior. They were afraid to leave him with a sitter and yet were afraid to take him with them for fear of being embarrassed again.

Joey is typical of an Oppositional-Defiant Disordered child who can be helped by participating in play therapy. He will need some help in controlling his behavior and resolving his internal conflict. This will be discussed at greater length in Chapter 6, *Testing for Protection.*

Anxiety Disorders: The Over-Anxious Child and Separation Anxiety

Play therapy is greatly beneficial for children who experience Anxiety Disorders. This includes the over-anxious child who tends to be worried constantly when there seems little foundation for concern. These children may repeatedly make comments such as, "Gee, I'm afraid I didn't do my homework right," or, "I'm not really sure," or, "I don't think so-and-so likes me," or, "I worry about my little sister because she cries a lot." This child tends to exhibit tension and an inability to relax due to constant apprehension.

As the term separation anxiety would indicate, these children are afraid to separate from their primary caretaker because of a fear that something will happen to the caretaker while they're apart. Once again, the primary factor here is the apparent unwarranted basis for the child's level of foreboding. In the playroom, this syndrome can produce some awkwardness due to the child's resistance to separation from her parents in order to come into the playroom.

Traumatic Stress

There are two types of traumatic stress. One is chronic stress (e.g., a child is being habitually physically or sexually abused on a routine basis). Perhaps this abuse started at birth and continued until age 16 when the child ran away from home; or it may have closer parameters (i.e., starting at nine and continuing until 12). Play therapy is beneficial in helping this child learn new ways of relating to adults and, consequently, improving the child's mental health.

The second type of traumatic stress is acute. In this case, the child may have either been involved in or seen something occur that has been very traumatic such as an airplane crash, an earthquake, or a parent die or be killed. With these children, therapeutic work may proceed intensely until a plateau is reached. At that point, the child's life appears to be moving along smoothly — the child appears happy, the parents are satisfied, and the child's behavior has moved to within normal boundaries. It is apparent that the child has come to a resolution for herself. Under these circumstances, it seems appropriate to suggest terminating therapy. However, there may be issues that are necessary in trauma work that have not yet surfaced for the child. In that case, it is prudent to advise the parents that while the child has accomplished considerable gains, there are still aspects of the trauma that most likely have not yet emerged for the child since they have not yet been addressed in therapy. When these issues do surface, the parents may begin to see some regression in the child's behavior. This is not to indicate that therapy has been ineffective, or that it is now necessary to return to therapy in order to start all over again. Rather, it is simply an indication that the child is attempting to communicate her unsettled state in the only manner she knows.

The issue resurfaces for several reasons. Something may occur which triggers an unconscious memory and precipitates an emotional and behavioral reaction in a child, or the child has reached another developmental stage. Along with the more advanced developmental stage comes a new maturity in cognitive and motor skills, in emotional and moral development, and in perceptions of the world. With the more advanced skills, it becomes necessary to reprocess the issue and come to a new level of acceptance based on the more mature level of experience and knowledge. At this time, the parent may want to take the child back for a period of therapy to facilitate the reconciliation of the old experience with the new feelings and cognitions.

Covington (1988) depicts this recurring type of treatment as a cycle of recovery. Oaklander (1978) calls it *intermittent longterm therapy*. Regardless of the term, when working with children or adults who have experienced traumatic stress, it is necessary to inform them that there may be cycles to their recovery. Each time the child goes through a new developmental stage, she will have to confront this issue on the new level.

Incidentally, development and developmental stages do not terminate magically at adulthood, so this issue may resurface at periodic intervals throughout adulthood as well. It may not be traumatic every time. It may just be a feeling of being uneasy about something. It may not even be apparent that the current state of discomfiture is due to the original situation. When the reaction is mild, a new look at the current agitation in light of the new developmental stage, new experiences, and new skills will take some time and thought but can be resolved by the individual alone. There usually comes a new perspective on life once one gets into her thirties, forties and fifties.

Because of this recurring theme of recovery, it is important to let both the child and parents know that even though they are ready to terminate for the first time, there may still be issues to deal with in the future.

Heather was a little girl who first went to a therapist when she was four years old. She was in the custody of her paternal grandparents following the death of her mother. She and her younger sister were the only two witnesses to their mother's murder. Numerous police officers and social workers had questioned them, attempting to get them to disclose the identity of the murderer, or at least give a description or some clue, but they couldn't do that. After being in treatment for about a year, Heather grew to be accepting of the fact that her mother was gone and would not return. She also had worked extensively on her rage about the situation, the helplessness she felt to alter the events, and the resulting dramatic changes in her life. After this time, her behavior reflected the gradual improvement that had evolved along with her resolution of this issue for herself.

When Heather was nine, her grandparents moved her sister into their home. At this point, she began to experience sibling rivalry issues and was faced with the memory of the last time she and her sister had lived together. For Heather, this reawakened memories of her lost mother at a time when her own femininity was beginning to blossom. The memories and resultant confusion led her back to the therapist's office. Her behavior had, once again, become of concern to her grandparents. Treatment during this interval was more succinct. She was able to move into playing out her themes much more quickly this time and her

*play was focused more on the primary issue rather than periph-
eral issues.*

*At 14, Heather began to be resistant to the grandmother
enforcing rules or routines. (At this age, in general, it becomes
necessary to establish new maxims for the novel, independence-
seeking behaviors children are suddenly empowered to accomplish.) Heather was refusing to be bound by any new regulations.
In fact, she was resisting the old ones as well. As the two of them
began their initial session of this, their second return following
the first termination, the grandmother related how Heather
resisted every long-established rule the grandparents had
imposed. At this disclosure, the therapist shifted her gaze to the
young lady and said emotionally, "She's just not Mom! Mom
should be the one setting the rules." The girl burst into tears, and
once again the focus returned to the issue of Mom not being
there. The grandmother had tried to be a mom for her; but
although she had fulfilled the role in all respects, she just wasn't
Mom.*

Somataform Disorders

Occasionally, a child may be referred to a psychotherapist after a visit to
a physician has not identified a physical basis for the child's complaints.
Most commonly, the child has complained of headaches, stomachaches,
or some other nonspecified pain. An important characteristic of this disorder is the ability to identify an emotional stressor which has occurred in
close temporal proximity to the initiation of symptoms. Play therapy is
also effective for treating this disorder. In the play therapy process, the
child is enabled to enter her fantasy, discover the etiology of the pain and,
through her own play metaphor, resolve the dilemma.

Adjustment Disorder With Depressed Mood

The diagnosis of Adjustment Disorder With Depressed Mood is appropriate with a child who displays situational types of moodiness or sadness that can be associated with an environmental situation. This sadness, or the blues, can be manifested by the child becoming more withdrawn, losing interest in surroundings, and changing sleep patterns. Often, these children become lost in their environment since they are not acting out and demanding attention. This child is often allowed to sit alone in her sadness. Seldom will parents seek out a therapist and say, "I think my child ought to see you because she is just being too good," or a teacher say, "This child is just too quiet!"

It is important to recognize when a child has shifted from being bright, outgoing, and enthusiastic about life to becoming lethargic and appearing uninterested in her customary activities. Play therapy can be a terrific avenue for these children to explore their concern and sadness about their living situation. Through play, the child can enact the precipitating event, as seen from the child's perspective, then progress to an understanding and/or acceptance of the residual feelings and situation.

What appears as Major Depressive Disorder is different from Adjustment Disorder With Depressed Mood, of course. However, the appearance of Major Depressive Disorder with psychotic features may also be situational. Children who have been sexually abused by a family member with whom they felt a close relationship may evidence a major depression that develops insidiously over a period of months (Livingston, 1987). The play therapist would be wise to be particularly alert for this disorder in children who have been sexually abused and to differentiate it from a depressed mood and childhood schizophrenia.

Developmental Issues[5]

Many of the children seen in play therapy are those children who have no overriding pathology but, rather, are simply struggling with adjusting to

---

5. These issues may or may not correspond to DSM-IV (APA, 1994) diagnostic categories of Adjustment Disorders or Bereavement.

the circumstances that life has cast before them. These circumstances could be familial, environmental, social, or developmental. Children may make statements like, "You know, I'm working on growing up; and it's just tough," or, "Going from being the youngest in the family to being the middle child is just not fair," or, "Why did my dad have to marry her?" Perhaps they have experienced a move across the country, or even from one home to another home in the same community. Children thrive on routine and consistency. Anything that creates a change (from hurricanes and tornadoes to loss of a favorite toy) is going to create an upset for children. Play therapy allows an opportunity for these children to examine their angry, frustrated, betrayed, confused feelings about situations over which they have no control.

When there has been a death in a family, whether that be a sibling, a parent, a grandparent, or even a pet, there is a delay in a child's adjustment to and understanding of this new loss. The young child is not yet equipped with the cognitive development to understand the concept of death. (Indeed, many adults continually question the concept of death and afterlife.) The child doesn't understand that vital organs are no longer functioning and, therefore, the individual no longer meets the scientific requirements for status. She grapples with acceptance of the fact that this could happen to anyone, including herself, at any time. When parents are in the midst of their grief, it may appear to them that the child is handling this crisis very well, causing many parents to think there is no need to be concerned or to consider counseling for the child. Then, about the time the parents have begun to acknowledge the loss and accept it, the child goes into grief, and her behavior begins to change. Because of the time that has elapsed since the death, the parents are unable to make the connection between the child's behavior and her recognition of the loss.

Developmental Deviations: Insomnia Related to Abuse; Elimination Disorders; Eating Disorders

Another symptom children often present is difficulty with sleeping. This is not to be confused with Sleep Terror Disorder, because research has shown evidence of neurological involvement with Sleep Terror Disorder (e.g., Murray, 1991; Sheldon, Spire, & Levey, 1992). Rather, reference here is to the child who is afraid to go to sleep, or wakes up in the middle of the night and can't go back to sleep for reasons that are not physical. This may also include Nightmare Disorder.

Another developmental deviation to be considered is bowel or bladder control problems. It is important with these children to appraise the etiology as well as necessary to rule out a physiological basis for the enuresis or encopresis. Questioning the parents concerning a family history of this nature or consulting with a physician can determine the existence of any physiological basis. Once a physiological basis is ruled out, play therapy may be utilized to help the child with this disorder.

Individuals diagnosed with Eating Disorders are predominantly adolescent or young adult females. The Childhood Onset Anorexia Nervosa that has been researched has considered largely prepubertal and pubertal children, ages 10-14 (Fossen, Knibbs, Bryant-Waugh, & Lask, 1987; Lask & Bryant-Waugh, 1992; Maloney, McGuire, Daniels, & Specker, 1989; Treasure & Thompson, 1988). However, the play therapy population consists of even younger children. Typically, the symptoms presented by young children do not meet all the necessary criteria to be considered Anorexia Nervosa or Bulimia. More often, the young child will manifest a few of the symptoms considered indications of an Eating Disorder or they may merely exhibit some unusual eating patterns. The following are generally considered atypical Eating Disorders in childhood: Food Avoidance Emotional Disorder (Higgs, Goodyer, & Birch, 1989), Pervasive Refusal Syndrome (Lask, Britten, Kroll, Magagna & Tranter, 1991), Selective Eating, Food Fads, and Food Refusal (Lask & Bryant-Waugh, 1992).

A clear picture of etiology of eating disorders has not yet been achieved, but it seems to be an interaction of genetic, biological, personality, and family factors which vary with each individual (Lask & Bryant-Waugh, 1992). Treasure & Thompson (1988) suggest, however, that the prepubertal group is atypical with more adverse life events precipitating the illness and an increased number of family and personality factors.

Psychological treatment of these children has primarily consisted of family therapy. Indeed, family therapy is indicated since so many family factors are predisposing to this disorder. However, play therapy can also accelerate the young child's progress in the areas of self-esteem, trauma resolution, and coping styles.

Dysfunctional Family Setting[6]

The term dysfunctional family is not a dichotomous situation. One is not either classified as purely dysfunctional or functional. Rather, dysfunctionality might be considered along a continuum and discussion could focus on the level of dysfunction. Most families are dysfunctional to some extent. Consequently, the great majority of children seen in play therapy will be from moderately to highly dysfunctional families. In their own way, they are attempting to find a manner of functioning within a maladaptive setting.

It often follows in these situations that the child is referred by an outside agency, and a certain amount of pressure is brought to bear upon the family to seek therapy for the child. It is not uncommon, however, for the adults in the family to view the child as the problem and to bring her in with instructions to the therapist to fix her — in essence: *make her more like us.*

> *Susie is the seven-year-old daughter of two attorneys. Her mother took her to a therapist after a parent-teacher conference where the parents were informed of the teacher's recommendation that Susie be retained for another year in the second grade. The teacher recommended therapy for this child because she was very withdrawn and refused to even attempt to do any of the school work. The teacher had been unsuccessful in her attempts to solicit any interaction with Susie.*
>
> *The mother took Susie in each week for play therapy. This child was very constricted in her play, almost fearful of exploring the room. She repeatedly questioned what the therapist wanted her to do. Finally, after many reassurances that she could play in any way she wanted with any of the things in the playroom, she began to play, at first mechanically, but more and more creatively as time went on.*
>
> *After Susie had been in therapy for about a month, the father asked to meet with the therapist. He wanted to see a report of all symptoms, a plan of treatment, and the estimated length of ther-*

6. This is not a DSM-IV (APA, 1994) diagnostic category.

apy. Each month thereafter, he demanded the same report and accountability from the therapist.

Susie's father had been upset for quite some time about the fact that Susie did not function more closely to his expectations of perfection. When her teacher recommended retention, he saw this as further evidence that she was not following his dictum. His goal for Susie's treatment was to make her more like himself.

While Susie's case certainly does not illustrate the degree of dysfunctionality evident in many families, it does point out how Susie was reacting to the world as she reacted to her father's expectations of responsible behavior. She was not allowed to be a child, make mistakes, and/or be careless. Everything she did had to have forethought, purpose, and planning.

One frustration that develops when working with a child from a dysfunctional family is the question of the efficacy of individual treatment of the child as opposed to family therapy. Can treatment be effective when a child is seen in individual therapy for one hour a week and then sent back into a dysfunctional home setting? How much of an impact can a therapist make in the life of an individual given the limited amount of time the therapist has with her during her childhood?

Since the last decade has brought much openness in talking about the abuses which happen during childhood, research data is now becoming available. One very important factor that appears to make the difference in the adult level of healthy functioning is whether or not an individual had someone in her lifetime, whether in childhood or adulthood, who accepted her unconditionally (Garmezy, 1986).

Moustakas (1959/1992) describes unconditional acceptance as: "... one person, a direct, human-loving person, a unified personal and professional self, meets another person, a loving or potentially loving child and through a series of deep human encounters, waits for and enables the child to come to his own self-fulfillment" (p. ix). If these dysfunctional, abused children find anyone to accept them in this manner, it does make a difference!

Selective Mutism

Since play therapy is a therapy of metaphors, it is not necessary for a child to speak in order to participate. Play therapy offers the child an opportunity to express, through metaphor, a reaction to any trauma that may have been a causative factor (Axline, 1964). It also allows an opportunity to address any fears of abandonment or feelings of social inadequacies and shyness. Here, the therapist may find it necessary to initiate family therapy in order to alleviate the abuse or violence that is present in the home. It may simply be necessary to instruct the parents on facilitating the child's independence and risk-taking.

Lack of Empowerment[7]

Another issue, experienced by some adults and almost all children, is the feeling that occurs within a child when she senses that, "Everyone in the world is older, knows better, and is always telling me how to do something." The child tries, but, "It's difficult to do so many things well because there's just so much to learn!" Sometimes, the child's hands, arms, and feet just won't move the way she wants them to. The feeling elicited is, "I'm not as good as other people," or "I'm not as good as I would like to be." Then, the child begins to question her self-worth and finds herself feeling inadequate and powerless. This child responds well to play therapy. Low self-esteem and lack of empowerment is not classified as a disorder but is certainly painful to those caught in the throes of the questions, doubts, and shame inherent in the process of constant self-examination.

Ashley's parents called for help with their seven-year-old daughter after the spring parent-teacher conference during which the teacher had recommended that Ashley be retained in second grade. Having never experienced anything like this in their family before, the parents were concerned about how to manage the situation appropriately. They also were concerned

---

7. This is not a DSM-IV CAPA (1994) diagnostic category.

about allowing Ashley to maintain as much of her self-esteem as possible through the process. After spending time working with the parents on a consultative basis (i.e., talking about their daughter in particular and children's self-esteem in general, and giving them articles to read), sessions began with Ashley.

When Ashley went in for the first session, some typical intake queries and activities took place. She was kept busy the entire first hour with drawing and answering questions.

Toward the end of the intake session, the therapist said, "Well, Ashley, I've kept you really busy today. I appreciate your doing all the things I've asked you to do. I'll tell you what: The next time you come in, we'll just do whatever you want to do. It will be your choice."

Ashley said, "Okay," and then left.

In the next session, she sat down in the playroom and crossed her hands in her lap and sat there very pristinely. The therapist reminded her that from now on they could do whatever Ashley chose — "I'm here, and whatever you want to do, that's what we'll do."

Ashley looked up at the therapist and said in a small, almost fearful voice, "Well, what is there to do?"

The therapist responded, "Oh, there's lots of things in here. There are games and paints and ..." and she named a number of things available around the room.

Ashley was quiet for a minute and then said, "Well, what would you like to do?"

Once again the therapist responded, "There are many things we can do in here, and I would be happy to do anything with you that you choose."

For the next 45 minutes, Ashley and the therapist sat in silence, which is by no means easy to do. Every five minutes or so, the therapist would make a comment like, "Boy, it's just really hard to decide what to do," or "You're just not sure what you want to do," or, "You're just not used to having an adult say 'We'll do whatever you want to do.'" After a while, the therapist was repeating the same comments and not wanting to, so she wound up just quietly sitting there as well. It was a long 45 minutes.

When Ashley went back the next week, she and the therapist again sat in silence. After about 10 minutes of this, Ashley looked up at the therapist and meekly asked, "Could we take a walk?"

The therapist responded, "Yes, of course we can!" And they took a walk!

It took a lot of courage for Ashley to ask this because it wasn't something in the room. As they walked that day, the therapist found every reason in the world why that was the best possible thing they could be doing on that particular day. Ashley was verbally bombarded with empowerment, and that was the course of treatment over the next six months.

The context of the empowerment changed as Ashley grew more courageous about exploring the playroom and playing out her issues. She was seen throughout the spring and over the summer. In the fall, the therapist consulted with her new teacher. Together with the parents and Ashley's newfound confidence, they got her off to a good start. Around November, it was agreed that just before Christmas would be a good time to terminate. On her last day, she bounced into the room saying, "Today I want to play a game, tell a story, take a walk, and draw a picture!" It was a busy day!

Identity Problems

Play therapy is an excellent arena for the child who is having difficulty adopting a life pattern. What better, safer, more accepting place could there be for this child to try on different identities in order to help her find one that feels consistently comfortable? Decision-making becomes taxing for this child since there is no personal foundation upon which to base choices and preferences. Consistent values and morals, an intact sense of self, and congruous patterns of functioning have not yet been achieved. Certainly, childhood is a time of experimentation with different styles of functioning. However, when children are provided consistency in their family of origin, their sense of self initially assumes patterns similar to those of their parents. During adolescence (sometimes sooner) and early adulthood, as the child moves away from the family, these patterns will be tested. However, the child who lives in an environment without this consistency has no model to follow and nothing to provide the initial foundation.

Dissociative Identity Disorder

Dissociative Identity Disorder [formerly Multiple Personality Disorder in DSM-III-R (American Psychiatric Association [APA], 1987)] is generally assumed to begin in childhood (Courtois, 1988; Kluft, 1985). In retrospect, many adults diagnosed as Dissociative Identity Disorder say their alternates began forming between the ages of four and six (Courtois, 1988).

Dissociation may be manifested by the child who is in a trance-like state and experiencing amnestic periods, with fluctuations in behavior and functioning, or it may be as unpretentious as a short period of spacing out. Brief periods of age-appropriate dissociation is not considered a disorder (Putnam, 1991). However, when the level of dissociation reaches the point where the symptoms begin to effect the child's day-to-day functioning, it may appropriately be considered a disorder. Play therapy enables the child or child alters to express themselves in metaphor and allows the therapist to assist in integration of the alters (Fagan & McMahon, 1984).

Obsessive/Compulsive Disorder

Play therapy is effective with obsessive/compulsive children, although the play therapy may have to be adjusted somewhat in order to demonstrate to the child that rituals are not necessary in the playroom. The atmosphere in the play therapy session is so accepting of the child's demonstrating her issues in her own way, that the child may initially struggle with the lack of structure. Given time, however, she becomes more empowered to be free in the expression of her metaphors. Having a sandbox in the playroom and communicating the acceptability of spilling the sand is one way of demonstrating to this child the acceptability of her inner struggles.

Narcissistic Children

Narcissistic children love to be the center of attention. What better place to feel special than in play therapy? An inherent difficulty in working with the narcissistic child, however, is the establishment of the relationship. Since these children do not trust others, it takes time, patience, and persistence to develop the relationship to a point where the child can feel safe enough to disclose through play. Other initial difficulties in relationship-building include the narcissistic child's rationalization and prevarications utilized to justify perceived deficits or defeats, her intense envy and devaluation of others, and the omnipotent control employed in interactions with others (Kernberg, 1989). Progress toward emotional well-being can be expected to be a lengthy process for the narcissistic child.

Client Disorders Where Experiential Play Therapy Will Have a Limited Effect

The following disorders can be expected to have limited, if any, success utilizing a pure form of experiential play therapy. If play therapy is utilized with these disorders, some adaptation to the play format will be necessary. This broad category of disorders includes those that have an organic or biological etiology.

Mental Retardation

Play therapy can be used with these children in addressing the emotional issues surrounding their delay. While they may also be impaired in social functioning, they still have emotional reactions to the painful and sometimes humiliating comments of others. Play therapy is ideal for the child who is struggling with feelings of social rejection. The interpersonal relationship with the play therapist is inherently enhancing for this child (Leland, 1983). In the case of mental retardation due to a lack of psychosocial stimulation, play therapy may be one of a number of treatment modalities utilized in an attempt to bring about improvement in the child's social and intellectual functioning. However, it would be unrealistic to expect play therapy as the sole method of treatment to improve intellectual functioning.

Pervasive Development Disorders: Autistic Disorder and Asperger's Disorder

There have been some forms of treatment with these children that have been called play therapy which have been somewhat successful (Bromfield, 1989; Lowery, 1985). It would not be circumspect to totally eliminate the possibility of using play therapy with these children, but it must be understood from the very beginning that it will not be a typical case and will probably need adaptations. Imaginative and symbolic functions (i.e., play) are deeply affected in these children (Dulcan & Popper, 1991). Children with these disorders perform rituals and stereotypies, such as spinning objects or rocking, and generally lack social awareness (Weiner, 1982). Since symbolic play is where the therapist studies patterns and symbols in order to gain an understanding of the state of being and issues confronting a child, autistic children are not recommended for experiential play therapy as the initial form of treatment.

Childhood Disintegrative Disorder

Children experiencing this disorder may respond initially in a manner similar to the mentally-retarded child. However, once the child loses her capacity for play, the relationship with the therapist becomes the primary, and perhaps sole, benefit to the child.

Schizophrenia — Childhood Onset

Although these children do demonstrate ability for symbolic play, there appears to be no pattern in their play. The ability to distinguish repeated themes is necessary in order to use play therapy effectively. Similar to adult schizophrenics who have tangential speech and loose associations, childhood schizophrenics have tangential play and loose associations. Their play may be more ritualized, with stereotypies such as those found in Pervasive Developmental Disorder. Visual hallucinations are more common with children than with adults (Dulcan & Popper, 1991). Therefore, it is difficult for these children to separate fantasy from reality.

Sometimes, children manifest schizophrenic symptoms or appear to be psychotic when, in fact, they are not. Rather, they are children who have been so severely abused that they have assumed these symptoms as a means of protecting themselves from the trauma. Protective mechanisms may include dissociation, problems with memory, blank spaces, nightmares, and confusion (Einbender, 1991; Gelinas, 1983). Children may also self-injure in an effort to recover from dissociative experience by feeling pain or blocking feelings of derealization (Gil, 1993b). A thorough assessment is necessary to differentiate this severe, abuse-adaptive syndrome from schizophrenia.

If therapists are in an inpatient setting where they have continual accessibility to the child, they can determine when the schizophrenic child is functioning on a higher affective level (i.e., more lucid and capable of communication). Under these circumstances, the child is capable of engaging in play therapy because she is playing symbolically and patterns are evident in the play. While she is capable of interacting with other individuals on a social and emotional level and functioning in reality, play therapy can be effective. However, it will only be effective with these children at this time. Because this is certainly not an occurrence which is predictable, it is difficult to facilitate a scheduled time for a play therapy session.

Attention-Deficit/Hyperactivity Disorder

The pure form of experiential play therapy is not recommended as a modality of treatment for Attention-Deficit/Hyperactivity Disorder. Cognitive and behavioral techniques tend to be used more often with these types of disorders. However, structured or directive play therapy is also gaining in popularity as a treatment style.

Active children are often misdiagnosed as hyperactive (Budd, 1990). Also, children who are experiencing life events that often result in a depressed mood will frequently become active and acting-out rather than lethargic. These behaviors, taken in isolation, frequently lead to a misdiagnosis of Attention-Deficit/Hyperactivity Disorder. However, if a child is truly hyperactive and on medication, the child will manifest as Oppositional-Defiant Disorder. When this is the case, experiential play therapy can be effectual. Once again, play therapy with these children cannot be expected to change the child's physiologically-based hyperactivity but will assist the child in the emotional struggles surrounding her activity level.

Reactive Attachment Disorder

Reactive Attachment Disorder represents a significant portion of the clientele of many child therapists. If a child begins manifesting Attachment Disordered symptoms after infancy, the child is frequently diagnosed as Oppositional-Defiant Disorder or Identity Disorder. These are children who have failed to bond with a caretaker for various reasons (i.e., severe abuse, neglect, or impaired caretaking). The symptoms which manifest in this disorder may include sadistic cruelty. It is common for caretakers to express great concern about some of the actions these children want to inflict on animals or a baby brother or sister.

At first, the Reactive Attachment Disordered child appears to be very charming; this charm, however, is superficial. Because there has been a lack of deep, intimate bonding with a primary caregiver, this child will superficially bond with anyone (Delaney, 1991).

A common statement made by parents, especially when they are adoptive or foster parents, is, "When my neighbors and friends meet my daughter, they all say, 'This child is absolutely charming! I don't believe all those terrible things you've been saying about her!'" The parent, usually the mother because of her role as primary caretaker, begins to question her own perceptions and judgment, wondering if something is wrong with her instead of the child. This child has an amazing capacity for counterfeit emotionality, allowing only those people with whom she feels vulnerable to see the traits for which this child is so well known.

The unattached child is also a master at passive-aggressive behaviors, setting others up to express her anger and rage. A parent, attempting to understand and respond in a healthy, mentoring capacity, describes her daughter, saying, "You know, she just keeps on with these irritating behaviors. I try to teach her right from wrong, but it seems no matter what I say or do, it backfires. It's not really arguing. In fact, it's hard to describe what she does. She just keeps doing it and won't stop until I get angry and out of control. Once I'm angry, she actually seems pleased! In fact, it almost seems as though that's what she wanted all along! Then she'll be fine for a few days until it slowly begins to start again. We're caught in this spiral and can't seem to get out of it."

These children also display a defective conscience. Reasoning with them does not work because they feel no guilt or remorse. They are such masters at projection and denial that, in their minds, things that go wrong are because someone else made a mistake.

Although it is important with any disorder, it is particularly important with Reactive Attachment Disordered children to do a thorough job of intake. Many of these children have experienced some kind of a separation in their past. Some were abandoned and subsequently adopted. Others may have had to remain in the hospital after delivery. In being tended to by a number of different nurses, the child was unable to develop a normal attachment to one single caretaker. Perhaps the child's mother became ill and had to go to the hospital for a while. In any event, when a child has experienced a separation over a prolonged period of time, particularly in the first year of life, it is a good indicator of the possibility of Reactive Attachment Disorder.

These children view others as need-fulfilling objects. However, the unattached child is incapable of reciprocating in a relationship due to a lack of empathy for others and due to the anxiety caused by any vulnerability on the part of the child. Many of the symptoms manifested by these children are very similar to those of the Borderline Disordered adult and to that which has been proposed as a Borderline Disorder of Childhood (Bemporad, Smith, Hanson, & Cicchetti, 1982; Lofgren, Bemporad, King, Lindem, & O'Driscoll, 1991; Petti & Vela, 1990; Wenning, 1990). Because of the similarity to the borderline syndrome and the evidence of organic involvement in that disorder, this syndrome has been grouped with the Constitutional Disorders. Given only the cluster of symptoms described above, with a history similar to that mentioned earlier and no suspected organic involvement, play therapy would be most helpful to these children only in the latter stages of work with them — after they have abdicated the rigid control they maintain on themselves and others.

CHAPTER 2

TOYS:
THE TOOLS OF THE PLAY THERAPIST

How Children Personalize Expression
Through Toys

Over a period of 25 years, hundreds of hours of videotapes of play therapy sessions were viewed, analyzed and critiqued in order to ascertain metaphors, themes, styles, shifts and direction in the play of children. In light of the patterns that soon became apparent, it was noted that when a child is given a variety of toys with which to play and certain toys are chosen repeatedly, it is because those specific toys have special meaning to that specific child. For instance, when a child chooses an airplane, he may have an underlying need to escape, or to maintain distance from the person(s) he is dealing with, or for speed to make sure that he can get away quickly. Therefore, it could be concluded that toys in play therapy are not selected at random but serve as a symbolic representation of a need or deficit.

Toys can be used in play therapy in a variety of modalities (i.e., fantasy play, artwork, therapeutic stories and/or sandplay). Consider the child who has seen one parent batter the other. Two significant individuals in his life are in conflict with each other. Since this child cannot talk about it, he draws a picture of a big cloud and a smaller cloud. He indicates there is rumbling and thunder going on in this big cloud. Then lightning strikes the smaller cloud, leaving dark spots all over it. As the smaller cloud feels the pain from the lightning, it starts to rain. Although the child is talking about rain, in reality he is talking about the pain he is experiencing in this significant relationship. Since getting too close to reality is painful and overwhelming, he has to go outside of reality in order to examine it therapeutically. When he feels safe addressing the trauma with clouds, perhaps he will then utilize objects such as cars crashing or a truck and a car in an auto accident. Perhaps he will bring in animals, such as a bull and a cow, symbolizing a mom and a dad. From there, he might bring it into human figures, then to moms and dads, and then my mom or my dad. It may take all these steps in order for him to finally be able to talk about it — if he ever chooses to do so. If he misses a step and gets frightened, he may need to regress a step or two.

Understanding a child's play in therapy is similar to the scoring of the Rorschach ink blot test (Rorschach, 1921/1942) where a therapist looks for the quality of the response. The first high quality response is human interaction. From there, the hierarchy moves to animal form responses, objects, insects and bugs, and then vistas and horizons. After this, there are body parts and dismembered parts and blood dripping, etc. In other words, the degree to which one moves away from human interaction, or that first high quality response, is the degree of pain one is experiencing. A child who draws dismembered body parts or blood dripping or bones inside an x-ray is in considerable pain. Unless it happens to be Halloween, children do not usually draw these types of pictures. Children who draw them repeatedly are communicating their level of pain.

It is important not to verbalize interpretations of the material children reveal (Miller & Boe, 1990). If they bring it into reality, it is appropriate to stay with them where they go. If they choose to leave it in metaphor and resolve it there, then it is vital to follow their lead and leave it in metaphor. It is possible to retraumatize children by adding content to their play before they are ready. It used to be thought that the more a therapist could pull play into reality, the better the results. However, Milton H. Erickson discovered that it was possible to resolve pain from trauma through metaphor without knowing the content (Haley, 1973). Since children play out their trauma, verbalizing the details of a traumatic event is not important to the child — understanding the situation and resolving the pain is. Children accomplish this through their play. Then, afterwards, if they desire to put any of their work into words, the therapist can help them with content.

This chapter provides a list of *possible* interpretations of the use of the most common toys chosen by children in play therapy. These interpretations are provided for consideration only. The list is not to be used as an absolute, but with the understanding that these are hypotheses to be considered. As the child's play unfolds and the theme(s) becomes apparent, hypotheses can be eliminated, leaving one or a few to be validated in other play sessions. Before discussing these possible interpretations, however, it is important to note certain criteria that should be considered before placing a toy in the playroom as well as some practical guidelines in their use.

CRITERIA FOR TOYS
IN THE PLAY THERAPY ROOM

Toys Must Be Sanitary

The first criterion a toy must meet before being placed in a play therapy room is that it be safe and sanitized both for the child as well as the therapist. Consider, for example, a baby bottle. The first child that comes into the room and puts it in his mouth has just made that toy unsanitary for anyone else. Therefore, it becomes necessary to take the bottle out of the playroom, clean it thoroughly, place it in a ziplock bag, and then put it back into the playroom. As soon as it is taken out of the ziplock bag, it becomes necessary to take it out of the playroom and put a clean one back in its place. In order to accomplish this, it may be necessary to keep about a dozen baby bottles ready for use.

Another example is the use of wigs, which are often utilized with costumes. If a child has lice, then the lice are transferred to the wig and to the next child who uses the wig. Wigs should be periodically checked to assess if they need to be taken from the playroom and sanitized.

A sandbox is an extremely important part of the playroom. However, one cannot just dig up sand from the backyard. The best sand for the play room is purified sand. Frequently, sand needs to be replaced as children contaminate the sandbox with their coughs and sneezes.

Toys Must Be Relationship-Oriented

It is important to have toys that will enhance the relationship between the child and the therapist as well as elicit and facilitate work on the child's relational issues. Any toy that can be used interactively with another person would meet this criteria. Balls, telephones, swords and puppets are some examples of relationship-oriented toys.

Toys That Represent the Reality in a Child's Life

Toys are needed that will allow children to re-enact the events in their lives both in metaphor and in reality. For example, a house, human figures, cars, etc., are toys that are a part of everyday life (Landreth, 1987). In addition, these toys should be easy to manipulate. Bigger is not necessarily better. The size of a toy does not determine its value. Since children are small, the ability of a child to manipulate the toy determines the desirable size.

Toys That Elicit Projective Play

As mentioned earlier, given a variety of toys, children tend to choose toys that have specific meaning to them. This is one of the main themes in toys — toys elicit a projective pull from a child onto the toy. The child can then create a symbolic association for that pull. Certain toys will elicit an emotional response for some children, whereas other toys will tap a response in other children. Since it is not possible to know which toy will elicit a response from a child, it is necessary to have a wide variety. For this purpose, it is better to have toys that are not aligned with popular characters the child may be familiar with from cartoons, television or movies.

Toys That Enable Children to Go Into Fantasy Play

Toys should not be so reality-oriented that children cannot go into fantasy play because they are forced to focus on the reality represented by the toy (Esman, 1983). A good example is a rubber snake. If it is lying on the floor and the child cannot tell the difference between a real snake and the toy one, it could cause so much anxiety for the child that he would lose his empowerment in relation to the toy. More preferable would be snakes that are made of cloth and look friendly. There are times when a child wants a toy to be as frightening as it was for him. In this case, it may be necessary to have two varieties of snakes — one that looks almost real and one that obviously looks like a toy. Children know what they need and can ignore the toy that does not meet that need. They will choose the one they want to use. However, if the therapist has only one toy of that kind, it would be advantageous to have the more benign toy that the child can approach.

Toys That Encourage Decision Making

Toys that encourage problem solving, decision making, change, and closure are also important in the playroom. Legos and Tinker-toys are good examples. Puzzles and games provide these qualities and can be suited to developmental levels of the child. Occassionally, a model kit that interests a child can serve these purposes.

Toys That Enable Children to Create

Children constantly surprise us with their ability to be creative. Their perception of an experience gives them an awareness that, when combined with their creativity and experience, can cause the unexpected to happen. A teacher evaluated a child as being "very limited in his ability ... and unable to do very much." In the play therapy room, however, he exhibited creative and imaginative play. His teacher was amazed to learn this. Because the enriching atmosphere found in the playroom was missing in the classroom, she was unaware of his potential. Children become unlimited when confronted with media like sand, clay and paints. A cardboard box has activated the creative imagination of many children.

What to Do When Children Want to Bring Their Own Toys to Play Therapy

Whenever children ask to bring one of their own toys from home, the criterion that the toy be safe still applies. Of course, when a child does bring a toy, the therapist will have to determine its symbolic meaning to the child.

> *In working with a five-year-old boy whose father had abandoned him and his mother, therapy was progressing well when one day he came to play therapy with his G.I. Joe tank mounted with all the rockets. It was totally armored. The first impression of the therapist was, "Wow, something has really happened!"*
>
> *When the mother came in at the end of that session, the therapist queried, "Something in his life is not right. What's happened?"*
>
> *She replied, "Well, I moved in with this person ..."*
>
> *The therapist responded, "Your son doesn't like it. He isn't comfortable with this situation and, consequently, is on his guard. What do you think this is all about?"*
>
> *All she could say was that she knew he wasn't comfortable with the situation. By therapist recommendation, the next week she arrived home unexpectedly to discover her boyfriend sexually abusing her son.*

Because the child was able to bring his own toy into his session, it expedited this process. The child knew innately what it was that he needed in order to help him in his process.

What to Do When Children Want to Bring Their Pets into Therapy

Because pets are an extension of children, it is very important to give children the freedom to bring their pets into play therapy.[1] In fact, they will bring every imaginable pet from land crabs to snakes to dogs and cats. It usually works best for a child to bring his pet into the playroom during the last 10 minutes of the session. Most therapists prefer that a parent remain outside the office with the pet until time to bring the animal into the playroom. If the pet is brought in at the beginning of the session, the child tends to want to keep the pet in the room the entire time. Then attention becomes focused on the pet, and the child loses his play opportunity.

Since a pet is an extension of the child, it is very important for the therapist to honor the pet — even if it is a snake. In addition, when designing a genogram with the family present, it is helpful to also draw the pet animals into the genogram. Children love this because they feel as though they have been honored in that process.

Practical Guidelines for the Use of Toys

Purchasing Toys

Many toys can be purchased at garage sales for a fraction of their retail cost, although the process may be time-consuming. Some agencies, however, require new toys, the cost of which can be prohibitive. A list of basic toys that will be adequate until others can be obtained is found in Appendix A.

---

1. A philosophy of play therapy based on pet therapy was developed by Levinson (1962, 1964, 1965).

Waiting Room Toys

Recommended toys for a waiting room are those that enable a child to play passively while at the same time activate the child's internal processes. For instance, a water toy with objects that move around inside would offer a child the opportunity to access feelings lying outside the conscious mind. Another toy to include might be one with a magnetic base where metal pieces can be manipulated to different shapes. Toys such as these bring out the metaphor of restructuring or rebuilding, and activate the child's internal processes when he comes into the playroom.

Beads on a wire are good for younger children because the beads can be moved, an embodiment of making change. Magazines with *find-the-hidden-object* pictures allow children to open the magazine and search for something, which again is a metaphor for an internal process of the child. Although the Etch-a-Sketch is a little structured, it applies the same idea — a child sits passively working with it in a creative fashion.

Displaying Toys in the Playroom

Toys displayed on shelves are most effective. If a child is in an important part of his play and needs to add another element to that play by using a different toy, that energy can be diffused by having to take time out to find a particular toy. Therefore, toy boxes are not effective. Not only does it take time to find certain toys, but toys having other symbolic meanings are seen, which interferes with the focus of the child's play. Toys should be placed in the same area of the playroom so children can locate them easily. Some therapists prefer to place nurturing toys in one area while aggressive toys are located in another. Preference is up to the therapist, but toys should be consistently located in the playroom.

Plastic vs. Metal

There are advantages and disadvantages to both plastic and metal toys. Although plastic breaks more easily than metal, it is also not as painful if a child should use that object in a hurtful way. The laws of physics apply:

the mass of a metal car coming toward a therapist is greater than the mass of a plastic car coming toward the same therapist.

Replacing Toys

In play as well as play therapy, toys get broken or cracked or just worn out. It is important that the therapist only have toys in the playroom that he is not attached to so that when one wears out or is broken, the therapist does not suffer from the loss. Toys are tools of the trade that will be used over and over again. There should be a backup supply of the most common toys used. In fact, it is a good idea to purchase two or three, or even four, of the toys most valuable in the playroom.

When a toy gets broken during a child's therapy, even though a backup toy is available, it is not immediately brought into the playroom. This is a good opportunity to see how the child adjusts to the loss of that toy. It is important, however, to make sure that the next time that child comes to the playroom, the toy has been replaced. Otherwise, the child will be disappointed and may experience anxiety or other feelings regarding the loss of that toy. It is a good idea to replace the toy as soon as the session is over so that the next time the child comes in, the therapist can say, "I found a new toy like the other one you liked so much. I brought it to the room so it would be here for you."

Replacement toys do not have to be the same color or exact item, although some children may expect it to be so and find themselves anxious if it is not. If this happens, and it is apparent that the toy is vital to a particular child's therapy, it may be important to make every effort to get one as close to the broken toy as possible.

Anatomically Correct Dolls

Anatomically correct dolls are tools as well as toys. They are tools for a reason and can be in the playroom. Children know they are available, and if they choose to play with them as part of their fantasy play, they may be allowed to do so. However, they should not be forced on children.

Symbolic Meanings of Toys, Animals, and Environments

Following are highlights of some of the more common toys and their symbolic meanings. This list also includes animals and environments. (More complete lists can be found in appendices B, C and D.) Again, it should be noted that this list of possible interpretations of a child's use of a particular toy is provided for consideration only. It is not to be used as an absolute, but rather with the understanding that these are hypotheses to be considered. As the child's play unfolds and the themes become apparent, hypotheses can be eliminated, leaving one or a few to be validated in other play sessions. At the end of each session, it would be helpful for the therapist to write down the five toys most used by the child. Later, the therapist may look up the interpretative meaning of each of these five toys and check for similar themes within them. Perhaps it will be anger in a relationship or feeling devalued or afraid of being hurt. It is also recommended that these interpretations be memorized so that the therapist can see the themes as they unfold.

Airplanes

Airplanes symbolize the need for escape, distance from the issue, speed of escape, freedom from the tensions of an issue, safety in respect to being removed from the issue, protection from a possible perpetrator, or the need to search for something. The distance provided by an airplane can help a child feel as though he is getting protection.

In elaborating on this theme, as mentioned earlier, consider the child who has placed a pickup truck on the ground and then begins to fly over it in an airplane. When the child gets over the truck, he drops a bomb which blows the truck up, and then he flies off. Because he not only needs distance and safety but also a way in which to express anger, he chooses an airplane. If the child could confront the person directly, he would use a different form of play. By using an airplane, he can go down and bop the top of the pickup truck or crash the two together or land the airplane and have the two figures come out and argue or negotiate —

communicating the amount of distance he feels necessary in order to feel safe.

Attacking with the airplane indicates that he feels safe only from a distance, whereas two figures arguing or negotiating indicates that he feels more empowered to communicate on a personal level. It is important to honor a child's need for distance and not identify a character (e.g., his mom or the school ground bully or the perpetrator) sooner than he is willing to reveal at any given moment. Perhaps, it will be necessary to start off by saying something like, "The airplane dropped a bomb on the car," and leave it at that. Another example might be, "The airplane is angry at the car." This is as far as a therapist should go until the child is ready to reveal more.

Animals

Wild animals represent themes of aggression, fear, survival, power and strength. For instance, animals such as grizzly bears, wolves, lions, or animals with teeth (e.g., alligators) often represent perpetrators to children. Domestic animals, on the other hand, represent protection, family, relationships, vulnerability, compliance, dependency, and other more personal themes. These symbolic meanings will basically be the same whether played out using toys, such as puppets or plastic figurines, or modalities, such as acting, drawing, or talking.

Artwork

Artwork is another modality in which metaphors are used therapeutically. If a child gets stuck in his play, a therapist might gently direct his play by suggesting, "Why don't we draw a picture of ... the monster." Directive play, in its true sense, is inviting opportunity for a direction that children can go in if they have the energy and are so inclined. However, when some children are handed a piece of paper and told to draw a person, they are unable to do so because of fear. They still need a certain amount of distance from their core issue. In these cases, children must be provided structure and safety in a relationship before they can follow such a directive. Given the security of the relationship, they can then go to another level through the use of art and put that energy to work and yet still stay in metaphor.

Baby Bottles

Baby bottles symbolize themes of regression to an earlier stage of development; a desire for nurturing; the orality that is present in that first developmental stage where a child likes to put everything in his mouth; coping issues in the sense that it gives a child a release and a way to escape the tensions surrounding his issues; dependency in that it indicates the child's dependency upon someone or something else for his own feelings of safety or security; issues around a new baby in the family or the wish to be a baby; troubles with siblings such as a new baby in the family; or issues of enuresis, as pouring water out of a bottle could symbolize that stream.

Bottles are among the most frequently used toys in the playroom and are used in a variety of ways. For instance, children may play out a scene and then go over and pick up a baby bottle and begin sucking on it, communicating their stage of development during the traumatic event. Children don't tell time on a clock. Rather, they tell time by their experience. In other words, they associate their developmental stage and experiences with the traumatic event, and by so doing communicate the history and duration of the events that were associated with the abuse.

Content and developmental stage of trauma may be intermingled in a child's play. For example, children may take a baby bottle, play out one theme, such as abandonment, and be communicating, "This is what I wished I had received at the time." Usually, the context in which children put their play conveys the stage of development during the traumatic event and the fact that this is the type of nurturing they wished they had received.

Baby bottles can also be a phallic symbol. For instance, children use them as penises in squirting the water into the sand. Another way they are used is to communicate the child's need for comfort when facing the traumatic event.

Balls

Balls represent one of the most basic toys in the play therapy room. For instance, they give a child an opportunity to interact with another individual (i.e., the therapist). They allow the child to maintain feelings of safety by distancing himself from the therapist. Balls also help in building trust between the therapist and child. For instance, as the therapist makes a conscious effort to throw the ball back to the child as accurately as possible, the therapist communicates that he will be clear and consistent with the child, as well as trustworthy — not using any tricks. Because a child's motor skills are not well-developed, his efforts to throw the ball to the therapist may result in the ball going anywhere in the room. Sometimes children will use the ball in such a way as to compete with the therapist. He will use this competition as an empowering vehicle for himself (i.e., so he can win and feel more empowered).

During the initial sessions of play therapy, playing with a ball conveys important information about the child. Since a child is allowed to throw the ball at the therapist in any way he may choose, the ball can be used to communicate what it is like to be in the child's world. This is often one of the first things a child wants to communicate when coming into the playroom. For instance, the child may come into the room, pick up a ball, and want to toss it back and forth with the therapist. Immediately the child begins to throw the ball in a disrespectful way, communicating how he is treated in his world. The therapist will usually have a corresponding feeling, which is how the child feels when he experiences this type of treatment. The child wants to communicate not only his experience but how he feels about that experience. While tossing the ball back to the child in a respectful manner, the therapist could say something like, "I try as hard as I can, but it's hard for me to know where the ball is coming from next. I do the best I can to throw it straight, too." Metaphorically, this play and statement is communicating, "I know that sometimes people hurt you — and it's really scary. In here you're going to be safe, and everything will be predictable; but I know that people do things that hurt you, and you feel sad and helpless to do anything about it."

These types of statements are very common in the first session of play therapy. Again, it is the relationship between the therapist and a child that makes play therapy effective (Landreth, 1993a). In the first few sessions, a child needs to know what a therapist is like. To him, the therapist is just a stranger, another human being like all of the others. This is when the therapist begins the honoring process by being present with the child, honoring what he communicates, and validating his experiences. "Yes, that's true. Your perceptions are accurate. What you have experienced in life, I accept just the way you are telling me." Children are drawn to this type of warmth and support.

Another way the ball may be used is to reevaluate the relationship between the child and therapist. For instance, some children will be deep into traumatic play and then suddenly stop and want to play catch. Essentially, they are indicating a need to stop and see whether or not the therapist still respects them. "Can the therapist be trusted?" "Am I still being honored?" "Is the therapist still willing to take care of me?" This might even go on for two or three sessions before they feel secure enough to go back into their play. The relationship with the therapist must be solid in order for them to feel secure enough to face their trauma.

Binoculars

Binoculars symbolize a perspective in the sense that the child can see what he is looking at in the way in which he so desires. In other words, he has control over what he sees, whether that be close or far away. Often a child will use the binoculars in the first several sessions while checking out the therapist. "Are you going to be the person I want you to be?" The child may even turn the binoculars the opposite way, communicating, "I want to distance myself from you."

Binoculars can also be used in surveillance. This allows the therapist to assess how safe or how threatened the child feels. For instance, a child may use them to look around the room, while saying, "I'm looking for tigers. I've got to keep an eye out for the tigers. You never know when they might attack us."

Binoculars may also indicate that the child is searching for something, as in searching for someone to love him or for his own identity or attempting to find his lost childhood. In addition, they can represent intimacy, as the child brings the object he is looking at closer. At times, binoculars can represent self-examination as when the child begins to look at his own body parts or at a toy that he has chosen to symbolize himself.

This is another toy that is often used in the initial sessions of play therapy. For instance, a child looks around at all the toys, examining them, and then picks up the binoculars. Now, he looks at everything in the room through the binoculars and then stops and looks at the therapist, communicating, "I don't know you very well, so I'm looking you over very closely. I want to know what you're like and how you're going to be in here, because I want to know if you are a safe person."

Often, children will rotate the binoculars and look through the opposite side of the glasses, scan the room, and then stop at the therapist. At this point, it would be appropriate to respond, "Now I'm smaller and further away. It's nice to know that you can make me any way you want me to be — big and close or smaller and further away. I'll be the way you want me to be in here," which is also expressing, "You have a say in our relationship. I'm going to attend to you and let you know that I will be present to the degree and level you want me to be."

Blankets

A blanket offers a child an avenue of regression in that he can take the blanket and use it as would an infant or toddler. He may be desiring comfort or security as he experiences feelings of insecurity in regressing to that stage. A sexually abused child may wrap up in a blanket as a way of protecting his body. It may also represent a child's attempt at establishing boundaries that, in the child's fantasy, cannot be violated by the perpetrator.

Blocks

Blocks offer a child an opportunity to establish strong defenses. For instance, a child can utilize them to build walls that serve as boundaries. They can also be used in construction to help the child in his fantasy play. Blocks can also provide closure for a child in that the child can use the blocks to enclose himself or build a structure, such as a fort, and in this way experience protection. They can also be used as barriers in order to protect one item from another. It may even be a way of protecting himself from a game of war he has set up on the other side of the barrier. In this sense, the child does not have to feel as vulnerable because he has the protection of the barrier.

Sometimes a child lives with a parent who not only sets up numerous rules, but is also inflexible in bending them. Used in this way, blocks are an abstract representation of the rigidity with which the child lives. However, a therapist would not consider that the child was using blocks to symbolize rigidity unless this style of play was done repeatedly.

Although wooden blocks can be used, foam blocks are preferable because they allow children to become more involved in their play. For instance, if a child builds a house or a wall and then wants to destroy it, wooden blocks can hurt if the child kicks them. Because bodily involvement by children means that they are moving toward their core issue, it is important to provide them with safe opportunities to do so. Foam blocks allow children to jump on them, kick them, explode them up in the air, roll on them, or stomp on them without getting hurt.

Books

Books can give a child a way in which to identify some of the issues with which he struggles. There may be a theme expressed in the particular book chosen by the child that represents something that has happened to this child in the past, or an occurrence he fears will happen in the future, or a representation of a current situation. The book may contain a story about a child who is emotionally and environmentally experiencing a situation that this child is experiencing, although it is a secret within this child that he has never been able to disclose. This can also be the case when a young child chooses a book that contains a character's diary.

Books can help a child in establishing an identity. For instance, a child may identify with a character in a story and want to have the story read to him repeatedly. While listening, he will identify with the traits of that character in order to gain those traits for himself to help him through his own struggle.

A child may communicate valuable information to th
merely in the books he chooses to have read to him repeatedly,
books also represent a way in which to acquire knowledge.

Children may use a book itself as a symbol of, for example, a special
time spent with a loved one while reading the book together. Perhaps the
story inside has special emotional significance. Usually if children store
a book and keep it with them, it represents a secret story or a diary of an
account of some event. It's the true story, according to them, as they keep
it in play. They have control of it — only they can read the story, so only
they know the story. In addition, books can be used for metaphorical storytelling. (See Chapter 8 for further discussion of metaphorical storytelling.)

Boxes

Boxes can be useful for a child to hide something in so that it represents
a secret — something that is unknown to others. They can also give a
child a way in which to establish a boundary, provide a place of containment for his emotions, or symbolize his struggles. During fantasy play, a
child may use a box to represent a gift the child is giving to someone else.
A child may also use a box to symbolize himself. For example, he may
take very good care of this box such as making sure it is placed in a location where it is protected and perhaps warm from the sunshine, etc. He
may also put items in the box that make it more valuable, communicating, "There is value in me that others don't see." It will be apparent that
the box or its contents has meaning to the child. However, the material
represented by the contents may be vague unless the child discloses them.

Boxes can symbolize a belief. This occurs when a child knows that
something is true but no one else believes him. The child will then put
the belief in the box and guard it as something important, letting it out
only when he is assured that the therapist will believe him. When that
belief is accepted by someone else, it is a confirmation of the child's
belief and, consequently, of the child. In the same way, a child may put
his dignity in the box, not letting it out until he is assured it will be accepted.

During a child's first session, there is an inner drive to communicate
where he is going in therapy. Sexually abused children, in particular,

want to disclose in the first session that something has happened to them. However, because a trust relationship has not yet been developed, they can't tell the content of what happened. It would be too frightening. Many times, these children find a box in the playroom, put something in it, and then turn to the therapist and say, "I've got a secret in this box, and you don't know what it is."

In this way, they are communicating, "I have control of this event." They know the content, and they can open up the secret in their own time. It belongs to them. They can wait until they have regained their dignity, control, and empowerment. It is very important to understand that they do the disclosing *at their own pace and in their own way.*

It is also important to have a place in the playroom where children can hide. Then they can hide and communicate, "There's a secret in this box!" Or a child can put a blanket over his head and say, "You can't see me, and I'm going to tell you something ..." That inner press to indicate where the child is going in therapy can then be expressed.

Broken Toys

A few broken toys in the playroom allow a therapist to observe how a child processes situations that are not ideal. For example, if the child tosses a toy aside because it is broken, he may be communicating that whenever he does something wrong, he feels as though he gets tossed aside. If a child picks up the broken toy and utilizes it in play or is able to replace it with something else that can be used in the same way, then he communicates that he has enough resources — creativity and self-esteem — to be able to substitute and feel comfortable with the change. Broken toys can also identify how children react to change as, for example, when a toy is intact one session and then the next session the child finds it broken.

Broken toys may also represent the self of a child. For instance, if the child has been abused in some way, he may actually feel broken. The broken toy then represents his identity — his feelings about himself. The child may utilize this toy to communicate the condition of his self-esteem and how he views himself. In the same way, broken toys can symbolize issues within the child with which he is struggling.

A child may also feel a sense of loss from a broken toy. It may remind him of a favorite item that has been broken or lost. It may even represent a loss in his own life such as his innocence.

In addition, when a child gravitates to the brokenness of a toy, there develops a double meaning. There is the symbolic meaning behind identifying with the brokenness of the toy and there is the symbolic meaning behind choosing that particular toy.

Camera

A camera can provide a child with a concrete example of a memory. Children can play that they are taking pictures with a toy camera as a way of communicating what they want to remember in a situation. They want to have something that confirms their memory or perception of an experience. A picture provides this reassurance. Playing with a camera could also represent proof and validation for a child in that a picture is proof that something actually did occur. The picture represents the truth. It can be used as evidence in proving the truth. It can also represent how things have changed. In other words, the picture provides knowledge about an event.

> *Billy is a little boy who went to his mom one day and told her that his dad was sexually abusing him. Believing her son's story, she confronted her husband who promptly denied it. She then called Child Protective Services who also confronted the father. Again, he denied it. Billy was then examined by a physician who couldn't find any evidence of the abuse. Since his mother had been questioning her commitment to the relationship with her husband already, she decided to initiate divorce proceedings. At this point, she took Billy in for play therapy.*
>
> *After the initial Exploratory Stage, Billy picked up a camera and a flashlight and turned the lights off in the playroom. Then, he picked up a doctor's kit, took everything out and filled it with everything of worth — play money, checkers, coinage, playing cards — and set it over in the corner. At this point, he said, "You're over there making drugs to sell."*

The therapist did as the boy requested and pretended to be making drugs. Billy then took the flashlight and shined it on the therapist while taking the camera and clicking a picture of the therapist, after which he said, "Now, I want you to take your drugs over there and sell them.." Again a picture was taken of this event.

At this point, Billy is giving some cues to the therapist about the abusive event — that what happened is a secret, and that it happened at night.

After the drugs were all sold, and the money was received, Billy said, "Spread the money all over the table."

The therapist followed Billy's directions. While shining the flashlight in the eyes of the therapist, Billy said, "Look at me. You are falling asleep."

So, the therapist pretended to fall asleep. Billy walked over to the therapist and took the money, laid it on top of the therapist's head, all over his shoulders, tucked some into his suspenders, around the waist of his pants, in his pockets and shirt buttons and lap and shoes — all over the body of the therapist!

Billy was putting so much emotional energy into this procedure that its importance was apparent. Yet the meaning of the metaphor was unknown to the therapist.

After telling the therapist to look at him, Billy shined the flashlight in the eyes of the therapist. He then took the camera and started taking pictures of the therapist as fast as he could.

As soon as he did that, it became evident that what he was communicating was the fact that all the evidence was there. "I can't lie my way out of this one, because you've got proof that I did it." Billy smiled and nodded his head yes.

It was also obvious that it was necessary for the therapist to communicate to Billy that he was believed. This had to be done before he could go on with therapy. He had just disclosed when and how his abuse had occurred. The therapist continued playing the role of the perpetrator as Billy captured him, took him to jail, and punished him.

Billy is a good example of a child's utilization of a camera to convince others of the occurrence of a situation when they were reticent in believing the child's verbalizations.

Costumes

It is important to have a variety of costumes available in the playroom (i.e., medical personnel, jungle characters, vampire with cape, fire fighter, police officer, fairy godmother, super-hero, astronaut space suit, pirate, robot, western outfit, ghost, soldier, witch, etc.). However, it may not be possible to have all of these costumes. For the therapist, there are two costumes that are very important: an adult male costume and an adult female costume. Sometimes children want to deal with the therapist as if he were a female perpetrator. In this case, the therapist may put on the female costume and play out the role of the perpetrator in the way the child wants it done. If the therapist happens to be a female and the perpetrator was a male, she may have to dress up as the male. By having these two costumes available, children can incorporate a therapist of either gender into their play.

Dinosaurs

Dinosaurs represent the past. This may also be the past history of the child's life. Children can recapitulate situations that have occurred in their past through their play. Dinosaurs are viewed as being very powerful. They are predators and create fear. They can also represent death because they are extinct. A child who fears death may play out these fears with toy dinosaurs.

Dinosaurs may also elicit conflict issues within a child. A dinosaur can represent the fact that a child's environment is one in which conflict is common, along with the accompanying need to struggle for survival. In this case, a child may use the dinosaurs to play out the actual battle that takes place in his life.

Children who are processing the death of a significant other choose dinosaurs more often than any other toy. This is also true of children who are experiencing a tremendous loss such as the death of their well-being.

After being asked to consult with a school district, the author spoke with special education teachers who worked with behaviorally disordered and learning disabled children. His goal was to help them recognize metaphors so that they could better connect with these children in order to effectively teach them. After a positive consultative meeting, the author met with the children and had them sit in a circle. The staff was asked to sit behind the children to observe. The author asked each of the students a number of questions such as, "What would you like to be when you finish your schooling?" "What would you like to be when you are an adult?" "Do you have a pet?" "Tell me about your pet." "How do you care for your pet?"

One young girl responded, "Well, when I get out of school, I'd like to be an archeologist."

The author responded, "Wow! Okay. That's really interesting! What do archaeologists do that interest you?"

"Well, they dig up old bones and find out what happened," she answered.

The author said, "Yeah, that's what they do," without pursuing it any further. With that information, however, he had gained clarity on the child's struggles. After continuing around the circle and then dismissing the students, he had a brainstorming session with the teachers in which methods of forming a relationship with each of the children and motivating them were discussed. When the group discussed the young girl who wanted to be an archeologist, the author asked if anyone were surprised at her response. Unanimously, they expressed surprise, not understanding it. The author then asked what significant person in the girl's life had recently died. The look on the staff's faces was one of collective disbelief. Finally, someone said, "Her father committed suicide five months ago!"

It was then explained that since the girl had no understanding of what had happened to her father, she wanted to be an archeologist in order to dig up old bones and find out what had happened to him. She had gone through the experience but had no organization or content to it. She needed someone to hear her pain, let her work on her issues, and then afterwards add some organization to it so that she could make some sense of it in her own reasoning.

Doctor's Kit

The toys in the doctor's kit include a blood pressure bulb, a syringe, a stethoscope, and a thermometer.

Blood Pressure Bulb. When a child plays with the blood pressure bulb, he may be examining internal issues such as anger, calmness, state of mind, internalized feelings, or a need for change. It is very similar to the thermometer — either the child is calm or angry or experiencing more feelings than being shown.

Stethoscope. A stethoscope can be used to assess internal status. *Internal* may represent both functioning organs as well as the feelings within the child. The stethoscope is one of the most widely-used items in the doctor's or medical kit. It is utilized in gaining access to internal parts of the body (i.e., a child's feelings). These feelings may be unknown or undisclosed to others. The child may initially convey to the therapist that these feelings exist, before he feels comfortable in letting the therapist know any details about them.

This toy is also representative of understanding the internal feelings in a relationship (e.g., closeness) and can be symbolic of opening up, feeling closer to the therapist, etc. It can also symbolize validation of an individual when the child checks to see that there are good things happening inside a person.

A child may take the stethoscope and put it up to his chest and listen. Then he may go over to the therapist and do the same thing. The child is doing this in order to assess the emotional state of the therapist — "Will you hear the emotions in me?"

Syringe. The syringe is usually utilized by a child as a means of inflicting pain. It represents times when the child may have felt physically violated, intruded upon, fearful, or penetrated.

Although a child may be told, "This is for your own good," when a child experiences an injection or other intrusive medical procedure that inflicts pain, he does not experience the beneficial nature. His memory is of the contact and impact which causes fear.

Many times, the syringe is representative of sexual and physical abuse. For instance, the child might say, "You need a shot," while at the same time conveying, "You're not going to want this or like it." In this instance, the child is communicating how it felt to be in his position. In the latter stages of the therapy process, after the child has confronted his pain and issues, he may be able to exhibit more of the standard medical model by saying, "Yeah, you need to have this shot because it'll make you better."

Thermometer. Similar to the stethoscope, a thermometer represents internal status. However, it conveys more information. For instance, when the temperature is high, the child is usually dealing with a person in his life who has a lot of emotionality (e.g., rage, enthusiasm). In essence, the attitude of the child is, "Boy, you gotta' be afraid of this person!" A low temperature, on the other hand, would be cold, frozen, contained, and stifled. In this case, the child is cautious, frozen, and/or hesitant in an area. In addition, the thermometer may represent sickness versus wellness, a need for help, a crisis, a need for change, etc.

Summary of Doctor's Kit. These toys symbolize an opportunity to heal and repair. They can also represent the power of healing or a powerful person, or they can symbolize pain that the child feels with a wish to be healed of that pain. Particularly for children who have experienced a crisis or a trauma, the toys in the doctor's kit can represent life and death.

These toys can represent positive change. On the other hand, they can also be viewed negatively as an intrusion or pain that has been inflicted upon the child by another individual. Sexually abused children have been observed playing out a scenario which demonstrates that being examined by a doctor after an abuse has occurred can be just as painful as the abuse itself. Although the doctor may have been very kind and gentle, this type of exam can be painful to experience.

A theme of body image can also be seen in playing with the doctor's kit. For instance, a doctor may make comments about various parts of the body as being healthy and others as being unhealthy or sick.

Many children with somatic complaints (i.e., headaches, stomachaches, pain in other parts of their body) will want to play with a doctor's kit because they are trying to communicate, "I store my pain somewhere in my body, and that's where it is." Many times, they will focus on an area of their body that has pain. The most common area is the heart, which represents their internal being.

During a training workshop, a mother and son volunteered to be involved in therapy. They were assigned to a therapist by the name of Bob. During these workshops, therapists first meet with the parent(s) for approximately 30 minutes for intake and then meet with the child. The mother went into this first session with Bob and, after sitting there for 10 or 15 minutes, finally said, "This is very difficult for me because, you see, the man who beat me so badly was named Bob and your name is Bob, and I just can't focus on what we're doing."

Bob quickly said, "You know, that should never have happened to you. I want you to know that. And I want you to know that even though my name is Bob, the "Bs" in my name are soft and gentle Bs."

In reality, this made absolutely no sense. However, to the right brain, it cut through the left brain's knowledge and within 90 seconds, she was focused on the interview with her son. At the end of this intake session, they walked out and the mother reintroduced the therapist to her son by saying, "This is Bob, and you can go and play with him."

All of a sudden, the son realized that there had been a shift in his mother's attitude, and that she was now giving him permission to play with this person — he's male and his name is Bob, but he's okay. So, the boy went into the playroom, picked up a foam ball, and played catch with the therapist the entire session. After Bob told him that they had five minutes left, he picked up a stethoscope, put it around his neck, and then proceeded to play catch the last five minutes. At the end of the session, Bob said,

"You know, our time is up for today. I've had a chance to play with you, and I really think it's been a great opportunity for me."

The little boy set the foam ball down on a shelf, put the stethoscope in his ears, put the other end on Bob's chest, and said, "Your heart is in the right place." He then took the stethoscope off, set it down, and walked out of the session.

First the mother adjusted to Bob and passed it on to her son, and then he adjusted to Bob. This therapist did an incredible job in treating this mother and son.

The three major uses of a doctor's kit include, (a) facilitating the getting acquainted process with a person at a deeper level, (b) assessing pain, and (c) demonstrating healing. Usually it is evidence of a crisis disguised as an emergency, possibly an accident or gunshot wound, indicating much internal pain in the body. This is especially true with physically and sexually abused children.

During the initial sessions of therapy, the toys in the doctor's kit will be used to communicate, "Will you hear my feelings? Will you experience my issues the way I have communicated them?" They may also represent getting to know the therapist and building that relationship. In the latter stages of the therapy process, after the child has worked through his issues, he begins to play out wellness exams, which is indicative of his own inner feelings of well-being.

Dolls

When a child plays with a doll, it is usually fairly clear that his fantasy play symbolizes both the child himself and what he is experiencing in his life. For instance, the doll may represent issues of identity, struggles with siblings, feelings of a competitive nature, closeness the child may feel with others, and/or the child's dependency upon his parents.

A child may also use a doll as a means of regressing. He may take a doll and use it in the way in which a two- or three-year-old would play with a doll, indicating the child is experiencing that particular regressive stage. Consequently, it is important to have dolls from infancy to toddler stage in the playroom so that they can be used to convey different developmental stages.

Doll House

The doll house can re-create the family environment. When a child plays in a doll house, the therapist can gain valuable information concerning the child's perceptions of his family, how his family interacts, and subtle attitudes that have been conveyed within the family.

Jimmy was brought in for therapy with the presenting problem of being obsessed with weather. He lived in an area where tornadoes were common. He was highly anxious and compulsive. His parents explained that from the time he got up in the morning until he left for school, and then again after school until he went to bed, he moved the dials on his radio up and down to hear every possible weather report. In addition, he believed that if he went outside, a tornado would come down from the sky and kill him unless he walked directly behind another person. Consequently, when he left his house to go to school, he ran out his door and quickly found another person to walk behind. People looked back at him, confused, because he stayed so close to them. When Jimmy got close to the school, he ran inside in sheer panic and as fast as he could run. If the person he was following started going in a different direction than the school, Jimmy quickly ran to find another person to walk behind. Jimmy only felt safe when he was indoors.

During play therapy, Jimmy set up the doll house until it was perfect. Then, because of his experience with tornadoes, he shook the house, knocked all the furniture over, and literally destroyed the interior of the house. In the middle of this play (representing the middle of the tornado), the telephone rang. He picked up the phone and went, "Yabba, jabba, jabba, jabba," and then slammed the phone down and began shaking the house again from the tornado. He played this three or four times during a session.

During one particular session, while the tornado was destroying the house, he picked up the phone and said, "Jibber, jibber, jibber, jibber. Okay, Mom." He then slammed down the phone. This was the first clue that Jimmy was fighting his mother's compulsive behavior.

Jimmy spent much time making sure the doll house was neat and well-organized. This represented his mother's compulsion to keep their house neat and organized. To her, Jimmy was an interruption to her compulsiveness. As a result, she became angry and yelled at him. Then she used guilt and shame to attempt to keep him under control. Rather than allow him to be a seven-year-old, she tried to make him perfect in the same way that she tried to keep everything around her in flawless array.

Later, it came out in therapy that his parents had taken him to a town that had been destroyed by a tornado. While observing the destruction, they said, "This is what God does when He is angry at you for misbehaving." This was the parents' style of controlling Jimmy. Since Jimmy was unable to be perfect and do everything just the way his mother wanted, he began experiencing feelings of shame, rejection, and abandonment in relation to her. He also began fearing that he would be destroyed by a tornado.

Figurines

Family Figurines. Play with family figurines can provide information regarding a child's perception of authority and power within the family or situation (i.e., who has the power, and how it is utilized); how nurturing takes place within the family; whether there is a possible perpetrator within the household with the resulting need for protection; whether there is any dependency or competition; how the child's relationships function as well as the status of those relationships; the security that is available to the child within his relationships; the acceptance or rejection the child may feel within the family; and family dynamics in general. In other words, play with human figurines is a direct correlation to the child's perceptions of a relationship with another individual.

Male Figurine. Play with a male figurine can illustrate any of the above mentioned issues with a father, brothers, uncles, teachers, sitters, or any male figure. It can also demonstrate modeling to which the child has been exposed.

Female Figurine. Play with a female figurine can also illustrate any of those previously mentioned under *Family Figurines*, as well as issues with a mother, sisters, aunts, teachers, sitters, or any female figure within the child's life. It can also demonstrate modeling to which the child has been exposed.

Girl Figurine. The girl figurine can represent the child herself, a sister, a sitter, or a friend. The child can also use this figurine to play out issues of identity, image, peer relationships, and social interactions.

Boy Figurine. The boy figurine can be utilized to represent the child himself, a brother, a sitter, or a friend. The child can also use this figurine to play out issues of identity, image, peer relationships, and social interactions, as mentioned above.

Baby Figurine. Play with the baby figurine can represent the child's desire for nurturing or for regression. It can also be utilized to play out issues related to the past or issues of competition and sibling rivalry.

Finger Paints

When a child enjoys finger paints, he may be communicating, other than the message contained in the actual drawing, that he enjoys the contact, or that he seeks involvement, grounding, regression, and/or security. He may also be attempting to communicate the emotional impact that a particular situation has had on him.

Usually children who want to finger paint are very tactile. They like to have contact with their struggles. They may be in conflict over their desire for contact and choose finger paints as a means of getting close to their issue. On the other hand, some children who are fearful of relationships and exhibit high anxiety will avoid finger painting. The touch may trigger a memory of a time in which they were touched in an uncomfortable way, or they may be hypersensitive to touch itself. The feel of the finger paints may have an unpleasant association for them. In the therapeutic process, a treatment goal for these children may be for them to feel comfortable while finger painting.

Other issues which finger painting may represent center around feces and smearing in the developmental stage of a two-year-old. Generally speaking, children who want to finger paint use their tactile modality predominantly and desire the physical contact.

Flashlight

Play with a flashlight may indicate a child's desire for control or a need to search, scan, or observe; or it may be an indication of secrecy, fear, or dependency; or it may be that the child perceives himself as a leader, and this is his guiding probe. (See *Lights*.)

Games

Although games are structured, they can elicit important information concerning the child. They may illustrate the structure and control that a child experiences in his life, or the control that he would like to have; a child's attitude toward competition; a child's empowerment level (i.e., does the child feel enough personal power to have the confidence to compete?); the manner in which a child processes situations of success or failure; whether the child is compliant; whether the child asks the therapist to explain the rules or simply jumps right into the game and asserts his own wishes; or whether or not the child is cooperative. Does the child resist the way the game is moving along and, consequently, change the rules in order to control the outcome to meet a need within himself? Changing the rules is not always negative. It may be that the child is simply creative and wants to play the game a different way. Is the child communicating: "You're doing well, and I'm not doing so well, but that's okay," or "I'm doing well, and you're doing well, and that's okay also." Games also reflect a sense of the child's own competency. If the child doesn't feel competent, generally, he will not approach the games made available. If he does, he will have a tendency to give up easily. Again, this is important information concerning the child's self-esteem.

Children often use games to reveal how the world deals with them. If, in the process of playing a game during therapy, it appears that the therapist is going to win, some children will change the rules in order to have a chance to win, communicating, "I have to turn my whole world upside down in order to have a chance." They will change the rules in order to have an experience with a positive, enhancing outcome. There is nothing wrong with this in play therapy because rules have no place in this type of therapy. *Children cannot cheat in play therapy.* Even though the game may start by the rules, those rules lose their meaning in light of a child's need fulfillment.

It is important for children to have the freedom to express their needs. If the child feels like life has cheated him, his play will include cheating because this is what he has experienced in his world. Consequently, the mood in the playroom should communicate to children that it is safe and permissible to express their needs and desires. It is permissible to meet those needs and desires in whatever ways are available. The purpose of all the games and toys is to assist children in expressing their needs.

Occasionally, a child will structure a game so that it becomes incredibly easy for him to win. This may be the child's way of communicating his perceptions of his world as being a place where he feels no personal power. Sometimes, a child will play a game and allow the therapist to win every time. This type of response tends to occur in children who come from alcoholic dysfunctional families. Because of the atmosphere in which the child lives, his attitude becomes one of being the caretaker. He has become accustomed to putting his own needs and desires last. These children are apprehensive about provoking anger in the adults in their lives for fear of being hurt themselves. The potential is there for both emotional and physical abuse.

These children become so focused on taking care of the adults in their lives that they're unable to feel their own emotionality. When they remain in this style of functioning in play therapy and are too fearful of taking the risk to do otherwise, it may be necessary to become somewhat directive in suggesting a different style of functioning within the framework of the play. For example, the therapist might say, "Let's do something different. I'll be you and you be me. Let's switch sides." Then the therapist might say, "You know, I have to make sure that you're happy, because if you were to get angry, I'd be really nervous. I've got to make sure you are taken care of. It's not important for me to win. I would rather you win." Even after the honoring stage has successfully built a trusting relationship, this type of intervention can only be utilized at a time when it fits in with the child's play of the moment and encourages the child to risk stepping outside customary safety practices. When a therapist offers a direct suggestion, it is important to note that the child always has the right to refuse.

Communication with the child in this manner frees the child to begin his play about protecting himself from the emotions of others. In this case, it is important to help the child feel empowered personally, but to do so in such a way that he still maintains his safe stance in the presence of his caretaker. It is necessary for him to judge, however, the safety of each new person and each new situation. The end result of this treatment is that the child can begin to put his energy into being a child and into recognizing that the origin of the difficulty lies not within himself, but within the adult.

> *Jason was a young boy brought in for therapy by his father who revealed that after he and his wife had divorced, his wife had moved to a different state some distance away and had taken Jason with her. His older brothers and sisters stayed with their father in their home state.*
>
> *One summer, Jason flew out to visit them. His older brother, who was 22, went to pick him up from the airport. On the drive home, the older brother noticed that Jason was very different from his last visit. He said to Jason, "What's happened to you?"*
>
> *"Nothing," Jason replied.*
>
> *The older brother persisted, "Jason, something has happened to you. What is it?"*
>
> *Jason said, "Well, nothing has happened to me. I don't know what you mean."*
>
> *Finally, the older brother pulled the car over and said, "No, Jason, tell me what happened to you."*
>
> *At this point, Jason began to share the following story. His mother was living with a truck driver. After school was out in June, the truck driver said, "Would you like to go on a trucking trip with me?" Thinking this would be an adventure, Jason had said yes. Rarely was he allowed out of the truck until it was time to go back to school the next fall. Every abuse one can imagine a child encountering occurred to this boy in that truck. He was sexually abused with a gun in his mouth. Knives were held to*

him. When the driver stopped to eat, he tied and gagged Jason and left him in the cab of the truck. Even his food was rationed. The only time he could get out of the truck was late at night at a rest area, miles from anywhere. Then, because it was dark and he couldn't run anywhere, he was allowed to get out and go to the bathroom.

When Jason called to talk with his mother, his calls were monitored by the truck driver so that all she heard was that he was having a good time and wanted to stay while they picked up another load and went somewhere else. The mother responded with, "Well, if you're having a good time, go ahead and go to ..." She was unaware that the truck driver had threatened to kill both Jason and his mother if Jason said anything about what was happening. Jason's entire summer was spent living under these circumstances in the truck.

The next summer Jason flew out to visit his brothers and sisters. The older brother, only 22 years old and not trained in any mental health field, was the first person to notice that Jason was different.

When Jason finished telling what had happened, his brother reached over and said, "Jason, this never should have happened to you. You didn't do anything to cause any of this to happen; but we have to tell someone. You need help in dealing with this."

Even though Jason did not want to go, the brother took him straight to Child Protective Services where he was interviewed. After struggling through telling his story, the social worker said that because it had happened in another state, their office had no jurisdiction. After telling Jason he needed to go to the district attorney's office and tell it all over again, Jason screamed, "No, no, no, no, I can't tell anyone."

At this point, his brother took him home. The next day, with the encouragement of his father, brothers, and sisters, Jason went to the district attorney's office. When they finished the interview, the person in the district attorney's office said, "You need some help and some therapy." At that point, Jason and his father were referred to Victims' Assistance where they were given the names of three counselors.

On Jason's first visit to the playroom, he was extremely frightened. To him, the playroom looked like the cab of an 18-wheeler. Because he was in a new place with a stranger, he began experiencing the same fears that he had experienced in the truck. Only this time, he was alone with a different stranger — the therapist. Aware of this potential, the first thing the therapist said was, "Jason, I know that a lot of people have asked you a lot of questions about the things that have happened to you; but I want you to know that I'm not going to ask you any of those questions. What I want to do today is just get to know you." They spent the session just getting acquainted with the room and with each other. As he was leaving the room, Jason saw the Monopoly game and said, "I just love Monopoly! Can we play Monopoly?"

The therapist responded, "Yes. The next time you come in, we can play Monopoly."

At the beginning of his next session, the therapist said, "Well, Jason, I remember that you wanted to play Monopoly. Is that what you would like to do?"

Jason said, "Yeah!"

The game was brought out, set up, and they started to play. Jason took the dice, rolled them, and moved his figure. The therapist then picked up the dice and did the same. Jason picked up the dice again and, as he was holding them in his hands, said, "Nobody knows how bad it really was in that truck." He then began to disclose what had happened. All of a sudden, his pain and anxiety became so intense that he could no longer talk about it. He rolled the dice and started to play the game again. The talking stopped. Then, after the therapist took his turn, Jason picked up the dice and said, "You know, the worst thing about being in that truck ..." and began talking about it again. When his anxiety became more than he could stand, he took the dice and began playing again. He alternated between playing the game and talking about his experiences on the truck. In this way, he was able to maintain control of the therapy process. The metaphor for the game Monopoly involved New York, Tennessee, Virginia, etc. In other words, it involved traveling from one part of the country to the other. Also, he chose the race car, a form of transportation, and used it as his mover. The game Monopoly

*was the modality in which he was able to replay that experience,
but this time with control and security.*

Because of Jason's experiences on the truck, one would think that he
would have chosen trucks and cars in the playroom to play out his trauma. However, Jason didn't do so. Rather, he went to the Monopoly
game. This game contains an exchange of money which represents value
and worth. The truck trip that Jason went on stole his value and dignity.
By playing Monopoly, he created a metaphor that enabled him to work
through his issues in his own way. Every child is unique in his choice of
a metaphor. The first time around the game board, the therapist was not
aware that, in effect, Jason was on the truck trip, playing out his issues.
However, every time a game is played, it is never just a game. It is always
a symbol of life. Because this therapist believed in the potential of the
child to direct his own therapy, the therapist provided Jason with enough
choices of toys and games to be able to design his own metaphor.
Children are brilliant in utilizing toys to create a metaphor that meets their
needs.

Grooming Utensils

When children play with grooming utensils (e.g., comb, mirror, lipstick,
etc.), they are communicating their attitudes about their self-image and
self-concept as well as any thoughts they have about a desire for validation, caring, or nurturing. Grooming items, when used to excess, along
with other indicators can be warning signs of possible gender identity
struggles and/or sexual abuse. These toys utilized appropriately in the
final phases of play therapy indicate confirmation or validation of one's
self-image.

Guns

Guns offer a child an opportunity to express his aggression, anger, hostility, need for power, and the need for some control in his life. They can
also illustrate feelings of being intruded upon, as with the intrusion of a

bullet within the body, both in the sense of the physical pain that occurs as well as the impact it has on the child emotionally. This pain could symbolize having been sexually or physically abused.

Guns can also give information on a child's attitudes about death, as well as provide an avenue for protection and boundaries. For instance, a child might say, "Don't come any closer, or I'll shoot you!" Some children will strap on a gun and wear it the entire session, communicating their need for protection. Other children will pick up a gun and shoot something in order to create death so that they can process internal issues with death.

Many parents are against their children playing with guns. However, once the purpose of guns in the playroom is explained, they are more tolerant. Whenever children play with guns under the supervision of a play therapist, it is different play than merely recapitulating the violence they witness on television each night. In the playroom the therapist is there to help facilitate resolution for the child on any issues he has attached to that gun. Once the issue is resolved through play, the gun will no longer be a necessary tool for that child. Then, if he has involvement with guns outside the playroom, he has a different attitude about them.

If the use of guns in the playroom is explained to the parent, and the parent is still not accepting of the use of guns in the playroom, it presents a conflict. The issue that surfaces between the parent and therapist is very likely the same issue with which the child is struggling. Since parents are part of the treatment plan, it is important for them to align with the therapist. If they cannot resolve the question of the use of guns in therapy, there may be conflict all the way through therapy, which will hinder the progress of treatment.

When children go into fantasy play, they unconsciously know that a traumatic event should not have occurred. It is important to allow children the utilization of every method they can create to return to that occurrence through play in order to regain their sense of empowerment, control, and dignity — even foul language or the use of toy guns. If this is not allowed, they will play their aggression repeatedly which ends up being rehearsal-for-life play and may lead to abuse of their own children or spouse, or to a pattern of violence. Rather, it is better to have a gun in play therapy in order to elicit the child's projections and then work with them using that gun than it is to eliminate the tool of resolution. By not allowing the child to play with the gun in play therapy, the message being communicated to the child is, "You cannot deal with emotions that are created by this event." Generally, however, if guns are not made available in the playroom, children will create one or something else of a similar nature, such as a fire where everything is destroyed. It is not possible to stop the expression of pain created from the violation of the child and the resultant energy created in the name of self-preservation.

Keys

Keys can disclose information about a child's need for containment for his own protection. In other words,

> *I need to contain this threat to me, and the way I do this is to lock it up. It gives me a sense of control in that I can have the ability to set a boundary. No one can get to me to hurt me.*

Boundary issues usually include keeping something contained that the child doesn't want out of control or keeping someone out who would come toward him without being in containment. In addition, keys may represent the inability to move into an area — not being able to go somewhere.

Usually, keys represent keeping something away from the child. It can also be the key to a secret or treasure or represent the unlocking of a new area of experience. Again, the child has control over how and when he confronts what is behind the locked door, or when he reveals the secret.

Kitchen Dishes

Play with kitchen dishes or a kitchen set allows the therapist to gain information as to the attitudes about the nurturing a child receives within the home environment, and the care he receives through that nurturing. It may also reveal whether the child is being neglected. This type of play also reveals information about the child's familial relationships — for instance, who does the cooking, who gets the food, and how mealtime is handled. The process of preparing the food and getting it on the table can also demonstrate emotional support. The person providing the food may be doing it in a very calming, reassuring, facilitative style of communication. The opposite may also be true. Since almost every issue will relate in some way back to a form of nurturing, the use of kitchen toys enables these types of issues to be addressed.

Nurturing issues often involve food. Children refer to poor nurturing as bad food (e.g., poison, bad, dead, yucky, icky, etc.). For instance, a child may say, "Eat poop." If, while eating the poop, the child is also playing a role and yelling at the therapist, he may be communicating not only about the poor nurturing but also about the emotional abuse he is experiencing.

When children have had good nurturing, they refer to food in a positive way (e.g., sweet, good, or preferred foods, such as pizza, hot dogs, hamburgers, etc.). One of the most soothing and caring acts with a child is to have a tea party, using the foods the child wants to eat. This will be played out later in therapy after the child has addressed his issues.

Knives

Knives provide a child with a means by which to express his aggression. In that sense, they could be called utensils. They also provide a means for the child to demonstrate his power. In addition, knives can provide a child with the opportunity of defending and protecting himself, and demonstrating his sexual violation, as well as the intrusion and pain he felt from that abuse.

During the first session with three-and-a-half-year-old Nicole, she found a teddy bear, picked it up, and held it close to her body. It was obvious that the teddy bear was an extension of herself. After caring for it, she moved it away from herself and laid it down. She then ran her fingers across a chalkboard and then took the chalk dust and sprinkled it all over the stomach of the teddy bear. The chalk dust represented dried semen on her stomach. At that point, she disassociated, grabbed a knife and, while the look on her face was one of intensity, stabbed the teddy bear repeatedly, symbolizing the pain she had experienced while being sexually abused. This all took place within the first 15 minutes of her initial session.

When a child does not take the time to build a relationship with the therapist but begins traumatic play immediately, this indicates that the abuse is still current. Immediately entering traumatic play without first addressing the issue of a relationship with the therapist is a child's way of crying out for help. This occurs when the pain from the trauma is greater than the need for a relationship. When the abuse is not currently occurring, a child can first build a relationship with the therapist.

Lights

Lights can be utilized by children to communicate messages of power and control. If the child is the one in control of the lights, then he feels powerful. He knows he is in control. It is important, therefore, to allow children to turn the lights on and off. In addition, children should have control over when the light comes on and when it goes off.

Lights can also allow a child to play out secrets. To a child, playing out a scenario in the dark is not necessarily disclosing the secret. This type of play may occur at a level where the child's consciousness will allow him to look at all the details at one time. Because the child may be too fearful to disclose all the details to the therapist, he can hide it in the dark. His play is more intense. In this way, the child can also use the dark as a form of denial. In other words, the child can play it out in the dark, turn the lights on, and then deny that it ever happened.

When the lights are turned off, it symbolizes nighttime. Many times, when children play out their sexual abuse, they will turn off the lights and play as though they are in a bedroom. This is the child's way of communicating that his abuse occurred at night in the dark. Since children are usually in their bedrooms at night, this type of play is a possible indicator of incest.

It is also important that flashlights be made available in the playroom, because they, too, represent power and control over a secret event.

Magic Wand/Crystal Ball

A magic wand offers a child the chance to be powerful. When he feels as though he is in a helpless situation, a magic wand can give him the power to make the changes that he would like to see made. In fantasy play, this toy also allows a child to achieve his wishes and goals concerning how he would like his life to be in the future. Usually a child will take the wand, hold it in his hand, and then play out a wish while carrying the wand around. He will let it be known that it's a wish that things were different rather than the way they are. They don't come right out and say, "I'm making a wish my life was better." That would be too direct. Rather, the child will take the wand, keep it with him, and play that he is taking a train to his grandma's home, and, "It's the best place in the world to be." The child is expressing a wish to live at Grandma's house instead of his own home. Then, if the train ride is bumpy or the train breaks down, the child will be communicating what is happening in his own family, what he is trying to move away from, and the fact that he wishes the problem would go away.

Model Cars, Planes, Etc.

When children will or will not spend time working on building models, it gives the therapist information about the child's consistency, motivation, focus, persistence, goal-directed behavior, need for validation, and desire for completion of a task. Then, as the child works on the model, the therapist can empower the child with the resultant improvement in self-esteem. Construction of models is seldom used in play therapy, however. It is more often used with children between the ages of eight and 11, and usually more in the occupational, recreational forms of therapy.

Money/Gold Coins

For a child who constantly struggles with empowerment, play with money or anything representing money can symbolize power, control, security, loss, or a sense of being cheated. How the child plays with money often represents his own feelings of self-worth and value. Some children will hoard money because they know that they're valuable but feel like no one else recognizes their worth. Children whose dignity has been stolen will rob a bank and steal all the money. It is also common for children to hide money in the sand, symbolizing how no one sees any value or worth in them. Then they like to find it themselves or later in therapy have the therapist find it, which communicates, "Now someone else is finding value in me." Then the child will begin to play a game of hiding it and letting the therapist find it because the therapist is the one seeing his value. As the money comes to the surface, the child is communicating, "You are seeing my value."

Children also use money as power. If they can control the money, they're in control of all the power.

There is an intense energy in the use of money. Later, after the child has faced his issues, the intensity will diminish and money will return to being used more casually. For instance, they may play store and use money simply to purchase everyday items.

Monster Figure

Not only can a monster figure symbolize a perpetrator, but it can also symbolize the child's fears, ambivalent feelings, fantasies, aggressive tendencies, conflict in relationships, and desire for revenge. It is the nondescript, nonidentifiable experience of the perpetrator or person in the child's life with whom he is having difficulty. The emotional connotation of this person is usually negative, difficult and/or fearful. The child feels out of control. It may also represent something in his life that is mysterious, unknown, secretive, or fantasized, that the child sees as representing a danger to him.

Musical Instruments

Musical instruments of all kinds offer a child an avenue for self-expression, communication, creativity, contact, and introspection. Because they can be played pensively, enthusiastically, quietly, loudly, etc., they represent the mood and attitude of the child. When a child is struggling and angry, he will not be gentle with an instrument. Instead, he will take the instrument and slam it down or, for instance, beat the drum or rake across the guitar, making a cacophonic sound. On the other hand, when a child feels nurtured, he plays gentle songs with soothing sounds (e.g., "Twinkle, Twinkle, Little Star"). Because musical instruments are a way of communicating feelings without words, they are an important addition to the playroom.

Paints

Children may use paints to distance themselves from their issue. In the painting, they may depict their pain without any content (direct awareness or disclosure) applied to it. Instead of indicating that it was painful when Mom beat him, a child may depict the pain without identifying that it was caused from a physical assault. Painting offers a means of expressing inaccessible needs, attitudes, and postures in the world.

Pillow

A large pillow in the playroom may become many different objects, depending on the child's needs and creativity. In that process, it can express safety and relaxation, or it may become a burden. It may symbolize territory, power, a parent, or a monster. The child may use it as the recipient of his aggression and frustration.

Playing Cards

Cards may be used by the child in unexpected ways. They may represent money, control, power, secrets, or even spontaneity. They also have the aspect of being relationship-oriented with therapists. Many times, children will play a game in which they will win because of the need to feel powerful. When children give all the face cards to themselves and all the numbered cards to the therapist, they are communicating that they have all the power and are in control. Sometimes, children will use cards as money. They may even throw them up in the air to celebrate or throw them at a target such as a waste basket.

> *When Jessica played with the cards, it was apparent that she had an issue with men. Every time the jack came up, she had an anxiety reaction. Yet there was no reaction to any of the other cards. She made the queen more powerful than the king. Then the queen was stronger than the king and the jack. The king was more of a father figure and the jack, an older brother. During therapy, she dealt with family issues and feelings of empowerment as a female that were not being acknowledged at home.*

Many times, children who are angry come into the therapy room and play the card game War. These children play out their ongoing feelings of conflict with relationships. Other children play highly competitively, having to win every game.

Some children will take a deck of cards, set the deck down, and only hand to the therapist the cards they want him to have. Then, they play War, and the therapist gets demolished. These children are really saying, "In my dealings with other people who are in power, I get demolished." At that point, the therapist can feed back the experience of being devestated: "Whoa, I don't have a chance! I think I'm going to win and, boom, I'm gone. Well, I won this little one, but it's not going to help me in the end." In this way, children hear that the therapist understands their experience.

Puppets

Puppets can offer a child an avenue by which to disclose information regarding his perception of his relationships. They can also disclose impulses within the child that create discomfort. By projecting onto the puppet, the child can disguise issues and feel as though he is maintaining a sense of anonymity. Puppets also give a therapist information concerning the child's communication styles.

Often, a child will pick up an animal puppet such as a lamb and, by the way he uses it, begin to let it be known that he identifies with it. He will either use it in dramatic play or relate to it (e.g., hold it and stroke it while commenting on its softness) and then transfer that puppet's characteristics into his play. The next common action is to put the lamb on the therapist's hand because the child wants the therapist to know what it's like to be him. For instance, a child might put a lamb on the therapist's hand, grab a wolf puppet, and come at the lamb. What this child wants the therapist to say is, "This shouldn't be happening to me; this really scares me! You make me do things I don't want to do, and it really hurts me!"

If a child takes a lamb and says to the therapist, "Why don't you take one of the other puppets," the therapist must be very careful in deciding what puppet to choose, realizing that animals such as grizzly bears, wolves, lions, or animals with teeth (e.g., alligators) represent perpetrators to children. Consequently, if the therapist were to take the wolf and say, "Hello," the violation has just been recapitulated, and the child may stop his play immediately. It is best to ask, "Which one would you like me to have?" By responding, "Take the wolf," the child communicates that he is ready to confront his perpetrator and feels the empowerment to confront this issue more directly. In this case, it would be appropriate to take the wolf.

The child may persist by saying, "No, I told you to take one. Just take one!" In this case, it is important to take a puppet that most closely matches the style of puppet that the child is using. For example, if a child is holding a lamb, the therapist might take a baby kitten. Because it is important not to take the play beyond the child's pacing to a point where the child becomes uncomfortable, the therapist should pick a puppet that is at the same level of empowerment the child is using in setting the scene.

A variety of puppets is desirable (e.g., human form, animal form, vampires, bats, spiders — all levels of distancing). Although it is difficult to find object puppets such as cars, it is desirable to have puppets representing as many different levels as possible — from human to domestic and wild animals to insects to monsters — so that the child can enter his play at the level at which he needs expression.

Puzzles

Puzzles may provide information pertaining to the child's problem-solving skills, need for closure, integration ability, and sense of or need for accomplishment. His approach to the puzzle also illuminates the child's level of confidence in his abilities. Decisions made in the process of completing the puzzle will illustrate problem-solving methods the child has had modeled for him.

> *Each time Shawn was in therapy, he would put together a puzzle but leave one piece missing. In every session, the missing piece was in a different place. He would never complete the puzzle. In essence, Shawn was communicating, "My life isn't complete. There's a hole in my life. A significant part of me is missing."*

Sandbox

Sand allows children to construct an entire world if they so desire. In addition, they can build a world and then destroy it. In this sense, children demonstrate their hopes and then how these hopes get dashed. Sand allows the therapist to evaluate how the child perceives his environment and community — for instance, his school, home, or neighborhood — as well as how these environments go through change. Sand provides a unique way in which to express one's creativity. It represents the child's emotional world — his feelings and the changes in his life. It is absolutely the most important item in a playroom. More children incorporate the sandbox into their play than any other single item.

Sand provides a wide variety of experiences for children — touch, texture, pouring, and smoothing, to name a few. In addition, more than any other avenue in the playroom, it gives a therapist mental status information about children. In fact, sand can be equated with a child's emotionality. For example, some children will take a container, fill it with sand and, in finding that it has a little lump of sand on the top, press it down, add more sand, and repeat this many times, displaying pressured play. Another example is that of the child who is highly anxious. These children often take a container, fill it with sand, and then wipe off the top of the sand until it is smooth. This will be repeated many times, communicating not only a high anxiety level but also a desire for their life situation to calm down. In some cases, children may be so anxious that they cannot tolerate the feel of the sand on their hands.

Tanya, a six-year-old girl, was very restricted in her play. During her first session in the playroom, she went to the sandbox and tried to get the sand as smooth as possible. In the next two sessions, she took a marble, hid it in the sandbox, and had the therapist try to find it. Then she would have the therapist hide it so she could find it. She was searching for her identity and worth. This theme began to ring clear in all her sessions.

Finally, she began pushing the sand out from the center of the sandbox toward its edges, while at the same time being very careful not to spill the sand. During one session, the therapist spilled a small amount of sand on the floor to see how the child would respond. Tanya almost froze. Then the therapist said, "You know, it's okay if the sand spills on the floor. It's okay in here."

Tanya continued to move the sand around, right up to the walls of the sandbox, but not over it. Again, the therapist spilled a little more sand on the floor outside the sandbox to see how well Tanya could tolerate it. After the therapist did this, Tanya said, "Well, you spilled." This time, however, the therapist noticed Tanya's anxiety over spilling the sand had lessened.

Over the next several sessions, Tanya started moving the sand right up to the edge of the box, yet not letting any go over the edge. The therapist began putting some sand on the edge of the sandbox. By doing so, the therapist was giving Tanya permission to do the same.

During her seventh session, Tanya put the sand right up on the edge of the sandbox but wouldn't let any spill over. She kept it within the boundaries of the sandbox by keeping her hand against it. During this session, the therapist decided to again spill some of the sand over the sandbox. The therapist played in the sand for a while and then again took her hand and spilled some on the floor. When Tanya looked at what the therapist was

*doing, the therapist said, "You know, sand can spill on the floor;
and in here it is all right."*

*During the next session, Tanya put the sand on the edge of the
sandbox and then knocked the sand off the outer edge and onto
the floor. During her last session, Tanya came in, started playing
in the sandbox, and then began throwing the sand out of the sandbox. She threw all of the sand out of the sandbox onto the floor.
That night, she went home and said to her mother, "I've got something to tell you. Daddy's been touching me all over my body;
and I want you to know I won't tell anyone because I know he'll
go to jail. But I decided to tell you."*

*She was so constricted, it took all that time to gain enough
courage to disclose. The entire process in the sand was a
metaphor for relaxing her control and fears. First, she smoothed
the sand, communicating, "Do I look all right?" Then she hid
the marble in the sand and let the therapist find it, which was her
way of asking the therapist, "Do you see value in me? Am I
worth hunting for and staying with and searching and seeing my
value?" When she asked the therapist to hide the marble, she
was saying, "Do you see value in me? I see value in me. Our
relationship is important, and the interaction is meaningful to
me." The next phase began when she broke the sand open and
pushed it to the outer edges of the sandbox. At this point, her
actions were a metaphor for, "I'm starting to open up to having a
relationship with you." The sand against the side of the sandbox
represented the pressure she was feeling internally with regard to
confronting a boundary. In the sessions that followed, she experienced putting the sand closer and closer to the edge and having
some spill over. Again, she was continuing to confront that
boundary as well as learn that it is okay to be messy — in other
words, "You can be messy and still be okay." When she threw the
sand out of the box, this was a metaphor indicating that she could
relax her controls and still be all right. Going through all these
stages gave her the courage and permission to tell her mother
that she was being violated. Prior to her disclosure, there had
not been enough input to know the abuse was taking place. Until
she added the content to supplement her play, the reason for her
constriction was unknown.*

A common question involving the use of sand concerns whether or not children should be allowed to throw it up in the air. Not only can sand get all over the playroom, but it can also get into people's eyes, hair, and clothing. In this type of situation, it seems most appropriate to use clinical judgment to determine if the possible damages are greater than or less than the possible gains to be made by allowing the sand to continue being thrown. If it is determined that the child is throwing sand to test for protection, then limits should be imposed. In Tanya's case, it was appropriate.

Sand-Bottom Bop Bag

How a child chooses to play with the sand-bottom bop bag provides a wealth of information about the level of frustration and conflict in the child's life. The child who uses the bag in an aggressive manner provides information concerning a relationship in his life. He is also communicating his desire for power and revenge. In addition, the bag may be a substitute for a perpetrator. On the other hand, it may also serve as a nurturing tool (i.e., a bed or a boat to get to safety). Similar to a pillow, the use of the bop bag depends upon the child's issues and creativity.

Sharks

Sharks symbolize an aggressive individual. A child may use a shark to demonstrate the fear that he feels from a person who he sees as dominant over him. It may be a perpetrator, or it may just be a person who misuses power.

> *One Thursday morning, Child Protective Services picked up a little five-year-old girl by the name of Kristi. She had arrived at kindergarten so badly beaten that her whole face was black and blue and her eyes were swollen shut. The service took her to the hospital where stitches were placed in her nose, mouth, and cheeks. They then interviewed her parents who denied having*

hurt the girl. In fact, not only did the mother deny abusing Kristi, but her father stated that he had not even noticed anything wrong with Kristi before school that morning. Kristi was placed in protective care.

The following Monday morning, Kristi was scheduled to see a play therapist. Upon arriving in the playroom, she went right into her play, rather than milling around and taking some time to get to know the therapist. (This indicated the abuse was current.) She picked up a little plastic child figurine and a frying pan. Then she picked up some clay and made it into eight or 10 balls and put them into the frying pan. After this, she picked up a shark and put it down beside the frying pan. After putting this all together, she picked up the child figurine and began to play. First, she went over and picked up the shark. The shark then grabbed the figurine in its mouth, shook it, twisted it, and then threw it down. Then she went over, took the first ball of clay, and stuck it in the shark's mouth. She repeated this until all eight balls were stuffed in the mouth. She had to press very hard to get all the clay balls into the shark's mouth. (This is a form of pressured play, communicating the intense emotionality related to the event.) After the shark's mouth was full, Kristi took it over to a make-believe bed, and the shark went to sleep. She played this scenario over and over until she was informed that it was time to stop playing and put the toys away.

Until this session, each time the social worker had asked Kristi who had hurt her, she would not answer. When the social worker consulted with the therapist regarding the session, the therapist explained that Kristi couldn't disclose who hurt her without breaking the family secret. However, from the associations, symbols, and metaphors in her play, it was possible to determine that whichever parent ate a great deal and slept much of the time was the perpetrator.

At this point, the social worker fell back in her chair. She then explained that not only did the mother weigh close to 300 pounds, but every time the social worker had been to their home in the last four days, the mother had been in bed. She immediately went and confronted the mother, who finally confessed that she had been the one who had beaten Kristi.

Through metaphor, Kristi spoke and was heard. Children communicate through indirect ways and, as therapists, we must understand that
language.

Soldiers

Soldiers allow children to express conflict, aggression, force, life/death
struggles, and fear of annihilation. This is similar to the manner in which
sharks are used. They may also be used to practice grouping or to show
group feelings.

> *Joey is a little boy who communicated about being emotion-*
> *ally abused by using a shark and toy soldiers. He picked up the*
> *soldiers and put them in the sand. He then took a shark and*
> *waved it over the top of the soldiers. Each time the shark went*
> *over the soldiers, he took his finger and pressed the soldiers*
> *down into the sand. He repeated this scene until none of the sol-*
> *diers could be seen. Essentially, Joey communicated that*
> *although no one could see the emotional abuse he was receiving,*
> *it had sunk deep within him, causing him a great deal of pain.*
> *He used the soldiers to communicate that the abuse was like an*
> *attack upon him.*

Space (Box, Tent, House)

An intact enclosure of some kind allows a child to be hidden, to demonstrate the need for boundaries, acceptance, trust, respect, and feelings of
shame, as well as a way in which to establish distance. A child can control his existence (object constancy) and any physical contact with others.

It is so important to have a place where children can hide that, if nothing else, a therapist could pull his desk approximately 18 inches away
from the wall so that a child could get down and hide behind it. Children
need to have a place where they have boundaries all around them —
where they're protected, and no one can see them. This can also be done
by providing a tent or a box in the playroom. Sometimes children will

crawl into a small box where they have to be in a prenatal position just to be in the box, and then ask that the lid be put on so they can hide. At times, providing space is similar in meaning to that of blankets.

Sword

A sword may be utilized to express aggression or to symbolize the need for defense, protection, and power. It may allow the child to gain some distance from his issue and to demonstrate his frustration with a particular conflict. Swords may also symbolize an intrusion that the child is experiencing. In other words, the metaphor is that he is always defending or fencing for his well-being in relationships where there is intrusion, pain, conflict, and clashing into one another. It should also be noted that when children play as though they are cutting off parts of the body, they are demonstrating their issues with relationships that cause them great distress.

Tape Recorder

A tape recorder allows an opportunity for a child to experience validation of his being. It provides reassurance of his existence — of his self. This toy also gives observation of a child's contributions to a relationship. When a child controls the tape recorder, as with controlling the lights, it confirms to the child that he does, in fact, have personal power and control. It also provides consistency for him in that each time the recording is replayed, it is the same.

Children love tape recorders because they love to hear themselves. It is very validating for a child to hear his own voice. Children with low self-esteem will sometimes get a little nervous or apprehensive around the recorder. They feel uncomfortable hearing themselves because they have had little validation in life. This may cause them to be very cautious. Some children will bring a musical tape to the therapy session and want to play it to soothe and comfort themselves. A tape recorder can also be used to record a metaphorical story for the child to listen to at home.

Targets

Targets can symbolize a child's level of confidence by how he approaches the target. For instance, if a child steps too close to the target, it may symbolize the child's feelings of wanting to look good to others while at the same time feeling a lack of competency. If the child steps far away from the target, it may represent low confidence and no expectations for success.

Play with targets can also communicate important information to the therapist concerning the child's style of setting goals. For instance, is the child setting an appropriate goal for his level of competency? Is he creating a self-defeating goal? Is he setting up a situation where he doesn't have to exert effort or take a risk? Changes in the child's style of playing with the target from session to session communicate his ability to adjust and adapt.

A child's play with targets is mental status play, the distance from the target indicating the child's confidence in his capacity for accomplishing a goal. A child who, for example, walks over to the target, takes the five darts off the board, and puts all five of them on the bull's-eye is a child who both fears failure and strives for perfectionism. Other children will stand a great distance from the target, throw the darts, and never even get near the target. This often indicates attention deficit-hyperactive children who are communicating, "I don't have a chance in life. Life doesn't give me a chance. It doesn't matter. As soon as I get these darts on, I'm finished."

A goal of treatment is to see each of these types shift and modulate to a point where the child is shooting at the target from a reasonable distance and succeeding one, two, or three times out of five. This is more typical of life — some successes, some failures, and acceptance of both. The boy who put all the darts in the bull's-eye during his first session might come in the next session, take a step back, and still put them all on the bull's-eye. During each session, he might adjust his distance, indicating how his treatment is progressing or regressing. His play, hopefully, will begin to move toward more realistic expectations.

After a child's play has become more adaptive, it may fluctuate from time to time. The fluctuation is dependent on the child's feelings about the circumstances in his life. So the distance between the child and the target will communicate to the therapist how the child is feeling about his world at that time.

Usually children will not play with targets repeatedly unless they are highly competitive. These children are in such a competitive battle that they appear driven to win at all costs. Even if the child is playing alone, he will compete against himself which puts the child in a double bind because he cannot feel completely satisfied with a win.

When a child is highly competitive he may put the therapist in the position of, for example, having a score of 35,000, while the child has a score of 7 million. Then the child will want to play this repeatedly. The therapist never wins because the child always structures it so he (the child) can win.

Because it is preferable to play non-competitively with a child, it is desirable for the therapist to reframe the situation so that the competition factor does not exist. This cannot be done until after the Dependency Stage where the child is confronting his issues. However, during the Therapeutic Growth Stage where the child begins to let the therapist win once in a while, the therapist can begin to reframe the game to eliminate the competition factor. For instance, the therapist may suggest that every time the child gets a number of points (for example, 10) and the therapist gets the same number of points, the child can add a zero to the end of his score (giving the child 100 points). In this way, the child still wins, but he begins to encourage success in the therapist. Now, the focus changes to a spirit of cooperation and support, encouraging a team style. Moving from the competitive to a more cooperative game shows that the child has gained integration and resolution in human relations.

Teddy Bears

Teddy bears, of course, are universally known for evoking feelings of warmth, nurturing, security, and companionship. They represent one's more tender internal security feelings. They may also be used as an alter ego, representing the child's beliefs about himself and his desire for protection. The teddy bear is often chosen by a tactile child.

Many times a child will pick up the teddy bear and play with it, relating to it. Then the child creates something unpleasant that happens to the teddy bear — some frightening or threatening incident. Whatever the child allows to happen to the teddy bear is what happens to the child in his world.

Telephone

The telephone is an important tool in play therapy, just as it has become a necessity in life. It offers the child a means of communication, yet with distance, safety, control, and power. It also provides him with the ability to disconnect whenever he becomes too overwhelmed.

> *During the Exploratory Stage, five-year-old Annie walked around the room, moving from toy to toy, when suddenly she picked up the telephone and yelled, "Help! Help! Help! Oh, they hung up." She then slammed it back down and moved on to the next toy. Immediately, the therapist was aware that Annie gave a clear metaphor representing a cry for help, although the content of her need was unknown. The therapist became alert to the pain and fear that Annie was experiencing. She also wanted Annie to know that she heard her cry and responded, "Well, that was a very important phone call."*
>
> *It is interesting to note that when Annie used the telephone, her call did not go through. This was a metaphor communicating that she had tried to tell someone about her abuse but had not been heard. Later, it was learned that she was being sexually abused.*

Another way children will use the telephone is to communicate with someone important to them and yet stay protected from their aggression. For instance, one little boy used the walkie-talkie to communicate with his father. He wanted to be close to his father, but his father was sexually abusing him. The telephone gave him the protection of distance.

Tinker Toys/Legos

Construction toys of this nature allow a child to demonstrate goal attainment and closure for himself. They provide a sense of structure for the child who feels he has none in his environment. In addition, when children are experiencing anxiety in the session, a structured toy will help them maintain their ability to manage that anxiety. Later in therapy, especially in the Therapeutic Growth Stage, children will use structured toys to communicate that they are nearing closure. Puzzles are also used in this way; toward the end of therapy, some children will want to complete a puzzle to show how much more complete, whole, and integrated they feel.

When a child wants to save what he has created, it is a good idea for the therapist to tell the child that he can't guarantee it. "If it is left the way it is, I can't guarantee it will be here when we get back together. In fact, most likely it won't be. But you can rebuild it because you know how to do that, and you have all your ideas in order to put it back together." In this way, the therapist can also empower the child. Then, if the therapist walks out of the room with the child and begins talking with his parents and another child rushes in and destroys it, the child is prepared.

If it is clinically significant to maintain that creation when the child leaves the room, a therapist can go back and put it aside. Then, before the next session, the therapist can put it back in place. Sometimes a child will build something out of toys which must be used for other sessions. The construction can't be saved. In this case, a Polaroid picture can be taken. If the therapist has time, he can reconstruct it before the next session.

Tools

Tools symbolize resources for a child and a chance for him to make an impact on his environment. They provide him with opportunities to make decisions and gain confidence from a successful outcome. These toys allow for change and problem-solving situations.

Many times, children will use tools to fix something that is wrong or broken. For instance, they may pick up a broken toy and try to fix it, perhaps identifying with the brokenness of the toy. It is very similar to the use of the doctor's kit, although the doctor's kit is more internal and relationship-oriented than the tools. Some children need to fix an object rather than a person in order to maintain their protective defenses. Perhaps, they will choose a broken car, a metaphor for the fact that they feel like they are an object, too, and are having trouble getting closer to their feelings.

Environments

The background in which play develops also contributes to the meaning of the play. Symbolism expressed with toys is enhanced by environmental symbolism. Environment sets the mood. Incorporating mood gives the therapist sensitivity to the comprehensive perspective of the content expressed in the play. Surviving the night in the jungle connotes experiences uniquely different from sailing on a ship in calm seas. Children convey intensity through the environments they create. The therapist utilizes all of the cues presented to enter the experience of the child.

Banks. Banks symbolize worth in the sense of where the child's value and dignity are stored or kept, how much there is, how it is treated, and who has access to it. Because banks also represent a place where others cannot have free access, it symbolizes secrets. In addition, a child's worth is so related to his family that banks also reveal the way in which the child's family treats him. If the child opens the bank and all the money is gone, or if the bank is robbed, it symbolizes a loss of dignity, security, or worth. In other words, when a child plays that a bank gets robbed, it often represents the fact that something or someone is stealing his dignity and worth. He has lost his value. This is a common theme in children who have been sexually abused — their dignity has been stolen from them.

Beaches. Beaches symbolize safety, freedom, playfulness, security, and childishness. A beach is rife with tactile experiences. It is one of the places where children can run, scream, throw sand, play in the water, and be totally child-like. It is tactile because the child can touch the sand and interact with it with his body. Beaches represent an arena of life in which the child is free to be himself. In fantasy, it is a place to go in order to relax and be secure. One can be passive or active, whichever is preferred. It is less formal and has the quality of giving permission to be more child-like or to move toward regression.

Bridges and Rivers. When children build bridges or exhibit the need to go across a bridge, one can see the need for transition, change, and the ability to cross a boundary the child has previously been afraid to approach. It can also represent the need to leave a place or get away from something. The child may be exhibiting the need to rejoin or connect with something on the other side. It could also represent the fact that something is missing, or the fact that the child is experiencing a void and cannot reach what is needed in order to bring completion. In the case of sexually abused children, it could represent reconnecting their bodies with their emotions. They can now think about their body without experiencing such emotional pain that they begin to experience high levels of anxiety.

It can also represent a path that leads to a place where the child has not been recently or where he desires to go.

If a child is going on a trail and comes to a river, he might say, "Well, I've got to figure a way to get across this river." Consequently, the river could symbolize power (i.e., the power to separate), a journey, boundaries, or entrapment. The flow of the river may symbolize conflict, energy, a struggle, a resource, a force, or a need for direction. If the child needs to cross a river, boundaries need to be crossed and conflicts resolved. There is usually a struggle to figure out how to get across — considering whether or not the water is too deep or the current too strong. Perhaps there is a need for direction because of a need to go up river. In addition, rivers may separate objects where connection is more desirable. On the other hand, the river may represent the fact that the child is aware of a need but cannot reach its fulfillment.

Haunted Houses. This is not a specific toy within the playroom. However, the child may build a haunted house or make reference to something as being haunted. When a child makes reference to a house as being haunted, it may symbolize secrets that are frightening to the child. It may also represent something unconscious in the sense that when the child concentrates or focuses on it, it evaporates. It may represent something happening in the home that may be difficult for the child to process directly; or it may symbolize something that may exist in the past as a vague memory. This is related to the extended family in that something frightening may have occurred while the child was visiting friends or relatives. For example, if a child visited an aunt and uncle and was sexually abused during the visit, the child may refer to their house as being haunted. Another example would be when a child was sexually abused by a parent and then the parents divorce and move. The child may refer to the home where the sexual abuse occurred as a haunted house.

Haunted houses can also represent issues that are unresolved and still haunting or gnawing at the child, as when an awareness of an experience creates fear. It is important to note that a child must have the empowerment to disclose at his own rate. If a therapist attempts to probe by inquiring about a haunted house before the child is emotionally prepared, the child will stop his play.

When children play haunted house, there is usually something troubling them at home. If children add ghosts to the haunted house, then there is probably a specific person they fear or a tremendous amount of fear or memories from the past or even a theme of revenge. In other words, there is more pain than simply what's indicated by the haunted house. Perhaps the child has lost something but can't identify the loss — they just know something is gone, pending, not complete.

Operations. When a child plays out an operation, whether it is with a set of toys prefabricated to depict an operation or whether the child designs his own set, he is playing out a crisis, an intervention, intrusion, action, risk, resolution, control, vulnerability, or healing. An operation represents the need for change, the crisis the child is in, or where the pain is located in his body. The type of operation, where the operation is located, and the level of pain within that operation will reveal much information regarding how the child is dealing with these issues. In fact, operating on the heart is the most common operation used by children. For instance, if it is a bullet wound to the heart, it is a direct, immediate pain; whereas, if it is a heart attack, it is usually a pain over events in the past which have accumulated in the child's memories.

Sometimes, when a child has undergone previous operations, he experiences anxiety or trauma related to those events. He will then operate on those areas of the body where he had his surgery in order to process his pain.

If a child has experienced emotional abuse and doesn't trust his own memories, or he has been called stupid, and experiences little self-confidence, he will conduct brain transplants or other types of work on the brain because he has no confidence in that area of his body.

Rainbows. Rainbows symbolize hope and change. In other words, "I know things need to be better, and I can get there." The child who draws a picture and puts a rainbow in it is communicating that he feels hope. This is in contrast to the child whose play revolves around a war zone. This child cannot see past the pain he is experiencing ("There's so much pain, I'm not sure I'm ever going to make it out"). Rainbows also symbolize that there is improvement, and that the child can make a difference. Even though the child is in a difficult situation, he can see the other perspective. If rainbows are seen in artwork early in therapy, and the child is very troubled, they usually represent covering up and trying to look good when there is great pain. A picture that includes both a rainbow and a sun is more positive. If rainbows are seen toward the end of the healing process, they are usually next to the sun, indicating that change is occurring and the child is feeling more hopeful.

For a list of basic toys necessary for a playroom, see Appendix A. For a list of toys and their symbolic meanings, see Appendix B. For a list of symbolic meanings of environments, see Appendix C. For a list of symbolic meanings of animals, see Appendix D.

CHAPTER 3

ASSESSING CHILDREN
IN THE PLAY THERAPY INTAKE

Introduction

The primary purpose of the intake process is to gain information concerning both the reason for referral and the presenting problem. After the therapist gathers this data from the child and family, it is helpful for her to provide the family with information that will assist them in understanding their child and her disorder. It is also important for the therapist to communicate to the parents how their particular family's life situation and style of functioning may be contributing to the difficulties their child is experiencing.

Through the information gained during intake, it may be possible to determine the etiology of the presenting symptoms. Establishing the etiology of a disorder, however, is not always as easy as it first appears. Nevertheless, as the following example illustrates, it is important to consider the etiology of the child's distress in order to determine the appropriate modality of treatment.

> *Nancy was a three-year-old who was referred to a therapist when she became mute shortly after witnessing her father beat her mother. Assuming this was selective mutism, the therapist agreed to work with her. However, during their first session, it appeared that Nancy was actually attempting to speak but was unable to do so.*
>
> *Seeing the possibility of a physical cause, the therapist began to explore various community resources in an attempt to ascertain whether or not a referral was in order. After the therapist described the events of the first session to a representative at The Community Center Foundation (whose centers are located in*

most communities), it became apparent that a referral was appropriate. Extensive screening and testing was initiated by the Center. It was discovered that Nancy had developed a brain tumor which was interfering with her speech.

The Initial Visit

Meeting With the Parents Alone

The initial process is best accomplished by meeting with the parents for the first session without the child. Often parents have information they would rather not discuss in the child's presence. Seeing the parents by themselves prevents the awkwardness of either leaving the child alone in the waiting room or putting the parents in the position of attempting to communicate with the therapist while at the same time keeping the conversation obtuse enough that the child, who is in the same room, doesn't grasp the import. If the child is in the room with the parents during the initial visit, it puts the parents in the position of having to be vague, frustrated, and/or confused. On the other hand, if the parents meet with the therapist without the child, they can speak more freely.

Each child born into a family is unique. There are many factors in the dynamics of a family that effect a child's development and that can change from the birth of one child to that of another. Perhaps the parents are more mature or more financially stable or unstable than when a previous child was born. The parents may be having relationship problems between themselves or be having difficulties with another child. Because of this uniqueness a wealth of information may be discovered by questioning the parents about the child's development from birth. The information gained from the child's birth order gives the therapist immediate understanding of some of the child's issues (Hoopes & Harper, 1987). For instance, if a therapist is conducting an intake on a boy and discovers that he has a slightly younger sister, the therapist can immediately begin to consider the possibility of a struggle with adequacy, since girls tend to develop faster than boys (Harris & Liebert, 1984). So while the boy, as the older child, is expected to strive toward perfection, this boy struggles for adequacy because of the overwhelming competence of his younger sister. He may very likely become discouraged and give up the struggle.

The parents' perceptions of their child are also important to ascertain in the intake process. For instance, "I've never met your child. Will you describe her for me?" Where one parent will give a physical description, another parent will demonstrate great sensitivity and awareness in describing the personality, strengths, and struggles of her child. In many cases, however, it takes parents awhile to feel comfortable in talking openly with a therapist. It may be necessary for the therapist to initiate probing questions in order to obtain the necessary information about the child and her emotional functioning.

If parents tell the therapist they don't know the best place to begin, a statement such as, "Well, you just start wherever you want, and if I have questions, I'll ask as we go along," can be helpful. Other questions might be, "Has your child always been this way?" "Can you tell me when you first noticed your child beginning to change?" Of course, there is always the parent who says, "Well, she just came out of the womb like that!"

Many times, a parent will reply, "She used to be so sweet. Then, about six months ago, she began to be grumpy and grouchy. This got worse and worse until finally she became this little monster!" This presents a good opportunity to explore the events surrounding the change in behavior. This often has the result of helping the parents understand that there may have been a precipitator. Determining a reason for the child's behavior often has the potential of facilitating the parents' patience, which will indirectly benefit the child.

How each of the parents relates to his or her child is another area to explore. What role does the child play in the family? Is she special to the parents in some way? Is the child the only son in a family of daughters, or vice versa? Is the child the first live birth following several miscarriages? This type of information is significant since it determines how parents treat their child and what expectations they have knowingly or unknowingly placed upon their child (Hoopes & Harper, 1987). An example is the family who has five children, one of whom is a boy who is midway in the family constellation, and upon which the parents have placed all their achievement expectations. Knowing this information will do much to explain the family dynamics as well as what may be seen in the child's play during therapy. Then, the therapist can explore how this particular child reacts to and feels about his family dynamics. Some little girls would love the opportunity to be the little princess of the family. On the other hand, being labeled as the high achiever in the family can place the child under constant pressure.

How parents relate to each other can also become an important determinant of the child's sense of well-being. Frequently children are brought into counseling with the attitude that there is something wrong with them when, in fact, the problem lies within the relationship between the parents. In these cases children may be put in the position of acting out so that the parents focus on the child instead of on their relationship. This communicates to the child that it is her responsibility to maintain the marriage and, in that way, keep the family intact. Although family therapy may be imperative, some parents are not always willing to admit the need for family therapy. Others refuse it or simply make themselves unavailable. Once a relationship has been established with the child and the parents, the therapist has an opportunity to tactfully suggest to the parents that the whole family be involved in family therapy in addition to play therapy for the child. This suggestion carries with it the possibility of alienating the family. Consequently, the therapist will have to use clinical judgment in determining whether or not she is providing the most help for the child by supporting the child within the dysfunctional system, or by suggesting family therapy because the system is so destructive. This is a delicate situation since children in dysfunctional families often do not have any emotional support from other family members.

This is not the only situation where a family is unavailable for family therapy. Sometimes the child has been removed from the family by the courts or has been abandoned and is in foster care. In these cases consultation with the foster parents is as important as consultation with the birth or adoptive parents. When dealing with issues of abandonment and rejection, the relationship between the child and therapist takes on even more significance.

It is important during the initial visit to establish rapport with the parents so that they accept a stance of cooperation with the therapist as a team in facilitating the emotional wellness of their child. If this does not occur, it may prove to be detrimental later in therapy when the child goes through a stage in the therapeutic process where she becomes highly dependent on the therapist. At that time, without the rapport with the parents, one or both of them can begin to feel threatened and want to stop therapy whereas, if they feel part of a team, their trust in the therapist will succeed in putting to rest their fears.

During this initial visit, many parents will ask the therapist what to tell their child concerning coming in for play therapy. This is when a book entitled *A Child's First Book About Play Therapy* (Nemiroff & Annunziata, 1990) is good to have on hand. It is a well-illustrated book that will give both parents and children an idea of what to expect.

Following is a list of questions that will provide additional information:

1. What is the historical resumè of the child's problems (i.e., an overview of what concerns them most about their child)?
2. What is the caretaker's assessment of the child's personality (particularly focusing on strengths)?
3. What is the family composition?
4. Has anyone in the extended family had a similar personality and/or problem?
5. What is the child's relevant medical history, starting with conception and birth?
6. What were the child's developmental milestones? (Note: David Looff, M.D., in his book, *Getting to Know the Troubled Child* (1987), includes an extensive Developmental Questionnaire.)
7. Have there been any physical and/or psychological stressors in the child's life (e.g., moves, separations, deaths, abuses, etc.)? During what developmental periods did these occur?
8. How does the child react to stress?
9. What are the parents' styles of discipline? How do they handle differences in their styles? How does the child respond?
10. What is the current family situation? How is alcohol handled in the home?
11. What roles have been overtly or covertly assigned to the child? How is this child the same and how is she different from the others in the family?
12. Does this child have special meaning to one or both parents?
13. What are the therapist's observations of parents during intake? How do they interact during the interview? Do they disagree on important issues? Which parent is the dominant or controlling

one? Is there positive sharing and agreeing? Do they offer insights for the interviewer regarding family alignments?

First Meeting With the Child

After meeting with the parents and gaining as much information about the child as possible, the therapist can then give her full attention to the child during their first visit. Just walking out to the waiting room and seeing the dynamics between the parent and child or children will give valuable information about the family system. Perhaps the parent is sitting on the sofa with another child, giving all her attention to that child, while the other is sitting in the middle of the floor playing alone. This scene may be typical of the child being ejected from the family system and becoming withdrawn. Then, as the therapist begins to work with the child, she can look to see if there is corroborating evidence affirming this speculation.

This first meeting will also give information about how the child interacts with a stranger in an unfamiliar environment. Some parents warn the therapist that their child will not want to go to the play therapy room without them. Invariably, these are the children who, when presented with the opportunity of going to a room with more toys, will be off and running. If at this point the parent says "Wait! Don't you want me to go with you?", the therapist begins to get a sense of to whom the separation anxiety belongs. If the child is truly afraid to go to the playroom with the therapist, the therapist can invite one of the parents to accompany the child. In this case the goal is to slowly remove the parent from the playroom to return to the waiting room.

When a parent does accompany the child, it is important for the therapist to focus on the child and not on the parent. A conversation between parent and therapist is not facilitative at this time. The child needs to know that the therapist is focusing on her, although only on a level that is comfortable for the child. This focus begins in the waiting room.

It is important for parents to respect their child's fear of separating from them. Too often, children are forced to submit to their parents' wishes. For instance, children are told to kiss relatives they don't like, do everything the baby-sitter says, or are required to go into new situations unaccompanied by a parent. Not being allowed the right to refuse such requests can cause unhealthy consequences for the child. Unless the child's reason for refusing to enter the playroom is purely resistive, the therapist should not insist that a child go to the playroom alone with her. Rather, it is important to respect the child's desire to protect herself. It is also important to respect the child's sense of comfort in determining both how to approach her in physical proximity and how friendly to be with her. She should be allowed to be silent and distant if this is necessary for her comfort level. This is a good time for the therapist to physically lower herself to the child's eye level and begin to make eye contact. Sometimes this can occur simply by looking at something the child is wearing and commenting on it or, if she is carrying a toy such as a doll, beginning a conversation about the toy (although from a distance, respecting the child's wish to remain safe and comfortable). It is important for the therapist to convey from the very beginning that she will defer to the child and will honor her wishes.

During this initial interview, some therapists are more comfortable with a structured type of interview. (See Appendix C, *Assessment Tools and Rating Scales of Child Psychopathology*.)

If a therapist is comfortable in a less structured setting, it is possible to obtain information directly from the child simply by making observations and asking questions. For instance, "What would you like to be when you grow up?" or "What kinds of things are you afraid of?"

Story questions can also be fun. For instance:

"Do you remember the story of Aladdin and the lamp? Well, Aladdin was this little person who went for a walk one day, and while he was walking, he found a lamp. This happened so long ago that it didn't look like a lamp that you might see today. It looked more like what we might call a teapot. It was all dirty because it had been hidden for a long time. As he was cleaning it, he rubbed it, and something wonderful happened. All of a sudden, there was a puff of smoke and out came a genie. I don't know if you know about genies, but they are magical creatures. Well, the genie said, "Oh, thank you, thank you, thank you for rescuing me. I've been in this lamp for a thousand years. I'm so glad to be out that I'm going to grant you three wishes. It can be anything in the world that you want."

"Let's pretend I'm the genie and you are Aladdin and you have three wishes. You can wish for anything in the world. What would you wish for?"

Most of the time, children respond with, "Oh, I'd like a new video game," or "I'd like some more super heroes." Surprisingly, another common response is, "I'd like to have a new house." During inquiry, the child will often explain that she would like a new house so that "Mom will be happy," which then gives the therapist an idea of the relationship between the child and the mother. Here, the child's sense of well-being seems to be dependent on the mother's positive emotional state. By asking these types of questions, the therapist can then inquire further into the child's response and gain even more information (e.g., "What would be special about having new tires for your bike?").

Animals can also be used in this type of questioning. For instance, "If you could be any animal, what would you like to be?" "Tell me what is special to you about being [name of animal]." Drawing can also give valuable information. Inviting the child to draw a picture of her family doing something together can provide good information about the child's family dynamics. It is always interesting to see a child whose parents have just divorced draw her family as if it were still intact. Sometimes, if the family is intact, the child will draw a picture with one family member over to one side and the rest of the family at the other extreme of the drawing paper.

Other possible questions in order to obtain information from the child include:

1. Identifying data (i.e., name, nickname, age, school, attitudes, and ideas about coming to see a therapist).
2. "Who is your best friend?" "Do you have a lot of friends, or a few?" "What do you like to do with your friends?"
3. "If you could change something about yourself, what would that be?" "Do you sometimes get angry with yourself? About what?"
4. "What kinds of things are you afraid of?"
5. "What do you want to be when you grow up? What do you like about that kind of work?"

6. "What are the things you like about yourself? Your mom? Your dad?" "What would you like to change about your mom? Your dad?"

7. "There are times when all boys and girls have daydreams. What are yours?"

8. "Will you tell me about a friendly night dream you've had? A scary one?"

9. "If you could change yourself into any animal, which one would you like to be? What would be special about being that animal?"

10. "If you were granted three wishes, and you could ask for any thing, what would you want?" (Inquire about each wish.) Optional: "If you could change anything about your family, what would you change?"

11. "What would you do if you found a thousand (or a million) dollars on the sidewalk?" (Looff, 1987).

12. "Let's pretend there's a rocket ship that's going to make a trip from down here on earth up to the moon and back. You're the captain. The rocket ship holds two people. Who do you think you'd like to take along with you?" (Looff, 1987).

13. Use an incomplete story to elicit certain themes. For example, to obtain information concerning the possibility of sexual abuse, a story might be: "A child and an adult went into a bedroom. The adult told the child they were going to play. What do you think they were going to do?" (Note: *The American Journal of Orthopsychiatry* for January, 1946, lists 10 *Despert Fables* which cover 10 themes significant to children (Despert, 1946).)

14. Utilizing the *Draw-a-Person*, the child might be asked the following questions about her drawing (Lord, 1985):
    a. "How old is this person?"
    b. "Does she go to school or have a job?"
        (1) If she has a job, "What does she do?"
        (2) If she goes to school, "How does she do in school? How does she like her teachers?"
        (3) "Does she have a favorite teacher? Why is that one her favorite?"
        (4) "Does she have one that she does not like? Why?"
        (5) "What is her favorite subject?"
        (6) "Which subjects doesn't she like? Why?"

c. "Is she married?"

d. "What is this person doing?"

  (1) "What does she like to do best? Why?"

  (2) "What doesn't she like to do at all?"

  (3) "What does she think is the worst thing to do? Why?"

e. "How many do you want to pretend are in her family, counting everyone?"

f. "Maybe she would never say this out loud to anybody, but which one in the family does she really like the best or a little bit the best? Why? Which one doesn't she like as much as the others? Why?"

g. "What is this person's biggest worry or problem?"

h. "Let's say that this person found a trunk. Do you know what a trunk is? Now, it is important that you answer this question just as fast as you can. Let's say that one day this person found a trunk filled with every kind of clothing that you could think of. Just for fun, she dressed up like ... Quick!"

i. "Let's say this person had a dream. It might have been a dream she had only once but never forgot, or it might have been a dream she had again and again. What was the dream about? What happened in the dream?"

j. "Let's say this person could be invisible. Where would she go? What would she do?"

k. "What is her favorite kind of story or T.V. program? Why?"

15. House-Tree-Person. Ask the child the following questions about the drawing of a house, a tree, and a person (Buck, 1966).

a. "What's the one special thing about this house?"

b. "What's the worst thing about this house?"

c. "What kind of tree is this?"

d. "Is the person a boy or girl?"

e. "What is she doing?"

f. "How does she feel right now?"

g. "What's the one thing she would like to change about the house?"

h. "Is there a scary place in this house?"

16. Kinetic Family Drawing. Ask the child the following questions about the drawing of a family (Lord, 1985):

a. "Name each member in the family."
b. "What is this family doing?"
c. "What is the one best thing about this family?"
d. "What is the one worst thing about this family?"
e. "Does this family have any secrets?"
f. "What kinds of things does this family do together?"
g. "If you could change one thing about this family, what would it be?"
h. "Who is the favorite person in the family?"
i. "How does everyone get along?"
j. "How does this person feel about herself?"

Certainly, the preceding list is exhaustive. It would be prudent to choose only those questions which seem appropriate to the child's circumstances, the child's temperament, and the presenting problem.

During this questioning style of intake process, a child may feel comfortable sitting and answering a number of questions or even exploring the playroom while answering them. Some children, however, will not cooperate in the question-and-answer format. In this case it behooves the therapist to allow the child to move directly into her play. Although it will come in its own time, the same information can be garnered from the child's play.

For intake purposes, observations during the child's play should include the following:

1. The child's attitude and approach to the toys. Is there any response latency? Are there frequent changes, avoidances of any particular toys, preferences, verbalizations, creative use of the toys, aggressiveness, energy, lethargy, or lack of ability to play without structure?
2. Whether or not the child's play age is appropriate.
3. If there are repeated themes in the child's play.
4. The child's type of play (i.e., does she examine the materials, use the materials in a functional way, or enter into fantasy play)(Sjolund, 1993).
5. The child's ability to start and stop play.
6. Any unusual observations.

7. Whether or not the child speaks as she plays. Is speech intelligible?
8. Whether the child approaches the therapist to involve her in the play.
9. The intensity level of the child's play.

Clinical observations to be made about the child during each session, but particularly during the first session, include:

1. The child's size and general appearance, her coordination, speech (amount and quality), and general intellectual functioning.
    Certainly this cannot be ascertained to a definite degree without utilizing more formal measures. However a general observation will provide an idea of whether or not further assessment is necessary or if a referral for further assessment is necessary in that area. It is very common, for example, for children in need of play therapy to also need speech therapy.
2. The child's capacity for human relations.
    a. How does the relationship between therapist and child develop?
    b. How does the child separate from the parent?
    c. Is the child friendly, aggressive, controlling, or showing a need for approval?
3. The mood or emotional tone of the child. Is the child fearful, angry, anxious, sad, apathetic, oppositional? What is the child's activity level? Does her play support her emotional tone, or is it incongruent?
4. The child's use of her environment. Does she only play in one small area or with certain toys? Does she always sit in the same place and play with the same toys? Does she relax once she becomes familiar with her surroundings?

An excellent assessment tool that utilizes play extensively is called the *World Technique* (Lowenfeld, 1939). It was originally developed in England by Dr. Margaret Lowenfeld. The *Erica Method* (Harding cited in Sjolund, 1981) evolved from the World Technique and is structured in a style similar to that of the Rorschach (Rorschach, 1921/1942). In fact, it could probably be called the Rorschach of play therapy because of the format of administration and the protocol that is utilized in the interpretation. The therapist uses the protocol sheet to describe the child's approach to sand play — the child's creation and the therapist's interpretation. It is important to have studied child development in using this technique since at different stages of development the same activity can have completely different meanings. For example, if a three-year-old pulls out five toys and creates her world, the meaning is very different from a 12-year-old pulling out the same five toys and creating her world.

The *Erica Method* (Harding cited in Sjolund, 1981) has prescribed toys which are placed in a cabinet. There are 360 miniature toys that represent components of a child's world. These miniatures are comprised of static toys, transportation toys, and representations of living beings. They are also grouped according to aggressive and peaceful categories. Specifically, the set is comprised of people, wild and domestic animals, transportation vehicles, buildings, furniture, fences, explosions, cannons, etc. There is also one broken toy. Facets of the child's personality are uncovered by learning how she relates to the broken toy. These toys are grouped and placed in 12 cubbies — domestic animals together, wild animals together, etc.

When the child enters the playroom, she is simply instructed to use the items in the cabinet to build whatever she chooses in one of the sandboxes. Instructions are kept to a minimum in order not to influence the child's construction. Since this is an assessment session rather than therapy, at this point the therapist doesn't actually get involved in the construction. Rather, the child is left to construct her own world while the therapist observes and takes notes about the child's behavior. For instance, did the child stand and study all the toys before deciding what to use in construction, or did she just grab all the toys out of one cubbyhole, dump them in the sand, and try to do something with them?

When the child says she has finished, or 45 minutes have elapsed, whichever occurs first, construction is stopped and the product is photographed. Then the therapist will do the inquiry (i.e., "Tell me about what you built."). Some children are capable of building a meaningful whole as, for example, the child who pulls the sand back, terraces it, landscapes it, and builds a castle up on a hill with a pond down at the bottom. At the other end of the spectrum is the child who merely dumps miniatures in the sand, causing half of the toys to be covered with sand. This gives the therapist a sense of the chaos in the child's world.

The constructions and observations take place during three consecutive sessions as closely related in time as possible. One session alone would not allow a complete picture, although some information would be gained (e.g., some children are anxious about new situations during the first session, and their constructions are effected). If three different creations occur, however, then the therapist can begin to see themes develop. These themes and their relationship to each other are what the therapist is looking for in making an assessment of the child. In addition, analysis of the formal aspects of the construction process is considered. The child's choices during the process and her type of play also provide further information about her functioning. For a more complete study of the World Technique, the reader is referred to Margaret Lowenfeld's book, *The World Technique* (1979); Margareta Sjolund's training guide entitled *The Erica Method* (1993); and the soon-to-be-translated *Handbook of the Erica Methods* (1986) by Allis Danielson.

Case History:
Initial Session With Juan

Juan, an eight-year-old Hispanic male, was referred for therapy by his elementary school counselor because of aggressive behavior at school — he extorted money from other children by telling them he would beat them up if they didn't give it to him. He was also oppositional with the teachers. Many of them confessed that their attitude toward him was such that they didn't want him in their classes. Throughout the school, Juan had a reputation for being the school bully.

Juan was participating in a children's group at school with the elementary school counselor. The group concentrated on identifying feelings. They also concentrated on how children might be expected to feel and react in different situations. It was apparent from some of Juan's statements during this intake session that he was learning from his group experience at school. However, the school counselor felt that he needed more intense involvement with a therapist.

The intake process is generally structured so that the therapist meets with the child, asks questions, obtains information, and then staffs the case. At that point, a diagnosis is determined, and treatment goals are established. Then treatment begins. The first session with the child is usually an exploratory time. However, in working with children, it is often necessary to be flexible in the intake style. Some children may be able to sit for an hour and answer questions, while others may not want to participate in that type of process at all. Any reaction between these two extremes may also occur. However the process occurs, intake information will be gained. If a child (particularly a very young child) only wants to play and doesn't want to sit still for any structured query at all, the material will be apparent through observing her play. It may take longer, but the information will be forthcoming.

The following excerpt is from the initial session with Juan. It is an intake session with exploration taking place concurrently. The therapist asks some questions of Juan as she gathers information. When he first comes into the room, Juan sees the bop bag, walks over and takes it in his hands, flips it down onto the floor, puts his knee into the neck of the bop bag, braces it there for a moment, and then lets it up. He says, "My dad is in the Air Force." During this session, there is a consistent pattern of proximity in occurrence between aggression and mention of his father, either one occurring first. Given this pattern, it would appear that this child is being physically abused by his father on a consistent basis or that it has occurred recently. The fact is, however, that Juan has not seen his father for three years. The memory of that abuse still arouses intense emotions in him. Aggression has been modeled by his father as an acceptable modality of relating to others.

Session	Comments
1. Juan: (Stands waiting for the therapist, swinging his arm, pounding the bop bag in the face. As he doubles up his fist and hits the bop bag right in the face, he says:) *I'm just practicing!*	1. As they first walk into the room together, the groundwork is laid for their relationship. Since he does not know what to expect, Juan is metaphorically demonstrating his perception of relationships. Hitting is his *rehearsal-for-life* play.
2. J: (Kicks the bop bag in the face and then punches it in the face. Whack!) *My dad always does like this to my back. He breaks my back.*	2. This is Juan's metaphor for his spirit and his sense of well-being that has been broken. The theme of shattered self-esteem is becoming apparent.

3. Therapist: *And that hurts you when he treats you like that.*

3. It is important to remain empathic with children as they reveal their struggles, even though at times it is very difficult.

4. J: (Repeatedly hits the bop bag in the face.) *I'm just practicing so I can hit someone in the face when I have a fight.*
    T: *So you want to hurt him now before he hurts you.*

4. Hitting is his style of human relations at this time.

5. J: (Picks the bop bag up by the head, squeezes it, then flings it across the room.) *My dad always does like this — a bear hug.*

5. Juan reveals his perceptions of family life, perceptions that have been garnered from his relationship with his father. When Juan is in his father's presence, his father is overpowering physically. He then abandons Juan and throws him off on his own.

6. J: *Ump, it's not bad at all.*

6. Juan makes this statement because, in his opinion, being physically abused by your father is better than not having a father. For children, having a relationship with an abusive parent transcends the abuse.

7. T: *Do you miss your father since you left him in Texas and moved here to Colorado?*

7. When a child is questioned about a perpetrator during intake, it triggers unpleasant memories for the child.

8. J: (Loses his concentration.) *It's hard for me to concentrate with my dad. Sometimes, I can't just get a hold of somebody else with my dad. I can't keep forgetting my dad.*
    T: *"Oh, you keep remembering him, and that makes it hard for you to think of anything else."*

8. All of a sudden, Juan's traumatic experiences with his father resurface and he becomes overwhelmed. Juan has never disclosed his abuse. When the therapist just happens to mention the perpetrator, Juan loses his orientation because the traumatic memory and resulting pain have been triggered. As a result, Juan becomes confused and begins to depersonalize. When this occurs, it is a signal to investigate

the relationship with his father and the possibility of abuse.

9. J: (Picks up the Slinky and uses it to strangle the bop bag.) *Sorry, sucker. You're dead meat, now.*

9. He structures the Slinky in such a way as to give a reflection of his internal pain.

10. T: *What is it like to be in your family?*

J: (Backs away.) *Being in my family is something tough to be for somebody else. Like when my mom gets raped by my dad, it starts hurting my mom's feelings.*

T: *When your mom gets raped by your dad, it hurts her feelings. I bet you don't like it when that happens.*

J: *Yeah. I get sad.*

T: *You feel sad that your mom is being hurt, and you wish your dad wouldn't do that to her.*

10. Because of the abuse that has taken place in his family, this question is very potent to Juan. He moves backwards in order to distance himself from the therapist and from the question.

As he staggers away from the therapist, he is communicating that he needs protection and distance from the pain. "... for somebody else," is Juan's confusion and depersonalization in relation to the pain of these violations.

Juan is disclosing the prevalence of violent relationships that abound in his family. (Rape is not a term that an eight-year-old would have known at the time of this taping.) So, apparently, he has heard someone else use that term to label what his dad has done to his mom. Whether he has observed the actual violation or not, his belief that his mother has been violated in that way by someone as significant to him as his father is excruciatingly painful for him. When two people for whom a person cares deeply mistreat each other, it creates an extremely uncomfortable situation for the person who cares for them both. That person experiences the anguish without the direct expression of anger to mask it. Juan is genuinely distressed. He is in tremendous pain from the dynamics in his family system.

11. J: (After slapping the bop bag repeatedly, Juan takes the gun and sticks it in the face of the bop bag.) *Stick 'em up, sucker.*

T: *It really hurts you when you see what happens in your family.*

11. This release of energy is his reaction to avoid the pain.

It is best to avoid taking children deeper into their pain until the relationship is established. It is important to maintain the emotional tone at a level that is determined by the client. This is not to imply that the therapist should emotionally abandon the client. Empathic responses are supportive and at the same time facilitative in building the relationship. In this statement, the therapist honors the child and communicates empathy, acceptance, and support.

12. J: (Spins the guns.) *When we lived with my dad, I didn't have to do chores. We did some fun things.*

T: *When you were living with your dad, some things were better, but you were sad about the way he treated your mom.*

J: (Points guns at the bop bag. Spins them on his fingers. Points them in the face of the bop bag again.)

12. Here he is reliving the experiences that the therapist is talking about (i.e., when he was living with his father), and his emotionality starts rising. He pulls the guns because he is back in his hypervigilant state. While physical appearance may not indicate that emotionality, it is present nonetheless and evident in his play. Pointing the gun at the bop bag represents the necessary hypervigilance in his father's presence. In an effort to compensate for the helplessness he experiences with his abusing father, he becomes expert at other symbols of power. His expertise in spinning the guns is an effort to demonstrate his assumed competency. He wants to look competent rather than feel the pain that he is experiencing.

13. T: *What is your favorite TV show?*

J: *Beauty and the Beast.*

T: *You like that show because you would like to be like the beast?*

13. The theme of the beast protecting and nurturing the beauty is inherent in Juan's selection of this as his favorite show. Children generally focus on being taken care of rather than caretaking. This interest on his part, therefore,

J: *I like him because he always takes good care of her and all that stuff.*

T: *You would like to be like the beast because he is powerful. You also like that he is sensitive and caring.*

issues a warning to observe him for the caretaking role in his home and with a chosen few of his peers. If, in fact, this is the case at home, this is a role reversal with his mother.

Notice that the traits of sensitivity and caring in Juan are not observed by the vast majority of people at school.

14. J: (Picks up a foam paddle and ball and bounces the ball in the air with the paddle.) *This is fun.* (Hits it about three times and then puts it down.) *I like that.*

14. This statement was the only spontaneous, child-like response made in the entire 45-minute intake session — and it only lasted 12 seconds.

15. J: (Goes over to the counter, takes two small animals, puts them two or three inches apart and then slams them together.) *You're dead!*

15. This is the same energy as if he had taken the bop bag and kicked it across the room into the opposite wall. Whether Juan is utilizing fine or gross motor movements, his feelings are expressed with the same intensity.

16. T: *Do you like any other TV shows?*

J: *Yep. I like the transformers.*

T: *You like how they seem real powerful ...*

J: *Yep.*

T: *... and how they get the bad guys?*

J: *Yep. The bad guys are the deceptacons.*

T: *Do you want to be one of the deceptacons?*

16. It is important for therapists to be familiar with the cartoons, movies, and characters that children relate to through the media. This will assist the therapist in understanding the nature of the character with which the child is identifying and the theme of that play. The therapist can also ascertain any deviations the child makes from the theme of the character.

17. J: *I used to, but I don't want to anymore. I used to want to be a deceptacon, but now I want to be an autobot. I want to be a leader of the autobots.*

17. What Juan is communicating is the fact that he is searching for his identity. In other words, although he has had a negative identity, he is working to move it toward a more positive one.

18. J: (Picks up the binoculars and uses them to look around the room.) *Christopher Columbus discovering America.*

18. Juan is metaphorically communicating, "Juan, searching for an identity."

19. J: (Runs a small car down the counter while making the sounds of a car braking suddenly.) *Bye-bye.*

(Picks up a dinosaur.) *Dinosaurs!*

(Picks up both a car and a cow.) *I like cars. I like cows.*

(Makes sounds of conflict while taking the car and the cow and ramming them together. The car kills the cow.)

T: *Your car got the cow.*

J: *No, this guy* [the dinosaur] *did.*

19. Here, once again, Juan is illustrating the violence that he has seen between his mom and dad. This time he utilizes a different context, however. He uses the action of the car and the cow. His statements that he likes cars and cows brings into consciousness the conflict with which he struggles. In doing so, he feels the pain. In an effort to avoid his pain, Juan denies the actions of the car. Unconsciously, he is entangled in his feelings about the relationship between his mom and dad. He doesn't want to bring those feelings into consciousness. All the relationships that he knows in his family are a continuing saga of one violent experience after another.

The more children display guttural sounds as part of their play, the more meaning that content has to the child, and the closer it is to his core issue. In trauma play, guttural sounds are common and indicate intense traumatic pain.

20. J: (Picks up a dart gun and waves it in the direction of the therapist.)

T: *Wow, wait a minute. I don't want you to ...*

J: (Points the gun in a different direction, shoots it, and hits exactly where he aims.)

T: (Claps her hands to indicate, "Nice shot!")

J: *Bingo! I even shooted* [sic] *sideways.* (Walks over and picks up

20. The therapist set a limit on him before she has had a chance to establish a relationship of safety, security, and trust. Not enough time has elapsed in this honoring process to provide the security for him. Consequently, she has set a limit before she is a trusted person to him.

This seems like a very mild limit. Juan, however, experiences it as he has experienced his limit setting of the past

the dart gun. As he is standing up, he sees himself in the [two-way] mirror. He loads the gun and aims it at his image in the mirror.)

T: *I don't want you to shoot the darts at the mirror.*

— he becomes fearful of physical reprisal.

21. J: (Takes the gun, turns it to the side, and discharges it at the wall.)

21. This looks like a simple act of respecting the limit that has been set. Juan, however, is shooting the gun to end the interchange. In this way, he does not have to be flooded with the emotions that he would have experienced. This response is an effort to protect himself from all that emotionality.

22. J: *I can use this guy* [bop bag]. *Bye-Bye.*

T: *You want to show him who's the boss.*

22. When a therapist defines how a child will play out his anger (i.e., "You want to hit him. You really want to kick him hard. You want to knock him all the way across the room," etc.), the statements become suggestions and may actually increase and condone the display of aggression. This is obviously inappropriate in therapy. To take the child's play to a behavioral level and then extrapolate to even more aggressive behaviors becomes evocative and may, indeed, lead the child toward the more aggressive acts.

It is more appropriate and beneficial to the child to stay with his emotionality in those intense situations. For example, you want him to know what it feels like to hurt, or you want him to know he can't hurt you anymore. Utilizing this style helps the child to discharge that energy.

23. J: *Yep. I got him just where I want him.* (Shoots the gun.) *I'm trying to get him right on the mouth.*

(Shoots the bop bag on the mouth.) *I'm trying to get him right on the mouth.* (Shoots the bop bag on the mouth again.) *I got him right there. "Sorry, you're dead."*

(Knocks the bop bag down. Aims the gun at the bop bag again.) *Like in Clint Eastwood — "Go ahead. Make my day."*

23. Now he is focusing on the mouth, which may indicate sexual abuse or the verbal abuse that he has received in addition to the physical abuse.

24. J: (Moves the bop bag back so that it is at a greater distance from him. Shoots and hits the bop bag on the head.) *Got him right in the head.* (Pause.) *My dad used to be a cop.*

24. By shooting at the bop bag at close range for such a long time and then moving it back, Juan is working through his relationship with his dad over time. First, at close range, representing when his dad lived with him. Then, Juan moved him back to represent the time since he moved away from his father. So, the next shot discloses the history of the relationship.

It is apparent from these excerpts that what Juan communicated metaphorically through play actually gave more information than the therapist would have received through a direct question-and-answer style of intake. In fact, in this case the direct question-and-answer modality reawakens his pain. Generally, when a child is questioned during intake, it is important to attend to the answer. However, even more important is to observe the shifts in a child's play. These shifts will disclose unconscious information. The nonverbal message is more accurate than the verbal (O'Connor, 1991).

In building a treatment plan for a child, it is important to maintain a consistent philosophy of children's inherent quests for resolution of internal conflict. The treatment plan will be carried out while the child maintains direction of the play. Opportunities must be grasped within the context of the play to insert statements or actions that address the child's treatment goals. For example, the child who fears the birth of a sibling directs the therapist to play the part of the child while she plays the role of the mother. Within that context, the therapist could, with the voice and actions of the child, request more time with the mother, express her fears of being unimportant, pout, hide the baby, etc. Some treatment goals, as in the case of Juan, are inherent in the play therapy setting (e.g., re-establishing trust in others).

In the case of Juan, there are a number of readily observable behaviors and attitudes that would support the teachers' view of him. However, looking beyond those, it becomes apparent that this child has some less obvious characteristics that, if recognized and nurtured, could set him on a more positive path in life. One of those attributes is sensitivity. While Juan has been participating in the children's group at school, he has begun to utilize some of the skills he has learned there. He understands the concepts being presented in the group because he is a sensitive, caring child. He does not yet feel comfortable, however, in utilizing that sensitivity in a manner which might leave him feeling vulnerable. In a one-on-one situation, where he is honored and respected, Juan feels free to interact with the therapist and begins to disclose aspects of himself that he would not disclose in an environment where he is expected to perform and be evaluated. Some of the disclosures he makes are unknown to him. These disclosures include the fact that he is sensitive, that he cares about what happens to other people, and that he is in pain (e.g., he "feels sad when his dad rapes his mom"). These are facts he has disclosed. Now, it is necessary to utilize this knowledge to assist him in his movement toward health.

A primary goal for all children is for them to feel comfortable in expressing their feelings in healthy ways. When they are expressed, the therapist can label those feelings and support the child in working toward resolution. Therefore, in the treatment plan for Juan, he would be encouraged to express his feelings, to explore them, and to develop his sensitivity into an attribute that he views as an asset. In his current functioning, because of his sensitivity, he experiences strong feelings. Then he manifests these strong feelings (i.e., hurt, shame, caring) as aggression.

A goal of play therapy is to assist the child in breaking the connection between these strong feelings and aggression. It is desirable to shift them toward a more positive response. Since aggression has been modeled for him in the past, his style of problem solving and interaction has been the misuse of power and aggression. He has also witnessed an attitude that women are objects of aggression. If he were to accept that attitude, an intimate relationship with a woman would be difficult for him to maintain. The goal, then, is for him not only to re-channel his strong feelings away from aggression but also to re-channel the potential object of that aggression. He will benefit from learning respect for females and revising his view to that of women being strong in their own way and possessing attributes that enhance a relationship. Juan's therapist is female, and in that therapeutic alliance, she is empowered as the therapist, will respond to his feelings, and will protect him. Because he does not have to take care of her, his view of women will be altered.

At home with his mother, Juan has been a parentalized child (i.e., he has been expected to provide emotional protection for her). Functioning in this type of role robs him of his childhood. When a child is deprived of his youth, he becomes a rageful adolescent. Alcoholism, violence, and gang behavior are common results of circumstances such as Juan's. Another therapeutic goal for Juan is to breach the parentalized role and allow him to regain his childhood so he can engage in spontaneous play.

Juan is at a crucial time in his development. While others may view him negatively at this time, he does possess some traits that can be utilized in either a positive or negative direction. In addition to the sensitivity previously mentioned, he also possesses leadership skills. This was disclosed when he stated that he wanted to be the leader of the autobots. It was also evident from the referral information that he dominated and controlled the children on the playground. The potential with his leadership skills has not been utilized in an affirmative direction thus far. If anything, it has being skewed in the opposite direction. It becomes apparent that if he assumes a negative identity, his leadership capacity will be utilized toward that end. The goal, therefore, is to shift this over to a positive identity. Then he will contribute to society in a positive leadership role.

By changing the way Juan responds to hurtful feelings from an aggressive to a nonaggressive style, by helping him utilize his sensitivity in constructive ways, and by redirecting the modeling that women are objects of aggression to feelings of being comfortable with females in a more egalitarian role, his leadership style will be aligned with his changed values. He will then be perceived as a more companionable, functional child.

In the playroom and with the help of the therapist, Juan will have the opportunity to work on his feelings relating to the loss of his father and on his reactions to hurtful situations. He will learn to accept his sensitivity and see it as an asset. He will also have the opportunity to regain his childhood and learn new roles for females. His therapeutic gains will be increased if both the school counselor and his teacher(s) are made aware of his strengths and are engaged as agents toward restructuring his behaviors by utilizing those strengths in more beneficial pursuits.

The therapist worked with Juan for about nine months in play therapy. Then, as occasionally happens, it became necessary for her to move and terminate with her clients. During their tenure together, Juan had made a number of gains toward his treatment goals. He had become comfortable with expressing his feelings, and the connection between negative feelings and aggression was severed. His aggression was diminishing, although it had not completely dissipated. Some gruffness still remained. However, he was no longer openly aggressive after experiencing negative feelings. He was learning to stay with a feeling, experience it, and express it in his play. Juan's view of women was in the process of changing. By allowing his therapist to care for him in the playroom, he was able to experience the normal child/caretaker role rather than the role he was experiencing in his home of being the caretaker of his mother's emotions. As his therapist respected and honored him, she modeled these attributes to Juan. Consequently, he began to honor and respect her. These new ways of relating to women were giving Juan an alternate view of the perceptions he was learning at home, demonstrating that women function in various styles.

When the time came for him to transfer to another therapist, the question arose as to which gender of therapist would be most beneficial to him. The gender of the therapist is actually a secondary issue, the primary issue being that children have the most effective therapist available. Regardless of gender, given an effective therapist, progress will be accomplished. For example, if a child has a male therapist, the treatment issues may unfold in a certain order and take a certain route, but the goals will be accomplished. With a female therapist, issues arise in a slightly different order and take a different route, but therapy is still accomplished. In other words, effective therapists will accomplish progress regardless of gender. Given a choice among an effective male therapist and an effective female therapist, then consideration can be given to gender issues.

As in the case of Juan, children of a cultural and racial background that differs from that of the therapist will create and be confronted with acceptance issues. Being a play therapist, the honoring process inherent in that role does not guarantee automatic acceptance. In the case of cultural and racial diversity, honoring the individual is not enough. An attitude where there are more similarities than differences is not enough. Racial and cultural identity provides character, security, validation, and acceptance for an individual. It is the individual's foundation. The child must know that her race and/or culture is also respected and honored. Once that is established, the child and therapist can approach the formation of their relationship, and the child can allow the therapist to protect her. It is important to let children know that their racial identification and cultural background are respected.

There are cultural centers all over the United States. If a child from a different cultural background is encountered and there is no familiarity with that culture, information may be obtained from a cultural center. A folklore story from one's culture would be both appreciated and therapeutic. Becoming familiar with some of the symbols in a child's culture will also facilitate understanding of that child's metaphors. It is the responsibility of the therapist to put forth the effort to honor the racial and cultural idiosyncracies so that the child feels that her uniqueness is accepted. Knowing this, she will also know that her pain will be accepted.

Progress Notes: Themes of the Day

An enormous amount of time can be spent describing everything a child does in play on a specific day. Realistically, few therapists have the time to accomplish this. This style of note-keeping can also lead to misinterpretation by individuals not involved in the therapy (i.e., case workers, attorneys, judges, or other psychologists involved with a litigation process). Therefore, it becomes more useful to examine the metaphors contained in the child's play and then incorporate that information into the child's progress notes. The alternative of writing a detailed description of the play leaves others who may not know the child to interpret its meaning within light of the adult's cognitions rather than the experiential world of the child. It is more efficacious to record only the themes of a child's play during a specific session. If there is one scene or one series of actions or even one quote that the therapist thinks significant, she can be more descriptive.

Commonly occurring themes in children's play include those of power and control, anger and sadness, trust or mistrust in relationships, rejection and abandonment, insecurity, and feeling intruded upon or violated. The need for protection, for boundaries, and for nurturing will be evident. Indications of a child's self-esteem and sense of (or lack of) self-empowerment will also be prevalent. A child will play out her fears and anxieties, her confusion, and her loneliness, as well as her feelings of loss, loyalty, and betrayal. Her struggle toward her own sense of identity and toward adjustment to change will also be apparent. It should be noted, however, that these themes are not mutually exclusive. Themes will co-exist in play as well as in life. Various issues that confront a child will be played out in fantasy play four to five times in each play therapy session. These issues may be played out in a number of different scenarios with a theme(s) of the issue being an element of each scenario.

For the sake of illustration, consider a young girl of four or five whose parents are in the process of getting a divorce. The young girl doesn't understand what is happening. In play therapy, she picks up some wild animals and begins to play as though they were out in the jungle, except that there is one monkey off in a tree by itself while the other animals are interacting with each other. Since children tend to only play three or four minutes on one setting, occasionally 15 minutes, and very rarely the entire session, she stops playing with the monkeys and starts to play with a doll family. She sets up a scene where the family goes on a picnic together and then returns home with one of them missing. Perhaps later she begins playing in the sandbox with cars and one of them gets buried, or she builds a wall with blocks and decides to pull one out at the bottom, illustrating her perception of her crumbling family. After the session, the therapist begins pondering to determine the common thread that ran through each of the play contexts in the session. Although the context was different, the pattern in each scene of one person or item being left out comes to prominence. The theme may vary from session to session, because one day the girl may play out her anger at the situation, and another day she may play out her fear of what is going to happen to her: Will she lose her identity in this process? In looking at the pattern of the themes, however, they all tie back to the central issue (Landreth, 1993b). Garnering the theme for the day takes practice. Doing so, however, helps bring focus and understanding to the therapist.

There may be periods of time when a child may enter into non-content play (i.e., non-fantasy play). Whereas fantasy or content play communicates important information to the therapist about the evolution of the child's issues, non-content play can communicate the child's feelings about the issue. While the child plays in the sand or colors (often nondescript forms) or plays ball, and the therapist observes or interacts with the child in these activities, the therapist must not only observe the child's style (i.e., does the child approach the activity with confidence or hesitation, etc.) but also monitor her own feelings during these interactions. For example, if the child asks the therapist to draw with her but continually criticizes the drawings of the therapist, the child is communicating her inability to please and her feelings of inadequacy and ineptness in her world. These feelings will be more pervasive for the child than simply when she is drawing. In fact, these feelings may not have been generated outside the playroom by her attempts at drawing at all. She is using the drawing as a modality of communicating the messages and feelings she encounters in her environment.

This is not to indicate that the therapist will be able to clearly understand everything the child is playing and tie it into a central issue each day. It is not imperative to always be cognizant of the child's theme in order to be facilitative. Fortunately, as previously mentioned, the atmosphere of respect, acceptance, and honoring inherent in the play therapy setting becomes, in and of itself, facilitative. The process toward growth and resolution is expedited, however, by the therapist being aware of the themes intrinsic to the child's play.

Consultation With Parents

Consistent, ongoing consultation time with the parents is vital to the child's therapy process. This time may be planned at the conclusion of the session with the child (e.g., the last 15 minutes of the hour), or at periodic intervals no less often than once a month. In essence, the parent owns the child's therapy. Unless the parent feels that the work with the therapist is helping the child and, consequently, the family, the parent may abruptly terminate the child's visits at any time. This potential exists unless regular visits have been mandated by the court. Even under those circumstances, unless the parents feel encouraged by the changes being accomplished in therapy, they may attempt to sabotage any therapeutic growth.

Time with the parents should be utilized as a consultation time for the benefit of the child. It is important that the therapist keep in mind at all times that the reason for meeting with the parents is for the benefit of the child. This time may be used to educate the parents on methods of disciplining their child appropriately. More commonly, it will be a time to give the parents information that will facilitate their understanding and acceptance of their child. It may also be a time to support the parents in their struggles with their child. It is extremely helpful for parents to become aware of the fact that all parents struggle with similar feelings about raising their children.

When parents experience this supportive relationship with their child's therapist, it is not uncommon for them to request that the therapist become their therapist as well. This is not recommended, however, because of the necessary conflict of interest inherent in that type of situation. Of course, in situations where the therapist is the only mental health practitioner in the area, it may be necessary to function in both roles. When this occurs, it should be kept in mind that there will be times when the therapist will have to use some of the therapy time to deal with the issues aroused by the duality of roles. For example, the child may become angry with the therapist and feel betrayed. The child may play out her anger during her therapy time. The astute therapist will recognize when the anger is precipitated by the child's sense of betrayal of his territorial rights.

The same issues, on a more intense level, will arise if the therapist begins seeing a sibling after she has already established a firm and trusting relationship with the first child. Unless the children begin therapy together and are seen together for group play therapy (with the siblings comprising the group), it is not in the best interests of the children for one therapist to see more than one sibling. If initial contact with the therapist is for family therapy, and later it is decided that both the child and family would benefit from the child having play therapy in addition to the family therapy, some of the same conflict of interest issues will become apparent, although not to the extent they are when another sibling becomes involved at a later date. Conversely, when a therapist begins as the child's play therapist, she cannot shift roles to family therapist because the new role is perceived as abandonment by the child. This feeling of abandonment will be expressed by the child as anger and confusion.

Recognizing the Play of the Healthy
vs.
Disordered/Abused Child

The Question of the Benefits of Unfacilitated Play

If a child lives in an environment that is supportive, play in and of itself can be therapeutic. Within this type of environment, children predominantly encounter adjustment-to-life situations only. Of course, there may be unusual circumstances such as the unexpected death of a parent. Even with this type of occurrence, though, the child and remaining parent will often provide comfort for each other. Similarly, in divorces, parents can be sensitive enough to their children to provide for the child's emotional needs.

If the child lives in an environment that is chaotic, abusive, or highly dysfunctional, or for several possible reasons, the parent is unable to provide the necessary support for the child, then play alone will not be enough. The parents' inability may be either situational and short-lived or characterological and long-term. When children grow up in a chronically dysfunctional type of environment, their emotional development becomes thwarted, as evidenced in all of the literature on the topic during the last decade (e.g., Kempe & Kempe, 1984; Putnam, 1991). Play therapy is needed to provide the child with a mirror to the world which reflects a more positive image.

*Whitney, who was nine years old when her appendix rup-
tured, is a good example of the therapeutic nature of play in a
healthy child. After the appendix ruptured, the doctors did not
realize what was wrong for almost a week. By this time, she was
so close to death and so full of peritonitis that she and her parents went through a horrendous ordeal in the hospital. After 10
days, she was allowed to go home because the doctors and nurses had done all they could. It was now up to Whitney's body and
will to live. It was nearly six weeks before she was able to return
to school.*

*When she left the hospital, Whitney took many of the items
that had been used in her room such as an I.V. bag, disposable
latex gloves, little bottles and pans, etc. When her mother finally went back to work and then returned home in the evening,
Whitney had put all the things she had brought home from the
hospital together with her stuffed animals in the family room.
Each one was bandaged in some way. Her mother said, "Boy,
you've had a busy day today! What kind of operations did they
have?"*

*Whitney replied, "Well, appendectomy, Mom. That's the only
one I know!"*

*About five days later when the housekeeper asked if she
should put the things away, the mother responded, "No, leave
them there as long as she needs them." The family then cleaned
and worked and lived around them for the next six months.
Gradually, things began to disappear out of the room. However,
even to this day, Whitney still talks about becoming a medical
doctor.*

For the most part, play in a healthy child will be rehearsal for adult
life (Lewis, 1993). Through their play, these children practice to gain the
necessary skills for adult functioning. This is often termed developmental play (Butler, 1978). As is illustrated in the example of Whitney, however, healthy children can also utilize their play to resolve a temporary
concern or confusion. For the child who is disordered, who comes from
a highly dysfunctional family, and/or has been abused, however, this is
not the case. Following is a comparison of the dynamics involved in the
play of a healthy child versus the play of the unhealthy or abused child.

Comparison of the Dynamics Involved in the Play of the Healthy vs. Disordered/Abused Child

The Healthy Child

The Disordered or Sexually Abused Child

1. Relationship With the Therapist

Healthy children will enter into a more open, direct relationship with the therapist.

They will engage in direct conversations, including eye-to-eye contact.

They will exhibit spontaneity, curiosity, and genuine emotions in their interactions.

There will be a willingness to talk about everyday life experiences and attitudes. For example, "Oh, yeah, last week we went to the zoo, and we saw the bears and the zebras. Did you know that zebras had stripes?"

Healthy children will interact in one or more of the following relational styles:

(a) Independent. They will be equally comfortable at playing alone or moving in and out of mutual play with the therapist. They will be happy in their play, often singing or humming.

(b) Co-operative. Although many children struggle with their self-

1. Relationship With the Therapist

Disordered or abused children will be aware of the therapist's presence but may ignore the therapist.

They will have little, if any, eye-to-eye contact.

They will manifest in one of two styles:

(a) They will appear uncomfortable in the presence of the therapist.

(b) They will simply sit and wait for instructions from the therapist. They become overly involved with the therapist immediately, before a rapport has been established.

Disordered or abused children will interact in one or more of the following relational styles:

(a) Dependent. They will wait for the therapist to do things for them, want to be told what to do, and tend to bombard the therapist with questions such as, "What is this?" "How do you play with it?" "What is it supposed to do."

(b) Competitive. Because of a lack of trust, disordered or sexually

esteem, and it feels good to compete and win, these children will be more likely to accept the fact that sometimes they'll win and sometimes they'll lose. Consequently, they do not exhibit strong styles of competitiveness or dependency.

abused children may want involvement with the therapist, while at the same time almost being driven to maintain control of the relationship. These children want to win every time and will do whatever is necessary in order to win, even if it means quitting before completion of an activity when it becomes inevitable that the therapist will be victorious.

(c) Interactive. These children will feel free to question the therapist. They may begin questioning the limits of the playroom right away.

(c) Aggressive. The play of these children will often be aggressive from the first moment of therapy, requiring the therapist to set frequent limits in the beginning of the therapy process. Once past this testing stage, however, the therapist will not have to set as many limits, although from time to time it may still be necessary. These children may even aggress against the therapist.

2. Flexibility in Play

2. Rigidity in Play

Healthy children will feel free to acquaint themselves with the playroom. They will utilize a wider variety of toys and materials. If they are working on building a scene and a vital part of the scenario cannot be located, they can be flexible enough to use a dissimilar toy and pretend that it is the desired toy. When finished playing out the scene, they may use the same toys to reconstruct a new scenario.

These children will tend to focus only on toys that enable them to reconstruct their world and the events of their abuse numerous times. Driven internally to play out the scene of their abuse, they are unable to use these toys in other scenes. If they cannot locate the exact toy to replicate the desired scene, they will give up on the whole scenario.

3. Intensity Level

3. Intensity Level

Healthy children will exhibit mild to moderate intensity toward their play or specific items within that play.

There is a high level of intensity in the play, movements, and speech of disordered and sexually abused chil-

They will utilize play as a means of exploring feelings and temporary tensions or conflicts that cannot be expressed easily or safely in school or at home.

They may occasionally play silently. Even in the silence, though, the atmosphere remains at a comfortable level of intensity. Their play simulates what these children observe in their world and becomes a rehearsal for life.

4. Openness

Healthy children will be able to express negative feelings and attitudes directly. This may occur in conversation or in play. If it occurs in play, the characters will express their displeasure with other characters openly. Since themes in play are focused expressions of the child's feelings, they are more easily discernable. These children will continue expressing such feelings until relief and satisfaction are achieved.

5. Integration.

Healthy children may express both negative and positive attitudes about the same person, issue, experience, or scene. For example, the sister doll and the brother doll are playing together and fight over something. Once the fight is over, they play together again, "Come on, why don't

dren. Although their activities may change quickly, the intensity remains inherent in the different play contexts. By the end of the session, the therapist may feel exhausted.

4. Diffuse Play

These children will exhibit more diffusion in their play (i.e., their play will not be a direct expression of their feelings). Fantasy play will be tangential, confused, with no order or pattern, or it will perseverate on one emotion only such as aggression. These traits make it difficult to identify any themes. Although this is frustrating to the therapist, it is important to keep in mind that it may not always be possible to translate the metaphor of the child's play into adult cognitions. Fortunately, this is not necessary in order to be therapeutic with these children.

5. Splitting

With abused or disordered children, the therapist will see splitting in their play characters. A character will be either all good or all bad. These children will not be able to see both good and bad within the same being (Shapiro, 1992). Also, there is often a pattern of play scenes with numerous

we go together and build ...", which is a more accurate reflection of real life. Their negative feelings also tend to be milder than those of the disordered or abused child — mild to moderate as opposed to severe.

bad characters, one victim, and maybe (as the child progresses in therapy) a character that is a hero(ine).

6. Dissociation

Some dissociation is a normal part of childhood and is not necessarily a prognosticator of Dissociative Identity Disorder (Putnam, 1991). Indeed, this may be the tool which allows children to engage in fantasy play in order to resolve internal struggles for themselves.

6. Dissociation

Abused and disordered children at times dissociate. This dissociation will be displayed in frequent shifts from one uncompleted activity to another, impulsivity or carelessness, amnesia for previously initiated play, an obvious trance-like state, or marked changes in behavior and play styles (Putnam, 1991).

The intake session is the time to determine, as much as possible, the character of the child and of her life situation. This will include a history, a presentation of symptoms and current environmental circumstances. It also must include information about the child's style of functioning and her approach to the world.

There are many ways in which this information may be gathered, including parent interview, child interview, observations, projective drawings or formal, structured assessment methods. By necessity, the therapist who works with children must be flexible enough to adjust her method of obtaining this information. Children will not always cooperate with the modality that is most comfortable or customary for the adult. If observations of a child's interactions and play are utilized, it is necessary to be watchful for repeated themes.

It is important to maintain a stance of cooperation with the caretakers in order to facilitate change for the child. Collaboration between caretakers and the therapist will enable both to better understand the child. The therapist can contribute the child's experiences and perceptions while the caretakers are able to place those experiences within a context. For example, after some time with the child, the therapist may be aware that the child is feeling overpowered, frustrated and fearful. The caretaker will be able to add the context of the bully in the neighborhood who has been tyrannizing her lately.

With a thorough assessment, a diagnosis may be determined as well as the most appropriate treatment modality and treatment plan for the child.

CHAPTER 4

REACHING A DIAGNOSIS

Introduction

Once the therapist has completed the intake and initial visits and observed the child's play, it becomes necessary to assign a diagnosis. Diagnosing children can be more difficult than diagnosing adults, primarily because children cannot give clear verbal descriptions of their symptoms. Therefore, it becomes necessary to diagnose children not only from information provided by the parents, caseworkers, and/or school personnel, but also from the information that the child presents in his play. Since play is the child's modality of communication, it becomes by necessity the style utilized to communicate the child's distress. Since this style of communication is not as succinct as verbal communication, understanding the child's message may require a somewhat longer period of involvement than is required with adults. Each disorder will present itself differently in the child's play. To ascertain the child's message, it is essential to take note of the recurring themes evident in the child's play.

Disorders

Conduct Disorder — Childhood Onset

Play of the Conduct Disordered child will be very similar to that of the Oppositional-Defiant Disordered child, with the exception being the lack of respect and aggression toward people and animals, the willful destruction of property, and a pattern of theft or deceit (APA, 1994). These traits will be described by the parents or foster parents as occurring in the home environment. In addition, they will be manifested in the play of the Conduct Disordered child as repeated aggression between the toys in fantasy play, with no preferred perpetrator as in the play of abused children. In other words, as the child recapitulates the abuse that has been perpetrated against him, there is no pattern in the aggressive play. The child may also necessitate an extended Testing for Protection period because of being destructive with the materials in the playroom.

A child with a history of physical or sexual abuse may display aggression toward others at school or at home and may be destructive, but in play it is possible to identify a perpetrator. This is in contrast to the Conduct Disordered child who does not identify a perpetrator. Also, many children will attempt to take home some item from the playroom. This is not theft. Rather, it serves as a reminder of the security they feel in the playroom. Therefore, Conduct Disorder-Childhood Onset may not be diagnosed based on this one criterion alone.

Because so many of the features of this disorder are similar to those of the Attachment Disordered child, a thorough history during intake is essential in order to make a diagnosis. A determining factor is a history of attachment between parent(s) and child. If, during any time of the child's first months of life, there was an extended separation of child and caretaker or a history of neglect on the part of the caretaker, Reactive Attachment Disorder would be a more likely diagnosis.

Oppositional-Defiant Disorder

The child with this disorder is one whose parents will describe as being stubborn, obnoxious, and/or disruptive. The therapist will get a sense that this child encounters so much cognitive and emotional defeat in his world that his acting out is an attempt to externalize the chaos and loss of control he experiences internally. With himself being the source of the chaos in his environment, he can manipulate its intensity and create emotional turmoil for those around him. In doing so, he does not have to concentrate on the turbulence inside himself. Utilizing this means of gaining some mastery over his environment, however, may create additional stress for the child since it is negatively perceived by other individuals in his environment. The additional stress creates subsequent feelings of defeat for the child who then creates more chaos. Thus, the cycle enhances itself.

This child will also be resistive in play and will test limits repeatedly. In addition, he will tend to be critical, finding fault with the status of the toys or the way he has structured the play. He may even have one of the characters in his play assume the role of a critical evaluator of other characters.

The oppositional child will not often choose to include the therapist in his play. If he does, it will be done in such a way as to demonstrate critical control over the therapist.

> *Josh was seven years old when his therapist first began working with him. One day during play, he told the therapist, "Here, I'll take the truck, you take the helicopter, and we'll meet over there." As the therapist was flying the helicopter, she began making helicopter noises. Josh stopped playing with the truck and said, "What are you doing? What's that noise?"*
>
> *The therapist explained that it was the helicopter, and Josh responded, "That's stupid! You can't do that! You drive the truck, and I'll fly the helicopter."*
>
> *The therapist then began to drive the truck, making truck noises. Josh stopped and said, "Where are you going?" After the therapist told him where she was going, he said, "Not over there, it's over here!" Although the child had seconds earlier directed the therapist to go to the spot where the truck was heading, she said nothing and did as Josh instructed.*
>
> *After numerous repetitions of scenes similar to the ones described, the therapist left the session feeling defeated and said to a colleague, "I thought I knew something about kids. Now I'm not so sure!"*

Playing with the Oppositional-Defiant Disordered child, under his control and criticism, creates in the therapist the same defeated feelings the child experiences in his everyday life. This is as it should be. If the therapist is accepting and honoring the child, as outlined in Chapters 1 and 5, the child will create his play and direct the therapist within that play so that the therapist will begin to perceive the identical affect that the child experiences every day of his life. It is common for therapists to wish to avoid experiencing these feelings because they can be very unpleasant. In working with adults, a therapist will talk with them about their feelings. However, because children experience their feelings rather than cognate about them, the therapist will also begin to experience them rather than think about them. As unpleasant as this can be, it is an important part of facilitating the child's movement toward well-being.

Anxiety Disorders

Overanxious Disorder. This child fears being overwhelmed by the world. His play will either be under-active or very active, moving quickly from one activity to another. This child's anxiety makes it difficult for him to concentrate on one activity for any length of time. This anxiety will manifest in one of two ways. One child will become unrestrained, moving quickly from one activity to another and asking many questions of a definitive nature (i.e., "What is this?" "How do I play with it?" "Is it okay to do this?" "Is it okay to do that?"). At the opposite extreme is the child who becomes constricted and inhibited in his movements. He will seem afraid to explore the room, initiate any play, or interact with the therapist.

The overanxious child has a predominant desire for approval from others. Consequently, his risk-taking behavior will be low for fear of making a mistake and facing the anxiety of disapproval and rejection. Since the playroom is a safe environment in which to experiment with taking risks, it is fitting that the therapist utilize this time as an opportunity for the child to experience this anxiety and take the necessary risks to overcome it. Without these necessary steps, the child will never know what it is to risk and be successful, which is a vital part of the growth process for this child.

Separation Anxiety. The Separation Anxiety Disordered child can first be detected from the parents' description of the fears their child experiences. Then, during the initial visit, the child will resist leaving the parent to go into the playroom with the therapist. In such a situation, it is appropriate to allow the parent to attend the session with the child. However, it is to be emphasized to the parent that he is there to provide emotional support for the child. Interaction between the parent and the therapist should be held to a minimum, with the child remaining at the center of attention. It is also important to note that the therapist must not force his attentions onto the child before the child is comfortable. In this case, the therapist should remain at a distance and begin interacting with verbal involvement. This can progress to more playful involvement as the child requests. The parent can slowly be moved out of the child's field of vision and eventually out of the room. NOTE: The child's permission should be requested before the parent leaves the room. The child must know what to expect from his parent and the therapist, and his feelings must be respected at all times. This process may require several sessions. Most important in this process is protecting the child's sense of safety and trust.

After the child feels comfortable being in the playroom alone with the therapist, an interesting phenomenon occurs. He begins to resist separating from the therapist. The evolving picture seems to be one of the child having difficulty with changing from one situation to another. Customarily, the end of a session is announced five minutes before the actual termination time. The child is advised that there are only five minutes of playtime left. With these children, however, it works best to give their five-minute warning sooner in order for them to have time to adjust to leaving. "We have five minutes left, and then it will be time for us to put the toys away and leave." It may even be necessary to give the five-minute warning when there are actually 10 or 15 minutes left so that the child has a chance to work through his separation anxiety while he is still with the therapist. It discounts the importance of the child and his feelings to allow him to leave in a state of anxiety about the termination. Parents are not always sensitive enough to the child's affective state to provide the necessary support. In defense of parents, however, they often have time constraints that do not allow them to be as attentive as they would normally be to their children's feelings.

> *Nicole was a little girl whose therapist informed her that they had only five minutes of playtime left when in actuality they had twenty. Nicole would then sit and rock back and forth saying, "Oh, I don't want to go. I don't want to go."*
>
> *With Nicole, the therapist would sit and rock and say, "Oh, I know. It's so hard, so hard. I don't want to do this." This would go on for 10 or 15 minutes before Nicole resolved her anxiety to the point that she could leave the room comfortably.*

After resisting, struggling with, and finally accepting the temporary end of her companionship with the therapist, Nicole was comfortable in leaving the therapist and the playroom to rejoin her caretaker.

Post-Traumatic Stress Disorder. The play of the Post-Traumatic Stress Disordered child will be similar to that of the Over-Anxious Disordered child. A child who has experienced a traumatic stressor, however, will demonstrate disempowerment in regard to anything he has associated with the stressor event. The disempowerment may be manifest as anxiety, anger or helplessness. Often a child will develop a form of coping to ward off the overwhelming anxieties related to the trauma (Terr, 1990). The child may choose one small part of the event and replay it repeatedly. Taken in isolation, the correlation between the repeated behavior and the trauma may not be readily apparent if the observer is unaware of the trauma. With stronger coping skills, the child may repeatedly reenact the entire event in his play in an easily recognizable format. Or the event may be in metaphorical form and not easily recognized as a recapitulation of the event. In this case, other symptoms must be utilized in making the diagnosis.

The parents will often notice an abrupt change in the child's behavioral patterns. The child may suddenly become fearful of separation from an adult with whom the child feels safe. He may withdraw from new experiences and may begin experiencing nightmares (Dulcan & Popper, 1991). He may regress in his development, becoming enuretic, encopretic or resort to regressive speech patterns.

In play, and in daily life, the child will struggle to regain the control that was taken from him by this unexpected, overwhelming event. This attempt at control may take the form of demanding rigidity in patterns of behavior. In play, there will likely be boundaries repeatedly established by the child. These boundaries may be physical, e.g., "You are Captain Hook, I am Peter Pan. Remember, we play it this way." When this is the case, this child will appear as Post Traumatic Stress Disorder with Obsessive-Compulsive traits. If this rigidity is coupled with a child's expression of anger and outrage, he may manifest as Oppositional-Defiant Disorder or Conduct Disorder-Childhood Onset. However, the play will differ in several respects. There will be themes of the stressor event in the play and there may be an identifiable perpetrator. While there may be violations against others by one being that could be identified as a perpetrator, there is, overall, respect for the rights of others evident in the child's play and in the relationship with the therapist.

Several characteristics differentiate between the child who has experienced an acute trauma, such as a car crash with fatalities and the child who has experienced (or is currently experiencing) chronic trauma, such as repeated sexual abuse.

The child who has experienced an acute trauma will be able to use the relationship with the therapist more quickly and effectively in his work. The child who experiences chronic trauma will struggle with the relationship in addition to the abuse. For this child, establishing trust in the realtionship is an integral part of the therapy. Even during the working stages, the child must continually monitor the relationship before he can use it as support in his work with the abuse issues. The acutely traumatized child will demonstrate a higher level of anxiety, whereas the child who has experienced chronic traumatic stress will manifest more depression. The play of the acutely traumatized child will change from his play prior to the trauma. It will enter a new arena of play as the child begins to reenact the trauma or parts of the trauma. Play of the chronically stressed child has changed previously at the onset of the abuse. He has been playing the changed style of play over the extent of the trauma so that the play style now appears as normal for him. The play has not been effective in alleviating his symptoms because it has not been attended to nor has the trauma been eliminated. His play and his life have incorporated the changes as dysfunctional adaptive life patterns.

> *Bobby was a seven-year-old boy who had been attacked by a pit bull. While walking around a parked pickup truck in an alley, he was attacked by the dog. It jumped over its fence and immediately began to maul him, leaving scars on his face. Not surprisingly, today he is afraid to walk around parked cars and is especially terrified of dogs.*
>
> *On the initial visit with his therapist, he was very quiet. After a brief question-and-answer intake procedure, the therapist told him it was time to play and they could play whatever he wanted. Bobby immediately picked up a flashlight, took the doll house, and started shining the flashlight up and down along the house. He was careful to cover every square centimeter of that house!*

The therapist, immediately recognizing this as unusual play for a first session, just walked over and sat down near the boy. After watching for a while, the therapist said, "Boy, you want to know all about that house." Several minutes later, she said, "You want to make sure there are no surprises." By the end of the session, her statement was, "You want to make sure this is a safe place for you to be."

Through his experience, Bobby had learned to question before he naively accepted any new situation. He demonstrated his insecurity with the new situation symbolically through his examination of the doll house. Notice the dialogue with Bobby. This therapist wisely did not start off with statements such as, "You want to make sure this is a safe place to be." Initially, it is important to give non-threatening statements that address the child's issue on a somewhat superficial level while still focusing on the child's feelings. For instance, a statement about his manipulations of the doll house is a good one to begin with. It is important to start off reflecting what the child is doing, then move to affective statements, allowing the child to set the pace. (See Chapter 8 for further discussion of appropriate responses during various stages of therapy.)

Somatization Disorder

The diagnosis of Somatoform Disorder will be apparent by the parents' description of the child's symptoms. Generally, the referral of a child experiencing physical symptoms follows a preliminary visit to a physician. Therefore, it is known that the etiology of the disorder is psychogenic. The play of this child will illuminate the stressor which has precipitated the psychogenic reaction.

Adjustment Disorder With Depressed Mood

Adjustment Disorder With Depressed Mood can be complicated in children. Their symptoms may be similar to those of adults (i.e., loss of appetite, loss of interest in usual activities, lethargy, etc.), or they may be paradoxically the opposite (i.e., the child becomes very active — acting out, irritable, and emotionally distant). Often, this results in the child being diagnosed as oppositional when in actuality the child is depressed, again emphasizing the significance of a thorough intake. The themes in this child's play will center around loss and grief, replaying the precipitating event, although it will be expressed in different play contexts. The loss may not be a tangible loss such as the death of a parent or the loss of a parent through divorce or forced separation. Rather, it may be more abstract such as the loss of the child's self-esteem or security.

The Suicidal Child[1]

Of more vital diagnostic accuracy than Adjustment Disorder With Depressed Mood is the Suicidal Child. In the play of these children, the therapist will see frequent themes of hopelessness, helplessness, and self-destructiveness. They will play out themes of sadness, loss, retrieval, and worthlessness. When these children see a gun or a knife in the playroom, they will take that toy and, rather than aiming it outward, as is more common, they will aim it inward (i.e., putting the gun to their own head or the knife to their own throat). They appear to lack regard for their own body. Sometimes, they will play the role of a superhero. Unfortunately, for the moment at least, they may indulge in magical thinking and believe it to be true. Consequently, the therapist must watch these children very carefully so that they don't attempt some superhuman feat and hurt themselves.

It has been observed, although not understood, that these children will frequently throw small toys out the windows of the doll house or throw things out the windows of their own home (Pfeffer, 1979). In feeling desperate, they want to let someone know their experience of hopelessness. Yet they feel as though nothing they do will have any effect on their environment.

Part of the therapeutic work done with these children will involve helping them to see that their actions can affect positive change in their own situation. Experiencing this cause and effect relationship empowers

---

1. This is not a DSM-IV (APA, 1994) diagnostic category.

them. In play, this is accomplished by bringing it to the child's attention every time change occurs as a result of a preceding behavior. For example, a child sets up a scene where children are playing together and one of them falls into a deep hole. The child (in the play) is frightened and fears he will never be able to get out of the hole. Even if the child does not allow the play child to get out of the hole, the therapist can still point out, "Even though he is not out of the hole yet, he is still holding on. He knows he is strong enough to hold on till he can think of a way to get out of the hole."

Play such as this would more likely be evidenced in the beginning of the play therapy process. Each play sequence over time would be expected to show progress along the evolution of empowerment. In the preceding illustration, for example, in the next play session, the play child may call for someone (very likely the therapist, or a character the child has asked the therapist to play) to help him out. Next, he will find something to assist him in pulling himself out, followed by his seeing the hole before he falls into it.

The sense of empowerment gained through this play process is incongruent with the feeling of hopelessness and helplessness (Gunsberg, 1989).

Eating Disorder

The central theme in the play of the Eating Disordered child will be power and control. Since these children feel they have no control in their lives outside the playroom, they will show their inhibited desire for control in the playroom where they feel safe and accepted. This child's play may be similar to that of the Oppositional-Defiant Disordered child, although it will be more constricted. For example, where the oppositional child makes demands of the therapist, the Eating Disordered child will show the control in his play rather than directly in the relationship with the therapist. Themes of eating may occur, but not necessarily so.

Identity Problems

Children with Identity Problems are very busy. In their play, they will experiment with numerous different roles and will even want their therapist to play various roles. Of course, what better place for them to do this than in play therapy? They enjoy playing dress-up, wearing glasses, playing Hide-and-Seek, etc. It will become quite obvious, however, that they have a difficult time making and maintaining a decision. Some identity confusion is to be expected during childhood and particularly during early adolescence. A good indicator of a child who has reached the point of excessive identity confusion is when the therapist becomes confused in the play because the child has repeatedly changed roles (both his and the therapist's), play scenes, and the play context.

> *During a session, Kelly asked her therapist to play the dad. Shortly thereafter, she wanted the therapist to play the mom and then the kid sister. Before long, the therapist began to think, "Wait a minute. I forgot who I am."*

The therapist in this session began feeling confused about the role she was assigned to play. When this occurs, it is a good indicator of the child's pervasive feelings. As mentioned earlier, children will often direct the play in such a way that the therapist replicates the role of the child, although it may be disguised as other characters. Therefore, by being active in that role, the therapist experiences the feelings one would experience if one lived that role. Again, this is the child's way of communicating his situation to the therapist so that the therapist can empathize with the child's feelings.

Reactive Attachment Disorder

Somewhat similar to the child with Identity Problems is the child with Reactive Attachment Disorder. In addition to the similarity in play, these children will show polarities of feelings which will fluctuate from session to session. For instance, one day these children will treat the therapist as though he were the most wonderful person in the world. The therapist will leave the session feeling that much progress was accomplished. In the next session, however, the therapist may spend the entire time trying to keep the child from hurting him. Additionally, these children may choose a theme, such as abandonment, and perseverate on that theme.

Most often, a modality which is much more directive than play therapy may need to be taken in working with these children. However, play therapy may be utilized as a medium of relating to the child. From the play, information may be relayed to the child about the effect of his behaviors on those around him (in this case the therapist), limits may be set, and the therapist can convey his caring for the child. By necessity, due to the nature of this disorder, this information is conveyed directly to the child in a firm and caring style. A disproportionate length of time in this therapeutic process will simulate the Testing for Protection Stage of play therapy. Once diagnosed, if the therapist wishes to utilize play therapy with these children, it will be necessary to adapt this special format, or refer them to a therapist specializing in work with this disorder.

Dissociative Identity Disorder

Dissociative Identity Disordered children may begin to manifest alters as early as four to six years of age (Courtois, 1988; Kluft, 1985). Indicators of children who may be Dissociative Identity Disordered include children who are known to have been abused but do not remember the actual abuse. Other indicators include the child who shows marked day-to-day or hour-to-hour variations in skills, knowledge, food preferences, athletic abilities, etc, which would be expected to be stable. Variations in handwriting, knowledge of arithmetic, use of tools, artistic abilities, etc., are suspect (Courtois, 1988). A parent or teacher is very likely to notice these differences. In the playroom, the therapist will notice distinct differences in personality style and very different play patterns between alters. For illustration, the child will make reference to a part of himself and may even want to be called different names on different days (e.g., wanting to be called "Bobby" one day and "Robert" another day). Also, he may want to dress differently, such as wanting to dress in torn, dirty clothes one day, and acting rowdy and boisterous, and on another day wanting to dress in clean, dressy clothing, and acting quiet, proper, and overly polite.

Dissociative Identity Disordered children seem unusually forgetful or confused about very basic things such as the names of teachers and friends, important events, possessions, etc. They may demonstrate rapid regressions in behavior or show marked variations in age-appropriate behavior (e.g., a 10-year-old using baby talk consistently or drawing like a three-year-old). Excessive lying or denying of behavior, even when the evidence is obvious and immediate, may indicate the alter performed the behavior and the host personality is not aware of it (e.g., "I didn't eat the cookie," when the cookie crumbs are still on his mouth).

In addition, the DID child may report conversations with an imaginary playmate when he is beyond age six or seven (Ross, 1989). It should be noted that one of these symptoms alone is not sufficient for a diagnosis of Dissociative Identity Disorder. More appropriately, it is necessary to look for a cluster of symptoms that indicate this disorder.

Obsessive-Compulsive Disorder

Play of the Obsessive-Compulsive Disordered child will be constricted. He will play prescribed roles rather than those that are rich with fantasy and symbolism. He will also prefer structured games, making sure he knows the rules and follows them precisely. It is difficult to get much interpretative value from the play of the Obsessive-Compulsive Disordered child. The therapist first has to model for the child that it is perfectly permissible to move outside customary parameters so that the child's play can become more expansive. If necessary, the therapist may even initially structure a situation so that it allows the child to experience the wider than usual parameters. For example, when the two are playing in the sandbox together, the therapist may "accidentally" push some sand out of the box and onto the floor. This would be followed by the comment, "Oh, that's okay."

The Narcissistic Child

The Narcissistic child will evidence a deficiency of compassion or empathy for anyone else's feelings. Whatever he feels on a given day, he will assume all others around him feel as well as at the same level of intensity. In fact, the feeling of the moment is all-pervasive and, at times, all-consuming. For instance, if this child comes into the session one day feeling cheated because the teacher wouldn't assign him the role he wanted in his class play, all his behaviors derive from this position. He views everyone he interacts with as if they were the ones who had cheated him. His assumption will be that the therapist will see the world in the same way. His feelings, of course, are not rational, but he will not be capable of observing the situation from a different point of view. His anger will be vented on anyone who may try to comfort him by using rationalizations or compassion for others. This is a sun revolving around the earth type of attitude.

Narcissistic children become easily bored and indicate a marked inhibition in play, rationalizing it as boredom (Kernberg, 1989). Initially, these children will move toward structured competitive games. Any defeat, however, creates intense anxiety and/or temper tantrums. This child's play will change from time to time, depending on his all-pervasive feelings of the day. It may be difficult to follow themes in his play because of the immense fluctuations in his perception of the world as being an accepting or rejecting place at that moment. These children will be demanding of the therapist, and that aspect of their character will pervade the play.

If there is a tape recorder in the playroom, these children love to tape themselves. They also enjoy performing on a stage, or putting on a puppet show, because puppets will focus attention on the child while, at the same time, distancing any display of affect or any chance of being perceived in error.

The Schizophrenic Child

Parents of schizophrenic children will describe their child as developing normally until around the age of three to five years. When other children's cooperative play began to flourish, these children began to withdraw. Their language may decrease to the point where they quit talking altogether or they may invent words. Their fantasies have a bizarre content; therefore their play, if they play, will have a bizarre content. For instance, they may fear another being will come and seize them in a symbiotic relationship so that they lose all control and sense of themselves.

Since many children have imaginary friends, which is not necessarily a symptom of a severely disordered child, parents may not realize at first whether or not the friend is abnormal. However, these children have difficulty coming out of fantasy and back into reality, or even knowing the difference. Therapists will not see patterns in their play, because it becomes loose and dissociated. Once this is diagnosed, it is time to stop using play therapy as a modality for change. Play therapy is most useful for these children when they are in a residential treatment setting and can be observed on a 24-hour basis. When they are observed to be in a more lucid state, they may be capable of communicating to a therapist through their play, their sandplay, or their artwork.

CHAPTER 5

THE EXPLORATORY STAGE

Introduction

Each child's development and experiences are unique. Consequently, the play of each child is distinct in style and content. As the play therapy process unfolds, however, certain discernable stages are similar for all children. Each of these stages will be described in terms of their similar characteristics in the play of children during the therapeutic process. Within these parameters, each child will manifest her own personality with her own issue(s) to resolve.

The first of these stages is the *Exploratory Stage*, so named because of the nature of the child's activities during this time. The purpose of this stage is twofold: (1) that the child become familiar and comfortable in the playroom; and (2) that the therapist begin to build a relationship with the child.

This stage occurs when the child enters the playroom and engages the therapist alone for the first time. This is very likely a new situation for the child, unlike visits to the family physician or pediatrician and unlike (although somewhat similar to) the child's time at school. In addition, it is very likely that the child's parents have not informed her about what to expect. As a result, this time will be utilized by the child in learning about the therapist and the play therapy process.

When the child enters the room, she will be intrigued by the room and its contents as well as by the therapist. It is very important for the therapist to allow the child to enter this experience the way the child approaches life — at her own pace. Some children will assume the safe path of awaiting instructions from the therapist, whereas other children will begin moving toward the toys. This is an opportunity for the therapist to inform the child that this room is for children and, as such, children can be the way they want to be in this room.

Initially, examining the toys is less threatening and more entertaining than interacting with the therapist. During this time, the therapist begins the formative level of the honoring process by accepting the child in any way that the child wants to present herself as long as it is not harmful to either herself or the therapist. The therapist shows respect for the child, accepts the style the child wants to present, and understands the child's need to present herself in her own manner, whether that be aggressive and resistive or shy and withdrawn (Axline, 1947b). This acceptance assists the child in learning that the playroom is an emotionally, as well as physically, safe place to be.

Initial Explorations

During the child's initial explorations, she may make comments about the toys to the therapist. These comments may range from a positive expression (e.g., "Wow, you have all these toys to play with!") to a more cautious or negative expression (e.g., "These are dumb or stupid toys!"). These early comments by the child are usually metaphors for how the child views the world and the people in her world as well as her need for protection and her capacity to trust in establishing this new relationship. It is the therapist's responsibility to accept the child's level of experience and be present with the child, however she chooses to present herself (Moustakas, 1959/1992). In addition, the therapist must honor and accept these expressions as being representative of the child's perceptions of the world. For example, if the child is frightened by a certain toy, the therapist must accept that fear as genuine and not attempt to dissuade the child from that experience. The child's feelings and behaviors are based on the child's perceptions. To the child this is reality and, as such, must be respected.

In addition, the therapist must communicate her acceptance of the child's perceptions while at the same time letting the child know she hears the message and accepts it. This is done by reflecting the protective needs behind the expression (i.e., "These toys want to know that they're safe when they play.").

During this Exploratory Stage, a child will continue to move around the playroom, exploring and selecting toys that intrigue her. The child will play with a toy for a few moments and then move on to other toys. Although she will make comments about a toy or its use, her expressions will be short, meaningful statements. A child will not maintain continuous play or develop a theme in this early play. These short comments, however, do contain meaningful content that identifies themes to be developed later in the child's play. The therapist should acknowledge these expressions with a reflection only, matching the child's expression in a given moment. For instance, the therapist may respond by saying, "That truck wants to show how powerful it can be," or "There are a lot of wishes in that magic wand that no one knows about." The therapist lets the child know that she is both listening and respectful of the child's expression; however, she does not initiate any direction in this Exploratory Stage, as is commonly done in an intake session. Again, the primary purpose of this stage is for the therapist to honor the child's expression of herself. In this way, the therapist begins to build a safe environment and relationship for the child. By establishing trust in the therapist, the child is able to engage in the next stage of play therapy — the *Testing for Protection Stage* — that is necessary for therapy to begin. (See Chapter 8, *Enrichment of the "Play as Metaphor" Process* for further discussion of appropriate responses during this stage of therapy.)

Common Questions Asked by Children During the Exploratory Stage

"Why Is This [Toy] Here?"

This expression is a metaphorical question meaning, "Why am I here?" The response of the therapist should be to the metaphor: "That's a very valuable [toy], and I'm glad that [toy] is here so that I can get to know it better." The relationship begins to build through the toys that are items of familiarity and security to the child. In fact, during this stage, it is very common for the therapist to talk to the toys rather than reflect directly to the child, which may be overwhelming or intrusive to the child. Reflecting through the toys allows the child to maintain her security and to experience the honoring expressed by the therapist. To the child, this conveys that someone is understanding the experience from a child's perspective, and that her expressions will be listened to, respected, and responded to as valid expressions that are meaningful to the child.

"How Do You Play With this [Toy]?"

Children know how to play. Consequently, this question's metaphorical meaning is, "How am I supposed to act when I'm in here with you?" The response could be, "That [toy] can be anything it wants to be in here. It can be a truck or a rocket ship or even fly to the moon if it wants. In here, things can be any way you would like them to be." This response allows the child to know that she can be herself in the room, and that her fantasy play is going to be accepted as it emerges in the Dependency Stage of play therapy.

"Do You Ever Play With These Toys?"

The meaningful level or metaphor to this question is, "When I play, are you going to play with me or not?" The usual answer is, "If the toys want to play alone, they can do so. If they invite me or want me to play with them, then I'll play with them." This conveys to the child that the therapist is available to join the play whenever she is invited by the child into the child's experience.

"Do You See Other Children?"

The metaphorical question here is, "How important am I to you?" When this question is asked, a good response on the part of the therapist would be, "Yes, and when you're in the room, you are the most important person." In this way, the therapist draws the focus back to the relationship in the room and keeps it focused on the child. This is very valuable.

"Why Do You Do This?"

This is a metaphor for, "Are you going to be on my side and see my view in what I tell you?" A good response by the therapist would be, "Because I care about children. When I was a child, life wasn't always the way I wanted it to be. Sometimes, big people don't have time for little people. I want to play with you and learn what you think about, and hear what is going on in your life." This communicates to the child that the therapist is child-oriented.

This is where a family in therapy and a child in play therapy differ. In family therapy, it is important to align with the parents, whereas in play therapy a therapist must align herself with the child. There is still an element of aligning with children in family therapy, but if the therapist over-aligns with the child's perspective then, through the child's view, the therapist ends up fighting the family as a therapist. This is where it is important to look at the system in which the child is functioning.

"Do You Live Here?" or "Are
You Always in This Playroom?"
This question is usually asked in a later stage of the play therapy process but may be asked toward the end of the Exploratory Stage. The metaphor to this question is, "Could I come and live with you? Could I be with you forever?" To the child, the therapist is such a security object that, in essence, she is saying, "I'd like to be around you all the time because I feel safer here than any other place in my existence."

An appropriate response to this question is, "I am always here when I see you, and I like being here with you."

Initiating Spontaneous Play

As this first phase of therapy continues, the child gains comfort and, if originally cautious, will begin to initiate more spontaneous play, showing less need to be guarded. This is important as it indicates that the child is experiencing the respect, caring, acceptance, understanding, and presence of the honoring process. The result is that she is able to express a sense of security and engage the therapist with more trust and less caution. It is not uncommon for children to express their liking of the first session. Common statements are, "I wish I had a room like this," or "I wish I could live here."

Leaving the First Session

The child enters the Exploratory Stage with the process of play therapy being a complete mystery. When the child leaves this first session, she feels inundated with respect and, therefore, likes the experience. This usually leads to a spontaneous decrease in the child's symptomatic behavior, and the child will show a temporary improvement. However, this will be short in duration since the child begins to use this newfound sense of security in therapy to confront the therapist in order to establish a deeper and more secure relationship. The child now knows the accepting and understanding components of this relationship and is ready to encounter and determine the therapist's acceptance and understanding level of the less acceptable parts of the child. This deeper relationship is created in the Testing for Protection Stage and leads to the working stages of play therapy.

The Exploratory Stage is represented from Point A to Point B on Illustration 1-1, *Therapeutic Stages in Play Therapy.*

Therapy Session With Maria

The following excerpt is taken from a child's first time in the playroom. The child is a six-year-old girl, Maria, whose mother asked that she be seen because of uncooperativeness.

Session	Commentary
1. M: (Walks into the room, goes to the sandbox and puts her hands into the sand.) *What's this?* T: *That's sand.*	1. As the child walks into the room, she's asking, *What am I getting into here? What is this all about?* Because the sand is the toy object she touches, another issue is, *Will you take care of my feelings?* (Also see, Chapter 2, *Sandbox.*)
2. M: *I thought it was.* T: *You were right.*	2. Maria is receiving confirmation that this is a place for children.
3. M: (Looks around the room and laughs nervously.)	3. She is experiencing the freedom to explore with some anxiety and hesitation.

4. T: *There's all kinds of toys in here, and you can play with them in any way you want.*

4. The therapist provides support and encouragement for the child's desire to explore and become familiar and secure in this new experience. The metaphor is, *You can be any way you want to be in here.*

5. M: *You've even got a board* [whiteboard]. (Laughs nervously.) *I didn't know you would.* (Looks around the room.)
   T: *Yes, we have a board.*

5. *You have things I like that I didn't expect to have available to me.* The focus on children in the playroom and the therapist's attitude of caring and acceptance toward her is surprising to Maria.

6. M: *You've got all kinds of stuff.* (Nervous laughter.)
   T: *The shelves are just filled with stuff.*

6. Metaphor for: *I can see that this is a place that will take good care of me; and I can tell you all kinds of things.*

7. M: (Turns back to the sand.) *This is nice and soft sand — softer than the stuff at school.*

7. She realizes not only that this experience will be safer than her experiences at school, but also that it will be different.

8. T: *You like the feel of it.*

8. Metaphor: *You like what you see here and how you feel here.*

9. M: *Only ... except it sticks to your hands.* (Brushes sand off her hands.) *You have to brush them off before you can go do something else.*

9. Metaphor: *I get stuck with a lot of feelings that need to be dealt with before I can move on to other things.*

10. T: *Yeah, you gotta' take it off.*

10. The therapist confirms the metaphor.

11. M: (Looks around the room.) *There's all kinds of stuff in here.*
    T: *Yeah, there's stuff over here and over there.* (Points to the other side of the room.)

11. Metaphor: *I have all kinds of feelings to tell you about, and I'm a little overwhelmed with this opportunity right now.*

12. M: *And there's play telephones.* (Picks up a walkie talkie.) *I like play telephones. My mom has one of these by my telephone, by my telephone book, the telephone cord thing.*

T: *So, you like to talk on telephones.*

12. Metaphor: *I have some communication issues that I need to talk with someone about. The person is my mother, and I want to feel more connected with her because she's more interested in other people than she is in being connected to me.*

13. M: *Uh-hum. These are only pretend.* (Turns it over and pushes buttons.) *Whenever you push one of them, all of them go down. That's weird. What is this? There's an alarm thing.* (Turns it over and examines it.) *This one is kinda' broke. This one ...* (Puts it back on the shelf and picks up another one.) *This one looks newer.* (Sees handcuffs. Says excitedly:) *Oh! Handcuffs! That's funny.*

T: *We even have handcuffs.*

13. She wants to have Mom focus her attentions on her [Maria] more often instead of spending so much time on the telephone. *That's my wish* [fantasy]. *Because my wish doesn't happen, I think there's something unacceptable or weird about me. I feel like there's a defect in me, and that I'm kind of broken [hurt].*

I have hope that things can change for the better.

An emotionally-charged projection to the handcuffs is created.

14. M: (Picks up key.) *This must be the key.* (Examines the handcuffs.) *These are weird ...* (laughs nervously) *... 'cause you can't ... how do you lock 'em ... to where they stay? Probably put this ... I put it in the wrong way.* (In a loud voice:) *Yeah, put it in the wrong way, Maria! Is that how you do it?*

T: *Hum, I don't know. It looks like you're putting the key in the right place — in the key hole. And you're doing everything you can to make things work right.*

14. The issue that the handcuffs represent is one of control (in a relationship with her mom). *How can I get my significant other to stay where I want her to be? She [Mom] has me locked in this relationship in the wrong way.* Maria is feeling like she does things wrong and has to be told what to do. *That's how I'm experiencing this relationship.*

15. M: *I did, but ... it's just not locking. Oh, I must have had the wrong key. I must have to get the key to the right one.* (Continues to struggle with the keys and handcuffs.) *Oops. Wrong key. This must be the right key. Now,*

15. *Yes, but it still doesn't work. So, when it doesn't work, I feel like I'm doing the wrong thing.*

NOTE: Therapy is only in the Exploratory Stage, and the themes are already emerging, although the play

I hope this will do it. It doesn't work! That's siwy [silly]. (Puts them back on the shelf.) *They make handcuffs and ...*

theme is not maintained with direction since the therapeutic relationship of trust has not been established.

Maria's regressive speech indicates to the therapist that the issue of this relationship has been experienced by Maria since she was an infant developing speech. She ends with an experience she can't pursue yet. The feelings of frustration and defeat in this relationship are now being experienced by the child. She goes to a deeper level of experience and blocks. This cue would take her deeper into her experience except that the therapeutic relationship has not been established to handle those experiences at this moment.

16. T: *It's important to know how to get these darn things to work the way you want.*

16. This is a metaphorical statement of the therapeutic issue of wanting her mother to change her control and be more available to Maria.

17. M: (Looking at the therapist:) *Yeah, they are.* (Looks around the room.) *There's a helmet. Ah! Play knives. That's weird.* (Examines the knives.) *They're dirty, though.*

17. *Because I don't get these to work right* [control], *I need protection from the experience of emotional intrusion that hurts me.*

This leaves me feeling weird ... [second time for this term] *... and feeling dirty ...* [ashamed and humiliated].

The knives are not dirty in the literal sense.

18. T: *Yeah, we have different knives.*

18. The therapist is confirming Maria's statements that things are weird, and she [Maria] feels different at times.

19. M: *This one got broke. This one is a big one.*
    T: *That is a big thing.*

19. *The big person in my significant relationship is broken.*

20. M: *Yes, they need a big one. They told us.* (Pulls knife out of holder.) *Yes, it's out, and it's a big, big knife.* (Puts knife back on shelf.) *Do you know how to spell my last name?*

20. *I need her, and she is very important to me. I have to know that she will be there for me.*

Do you know how to spell my last name, is a metaphor indicating that the person represented by the big knife is the person that determines my identity, and our last names are the same. It is surmised that the relationship between mother and daughter is enmeshed.

21. T: *Hmm, I bet you know how.*

21. *I want to know you in the way you want to present yourself to me.*

22. M: (Walks over to the white board.) *I do.* (Laughs nervously. Picks up a marker.) *Now what I'm going to do ...* (Maria writes her last name on the board saying each letter as she writes it.) *I print.* (Nervous laughter.) *I'm in first grade.* (Examines white board eraser.) *This is nice and soft.*

22. *I know how I want my identity to be. The identity that I've gotten and the one I want are not the same as I would like them to be.* This causes her some anxiety.

When Maria says, *Now what I'm going to do ...* and then pauses before saying, *I print*, she is telling the therapist through metaphor that she needs to be understood as the child she is rather than by expectations to be an adult.

I'm in the first grade, is a confirmation that she is still a child.

Her reference to the whiteboard eraser — *This is nice and soft* — indicates *I like the way you are with me. I feel safe and comfortable.*

23. T: *You learned to print your name.*

23. *You like being the child that you are, and you like being childlike.*

24. M: *Uh, huh. I know how to spell my first name too. It's spelled ...* (Maria writes her first name on the board.)

24. *I feel safe with you, and I'm going from the formal to the familiar with you since I feel safer.*

25. T: *Oh, you can do your first name and your last name.*

25. *You can tell me all about yourself.*

26. M: (Laughs)

26. The previous metaphor causes some anxiety in Maria. She feels somewhat exposed and fears that she may be moving too quickly into this relationship. This could cause some ambivalence about enjoying this relationship and what it could mean to her relationship with her mother.

27. T: *You can do your entire name.*

27. This is a response that leads the child further than she may want to go. Metaphorically, it is asking Maria to go further than she has already gone and resembles the type of expectations she is struggling with in her life.

28. M: (Laughter) *Except my middle name. I haven't learned how to do my middle name. My middle name is Gloria. I have a kid in my class named Gloria. I think it's spelled ... G ...* (Works at sounding out the name and writing it phonetically.)
    T: *It sounds just like that.*

28. *I'm willing to give you what I know, but I'm not sure how it all fits together. I'm willing to try what I can to tell you my experiences.*

29. M: *Yeah, it does. That's how I think it's spelled. You have a basketball hoop. Now, where's the basketball?* (Looks on the shelves.)
    T: *You can have any ball be a basketball.*

29. *I'll struggle to tell you who I am as best I can.* This experience has an association to adult expectations, so Maria changes the focus to adults by switching to basketball.

Basketball hoops give children the experience of dealing with an adult — someone taller and bigger than they are.

30. M: *This ...* (Picks up a foam ball.) *It's easy.* (Throws the ball at the hoop and misses.) *Oops, I forgot.* (Laughs) *It's kind of hard.* (Throws

30. Maria is feeling the confidence of the therapist being present with her in the playroom. This makes her forget how hard things can be. Then she

the ball against the wall under the hoop. Laughs:) *Oh ...* (Laughter) *Nice throw.* (Throws the ball and makes a basket.)

    T: *Whoa!* (Claps her hands.)

31. M: *Right in the basket!*
    T: *You got one!*
    M: (Throws the ball and misses two times.)
    T: *Almost a basket.*

32. M: *And ready.* (Jumps and throws the ball and misses.) *Sometimes, people try to do it jumping, but I can't do it.* (Shoots the ball and misses.) *Aw, almost a basket again.* (Shoots again and misses.)

33. T: *That was close.*

34. M: (Puts the ball away. Picks up a treasure chest.) *Now, let me see ... I think there's pretend money in here. Close your eyes.* (Opens the chest.)
    T: *Ooo-o-o! Lots of money!*

35. M: *Yeah, lots of money, I would say.* (Puts treasure chest back on the shelf.) *Oh, blocks!* (Touches colored foam blocks.) *Huh, I wonder ...* (Picks up a wallet.) *Ooo-o-o, there isn't anything in here!*
    T: *It's not what you wanted it to be.*

remembers that things don't come too easily. Note that she evaluates herself in a sarcastic manner and then accomplishes the task.

31. *Sometimes, I get things right!*

32. *I try and do things to please people* [a person]. *I keep jumping to see if I can do it right. I'm almost able to get it right, but it doesn't seem to be enough.*

33. This statement is encouraging but in the same style of expectation that she is struggling to overcome. More preferable would be, *You work hard to do things the way you want.*

34. Maria feels defeated that she can't perform at the level of expectation. She focuses on the treasure chest but makes statements that it is pretend money, a metaphor for a false sense of worth, which is her feeling right now. The closed eyes means no one can see her internal worth.

35. Maria isn't feeling very much self worth at this moment and, therefore, does not acknowledge its worth. She moves to the blocks. Then, her emotional flow is blocked. She switches back to value in the wallet and states that there is nothing of worth in it.

36. M: *Nothing.* (Puts the wallet back on the shelf and picks up a flashlight.) *Now, I wonder if there's any battery in here. How do you turn it on? There's probably a trick.* (Turns it on and laughs.)

 T: *Oh, you did it!*

36. Sometimes, Maria feels like she has no sense of self-worth in relation to expectations from her significant other — her mother. She then begins to feel empty inside and loses her confidence to do tasks that she would normally be able to do, believing that she is being tricked.

37. M: (Laughs and then groans as she shines the light on the wall opposite her.) *I can see it.* (Groan:) *Oh, I really can't 'cause it's not dark.* (Turns the flashlight off and returns it to the shelf.)

37. Anxiety and relief from the internal pressure to succeed. She starts to give some validation of success and then retracts the validation because it's not dark enough to see the light well. She has incorporated the self-fulfilled prophecy that she will fail anyway.

38. T: *We could make it dark.*

38. The therapist tries to break the prophecy by increasing the validation.

39. M: *Yeah, we can. Turn off the lights. How come that baby bottle is in here?*

39. She keeps the self-fulfilled prophecy by not acknowledging her success and by changing the association to the baby bottle to say that this prophecy has been in existence since she was a baby.

40. T: *To play with in any way you want.*

40. *You can be any way you want to be in here. Just like the way you wanted to be as a baby.*

41. M: *Aw, a puppet.* (Puts a tiger puppet on her hand.) *I'm good at puppets.* (In a high voice:) *Hello, I'm gonna' eat you guys u-u-up.*

 T: *You're gonna' eat us up?*

41. Maria hears the validation that she can be any way she wants to be in the playroom. This gives her some confidence, and she states that she is good at puppets. Since puppets are representative of human relations, she tells how aggressive relationships are for her. The high voice represents the anxiety this relationship causes in her.

42. M: (In a lower voice:) *Oh, no, don't eat us up.* (Puts puppet on the shelf and walks across the room.) *There's other ones over here.* (Picks up the butterfly puppet.) *What is this one? Now, where do you put your hand?* (Looks inside the puppet.) *Oh, there's a trick.*

    T: *Oh, yeah.*

    M: (Turns puppet inside out.) *Oh!*

    T: *He turns inside out.*

42. Maria pleads that the aggression not materialize. Her low voice represents a need for power to stop the intrusion. She picks up the butterfly puppet. When she can't find the hand slot, she assumes that it is trickery. Since this is her second reference to trickery, it is surmised that she has experienced repeated episodes of being tricked by significant others.

43. M: *Yeah, it turns into a ... a ... it's supposed to stick in there.* (Returns it to the shelf.)

43. As the butterfly turns inside out to become a caterpillar, she focuses on the Velcro strip that holds the puppet together. Her current experience is to get her internal feelings in control for now.

44. M: *Oh ...* (Picks up a bee puppet.) *... and there's a bee. Oh, I know how this works.* (Laughs)

    T: *You know a lot about puppets.*

44. The therapist validates her vast knowledge about puppets (her internal feelings about relationships with significant others.) Also, the therapist gives the message, *I will believe you.*

45. M: *I know.* (Struggles to get the bee's legs onto her fingers.) *There's too many hands, so you have to have one without a finger.*

45. *Sometimes, I feel like I don't fit right and have to adjust to another person's style whether I want to or not.*

46. T: *You need an extra finger.*

46. *You use all the effort you have to make things work right.*

47. M: *Well, just pretend like there's one. Buzz-z-z-z.* (Bee flies and lands on her shoulder.)

47. *I have someone close to me that looks friendly but could sting me if she wants.* The buzzing signifies her caution at this moment.

48. M: *Yep.* (Puts the bee puppet away, picks up a wolf puppet.) *Oh, the big, bad wolf.* (Puts the wolf puppet on

48. By switching to the wolf puppet, Maria indicates that while the person is a threat much of the time, this power-

her hand. In a low voice:) *I'm gonna' eat you guys up. My name is the big, bad wolf.*

49. T: (Cringing:) *Oo-o, that's a bad wolf.*

50. M: *I got big teeth. See!* (Opens the wolf's mouth to show the therapist.)
    T: *What big teeth it has.*

51. M: *Well, at least I'm nice and soft.*
    T: *It's a soft wolf.*

52. M: (Laughs:) *Yeah.* (Sets the wolf puppet back on the counter and picks up a different wolf puppet.) *Now, another wolf. Okay, now.* (Picks up the first wolf, puts one on each hand. In a high pitched voice:) *We are the big, bad wolfs. We have big, huge teeth. We are all nice and soft, and we eat very well. Our sharp teeth ... and we are very small.* (Smiles and swings her arms while still holding the puppets.)
    T: *They are soft, and they have big teeth, and they are small.*

53. M: *And they are going to eat you.* (Laughs as she places the wolves back on the counter. Walks over and picks up a sword.) *Ugh! What are these? Oh ...* (Examines the sword.) *I don't know how they work; but they are bats.* (Places it on the floor.)
    T: *They look like bats.*

ful person becomes verbally aggressive when the person isn't feeling well.

49. The therapist plays the cowering experience that Maria feels when receiving the aggression.

50. With the experiential acceptance of the aggression, Maria now shows that the threat of aggression is greater than previously indicated.

51. This reference to the external characteristics of the wolf is her way of saying that the person looks better than she acts.

52. Because the therapist acknowledges only the soft, external parts, Maria laughs and puts the wolf puppet down. When she sees another wolf puppet, she again experiences the aggressive nature of this relationship. Now, she joins the wolves with one being big and the other being small. *At times, we are nice, and at other times, you had better watch out.* Again, she is identifying with the aggressor.

53. The warning indicates that she never knows when the aggression will come. Because of the constant fear of aggression, she starts to question her own perceptions. She also fears her own aggression, which serves as a defense against her mother's verbal aggression.

54. M: (Picks up a hippopotamus puppet.) *Oh, ano-o-other one.* (Puts the puppet on her hand.) *I'm not going to eat you up. I don't have very big teeth. They're just nice and round.*
     T: *That one has round teeth.*

54. Maria returns to the less aggressive part of her relationship. This is the safe and less aggressive aspect of the person. *At times I don't look as aggressive as I am.*

55. M: *I don't have very many teeth, so you're going to have to help me eat. Eat very nice food. I always eat fish. I eat ... I live in the water.* (Puts the hippopotamus puppet on the counter.)
     T: *She lives in the water and eats fish.*

55. *Then, I expect you to take care of me and nurture me.* Note the role reversal in the nurture of the parent-child relationship. She believes she does a good job of caring for her mother. *I live in the water* means that one does not see everything that goes on privately in the life of this person.

56. M: *Yep.* (Picks up the shark puppet.) *Of-o-o, a shark! Oh, no! The shark!* (Puts it on her left hand.) *Wrong hand.* (Moves it to her right hand.) *I usually use this hand.* (Examines the shark's mouth.) *Oh, now I need this hand* [right]. *Actually, I need both hands. It has room for you to go like that.* (Pushes her hand in further and moves the shark's mouth.)
     T: *Yeah, you can make it work.*

56. She now reveals the aggressive side of the person that comes out of the water. She discloses her view that she can't do anything right, and she gets confused by the potential of the aggression that is directed at her and blamed on her performance or behavior. When Maria says, ... *I need both hands*, she is indicating that *It takes everything I have to deal with this aggression.*

57. M: *Yeah, it's hard, though.* (Takes the shark off her hand and puts it on the counter.) *It's hard. Now, who's this?* (Picks up the hippopotamus puppet.) *Oh, yeah.* (Puts it down and then points her finger, as if thinking.) *It's the one I tried out.* (Walks to the sandbox and begins playing.)

57. *I survive the aggression, but it's not easy.* She returns to the hippopotamus to indicate that after the intense aggression, the person [Mother] returns to her previous demeanor — the one others know. She moves to the sandbox to continue the experiences of her exploration.

Maria's Exploratory Stage is very typical of children who come to play therapy for the first time. While her movement from toy to toy was exemplary of this stage, the themes of her issues were unique to her situation.

The main purpose was to build a relationship with the therapist. At the same time, her conflict in relationship to her significant other emerged from the play. Maria was giving her view of relationships as she and her therapist were developing their relationship. An overture of the themes to evolve were shared in this first encounter; however, they were not developed nor intensified into the depth she will play in the Dependency Stage with her therapist. During this Exploratory Stage, Maria received the freedom to express herself in a safe and understanding environment.

CHAPTER 6

TESTING FOR PROTECTION STAGE: SETTING THE LIMITS OF SECURITY

The reasons that children are in therapy are as varied as the children themselves. Yet, there is one common factor — in some way, they have been emotionally damaged and need assistance in restoring their emotions to a state of well-being. It is at this point that the play therapist comes into the lives of these children. The child who has been sexually abused on a consistent basis may be terrified of being in a room alone with an adult [the therapist] because of the fear that someone else might abuse him. The child who may have experienced the death of someone significant may feel guarded about being vulnerable to another person who might also be taken from him. Regardless of the situation, when the child encounters the therapist for the first time, he suddenly experiences someone who acknowledges and honors him and speaks kindly, even soothingly, to him. For many children, this is completely foreign and, consequently, difficult for them to trust. Yet, it feels good at the same time, although perplexing because of the novelty of it.

A dilemma for the child lies in being resistant to reentering his pain, while realizing, on some level, that he must reexperience all those uncomfortable feelings in order to move beyond them. Before he can disclose this pain, however, the child must know that the therapist will believe and accept this pain that his insecurity has kept him from willingly exposing. Slowly, nurtured by appropriate responses on the part of the therapist, the child begins to trust the therapist.

At some point during these initial sessions, the child will judge that he is beyond the initial acquaintance period and comfortable enough in the honoring style of relating to be ready to move on to a deeper level of relating. He will begin to question:

"Do I really perceive correctly that I'm safe with this person? Let me test this out to see if this is really true.

"Okay, I've let him see all the nice things about me. Now, I'm going to let him see some of the not-so-nice things and find out if he's really as accepting as he appears to be. Will he really hang in there with me when I let him see all these other parts of me that other people don't like? Can he handle my emotionality and not let me get out of control?"

These doubts, of course, are unconscious. The motives, though, lead the child to begin testing the relationship. Indeed, in order to accomplish the progression of moving into a trusting relationship with the therapist, it is necessary for the child to test the therapist. Children want to know that they will be protected, and that the therapist will not allow them to get out of control, either with their behaviors or their feelings. At some level, they realize that, singularly, either their unleashed exhibition of powerful behaviors or their feelings could overwhelm them. Taken in combination, without protection, these powerful behaviors and feelings could be devastating.

Many years ago, therapists were taught to set limits as soon as the child entered the playroom. This created external boundaries that have authoritative meaning rather than allowing the child the opportunity to build trust and security in the relationship through testing the therapist. In other words, if rules are given at the beginning of the relationship, it puts the child in a paradox — he can't test the therapist to find out how the therapist is going to take care of him. Instead, he must resist the rules. It is by *resisting the therapist* that the child creates the relationship he needs in order to accomplish his therapy. The child must risk the relationship and, in doing so, experience the acceptance and understanding of the therapist. Again, this is necessary before the child can feel safe in disclosing his intrapsychic pain. Essentially, the goal of the child during this stage is to test the therapist in order to discover his safety and security within the relationship, and the goal of the therapist is to show to the child that he understands and accepts the child's need at that moment.

The most common way in which a child will test is to become oppositional in a way that is not personally related to the child's issue. For example, "I need this gun at home," is a child's way of testing the therapist. In addition, the child is communicating to the therapist that he wishes he had more empowerment. Although the actual toy may symbolize something related to the child's issue (e.g., a baby bottle for a child who wants more nurturing, or a magic wand for a child who wants changes to occur in his environment or, as in this case, a gun for a child who wants more empowerment), the act itself is not related to the child's issue. Again, this is executed by the child in order to have the therapist respond to him in an accepting and caring style as the child is being opposing or oppositional to the therapist.

Opposition can take different forms. It may be as mild as a child saying, "I wish I didn't have to leave today," or as determined as saying, "I am not leaving today!" Some children who are shy and passive may never test the relationship directly. Rather, they will do it passively (e.g., "I wish I could take this toy home with me."). Regardless of the level and manner in which the opposition is introduced, the moment the child introduces testing, a process begins in which the therapist must respond to the child in a very caring and understanding manner. The therapist must acknowledge the opposing demand and the underlying needs of the child. This is not a power play by the child but a request for respect as he expresses the autonomy of his being. Whether direct or indirect, mild or strong, the therapist must react to the child's individual form of testing in such a way as to communicate that the child has been heard, accepted, and understood.

While the expression may, on the surface, focus outside the play situation, the therapist must bring the focus of the interaction to the immediacy of the playroom and the relationship between the therapist and child. In essence, testing becomes a *here and now, I and Thou* situation so that the child gains confidence in the therapist to understand and protect. For instance, an appropriate response to the child's statement, "I need this gun at home," would be, "You want to know that you are safe and that you have all the protection you need." This lets the child know the therapist understands the need behind his request or demand and that these demands will be responded to in a caring, understanding fashion.

The following is an illustrative dialogue indicating appropriate responses on the part of a therapist.

> C: *I'm going to take this gun home.*
> T: *That's a pretty important gun, and you want to take it home with you.*

C: *I want to have this at home.*

T: *It's important for you to have a way to keep yourself safe.*

C: *No, I want to have this gun.*

T: *I can tell that's an important gun to you.*

C: *Yeah. And I want it for me.*

T: *I know how important that gun is to you, and we need that gun for the playroom so you and I can play with it here.*

C: *I wanna have it with me.*

T: *I know you want it with you, but we need it here so that when you are here in the playroom, we have a gun for you.*

C: *But I want it for me.*

T: *I understand how much you want the gun and how important it is to you. We just need the gun here so it will be here for you when you and I can play together again.*

C: *Can I hide the gun until next time?*

T: *You can put the gun wherever you'd like in the room.*

C: (Hides the gun behind the doll house:) *Will it be here when I come back?*

T: *I'm not sure if it will be in your hiding place, but yes, it will be here. Then you and I can play together and you will have the gun.*

C: (Moves toward the door.) *I get to come back in this many days ...* (Child shows five fingers.)

T: *That many plus two more fingers. And the gun will be here too!*

C: *Yeah!* (Child acknowledges, opens the door, and leaves the play room.)

Case History of Louie

With some children, however, testing for protection may be more complicated, as in the following example.

A boy by the name of Louie went with his father on a drive up in the mountains. His father was an older man and, while driving the car, he suddenly had a heart attack and died. The car swerved off the road and rolled down an embankment into a ravine. Louie was locked in the car with his father for an hour before anyone found them. Then it took another hour to get him out of the car.

Most parents would initiate therapy for a child who had gone through such a traumatic experience. In this case, however, Louie's mother was not even aware of the effect this traumatic event had on her son.

Almost a year later, Louie was riding in a car driven by his grandfather. Suddenly, his grandfather had a heart attack and drove the car off the road and into a tree. This time, Louie was able to climb out of the car and run for help, but not before his grandfather had died.

Still, the mother did not experience enough empathy for Louie to see the trauma he had experienced and she did nothing to help him deal with these two deaths. Six months later, she remarried. After four months, she couldn't understand why Louie was unable to build a relationship with her new husband, and she decided to take Louie in for therapy. At last, Louie's pain had impacted her life.

At this point in Louie's life, there was no way he could come into therapy and say, "Gee, you're a trained play therapist. I'm going to enter a relationship with you!" If he did, all his pain from the loss of his father and grandfather — the significant males in his life — would come roaring up inside him. It took four sessions before he was even willing to test the therapist. Finally, at the end of that fourth session, Louie became opposi-tional. He was playing with cars when the therapist said, "We have 10 minutes left." Louie began disengaging from his play. Five minutes later, the therapist said, "Well, we have five min-utes, and we need to start picking up the toys." Suddenly, Louie said, "I'm not going to pick them up!" He did not want to leave. In his play with the cars, he had entered his pain of the loss of his father and grandfather. He was feeling vulnerable. In order to regain his sense of control, he displaced the energy into being oppositional.

At this point, the therapist said, "I know it's hard to leave, but it's time to go. Before we do, though, we need to pick up the toys."

Then, Louie kicked a toy and said, "I am not picking them up!"

The therapist said, "I know you don't want to go. I'm glad you like being here; but, it's time to go now. If you kick the toys again, I will hold you to make sure you are all right."

Louie said, "No! I'm not going to," and kicked the toy again.

At this point, it became necessary for the therapist to hold Louie in order to stop the destructive behavior and help him regain control of his feelings. During this stage of therapy, verbal responses are usually enough. This case became more extreme, however, when Louie refused to stop kicking the toys. Since toys represent an extension of the child, when Louie began to kick them, it was like kicking himself. Knowing this, the therapist could not let Louie hurt himself.

When children have been honored appropriately by the therapist, it is rare that they need to be physically restrained. There are times, however, when it is crucial. Consequently, it is important that it be performed appropriately. In this case, in order to restrain Louie, the therapist approached him from behind and held Louie by crossing Louie's arms and holding them between the wrist and elbow, where no damage or pain would be created. Also, the therapist did not hold Louie's fingers. As children squirm and twist while being restrained, it can create pain if their fingers are being held, just as holding their wrists can pull a ligament or tendon. The whole point of restraining a child is to protect the child, not to be punitive.

If the therapist had approached Louie from the front, he would have entered Louie's personal space, causing the issue to exacerbate. When this happens, the core issue with which the child is struggling will literally explode between them. In other cases, such as with a child who may have been abused by the perpetrator approaching him from behind, this style of approach could also exacerbate the child's issue.

The therapist then turned his head so that his cheek was about a half inch from Louie's head, realizing that if Louie threw his head back, it would hit him on the face and hurt. As Louie leaned forward, the therapist leaned forward. In this position, Louie's ear was near the therapist's mouth. The therapist began using a soothing, comforting, protective tone of voice to speak to

Louie in order to redirect the energy Louie had kept inside himself for so long and was finally acting upon. At this point, if the therapist had entered into a power struggle with Louie, it would only have hindered therapy.

When restraining a child, the therapist can say to the child, "I'm going to count to 10, and if you are calm by that time, I will let you go." He then can begin to count by saying:

One. It's okay for you to be angry. That's all right. (Pause.)

Two. While it's okay to be angry, I'm not going to let you hurt me. (Pause.)

Three. I know you have feelings you want to share, and these feelings make you feel very angry. (Pause.)

Four. In here [playroom], you can tell your feelings as long as no one gets hurt and you're safe. (Pause.)

Five. I know you have important feelings to share, and I want you to be safe and know that you are safe in here [playroom]. (Pause.)

Six. I want to know all about your feelings. Sometimes, there are angry feelings that upset you. I want you to be able to play your feelings and know that no one is going to get hurt. (Pause.)

Seven. Now, you're feeling safer again, and it's okay to tell your feelings and play. (Pause.)

Eight. Now, you're going to be all right, and you're feeling better. It's going to be all right. (Pause.)

Nine. I'm going to let you go, and you're under your own control now, and everything will be all right. (Pause.)

Ten. Release the child.

In Louie's case, he did not calm down by the time the therapist counted to ten.

After counting to six, Louie kept squirming. On this particular day, the therapist was wearing a short-sleeved shirt. After holding Louie for quite some time, he sat down. At this point, Louie began to spit on the therapist's arm. Because this was a trained play therapist who had great empathy for children and

understood metaphors, his first thought was, "You know, this lit-
tle boy has so much pain over the loss of his significant males that
his spit really represents the tears he needs to cry and the sadness
he needs to experience." As a result, he let Louie spit and spit.
Although there are times when limits have to be set, the therapist
felt at this moment that it was important to let Louie spit.

All of a sudden, Louie moved his head down and put his teeth
on the therapist's arm. The therapist quickly said, "Louie, I know
how much it hurts inside and how sad you feel about the things
that have happened to you, but you don't have to bite me to let me
know how much it hurts. You don't have to do that."

Interestingly, Louie backed up and started spitting again.
The therapist felt that in Louie's own way, this was a sign of
respect because he didn't bite the therapist. The therapist again
started to count to ten. By the time he finished, Louie had calmed
down and was released. The session ended shortly thereafter.

Louie's opposition was a metaphor communicating both his fear of reexperiencing the pain from his trauma and his fear of entering into a relationship with the therapist. In essence, he was saying:

> *"If I enter into this relationship with you as a therapist [who is*
> *male], I'm going to have to reexperience all the pain from the*
> *loss of two significant males in my life. In order to accept you as*
> *a male, I will have to accept my pain."*

When Louie spit on the therapist's arm, he was communicating the tears he would cry and the pain he would feel if he opened himself up not only to the relationship with the therapist, but also to therapy itself. By calmly holding Louie and reflecting Louie's metaphor while counting, the therapist communicated that he would take good care of Louie in the midst of his sadness, pain, anger, and hurt. If, on the other hand, the therapist had refused Louie's metaphor by telling him to stop spitting as a means of control, it would have conveyed a power struggle rather than understanding. Then Louie would have closed himself off from therapy. Using power to control children's behavior will only inhibit the therapist's ability to conduct therapeutic work with them.

When Louie left this session, he was agitated and sad. In the next session, although he was still somewhat cautious, he picked up the toys and started right into his play. Because the therapist had taken care of Louie when he [Louie] had entered into a pain that was too difficult for him to handle by himself, Louie was able to enter into a trusting relationship with the therapist.

Basic Limits of the Playroom

For the safety of the child and therapist, there are basic limits in the play therapy room (Axline, 1947b/1969) that can be divided into three categories.

1. Absolute Limits. These limits are invariable and related primarily to safety.
    A. The child will not hurt himself as a part of the play.
    B. The child will not hurt the therapist as part of the play.
2. Clinical Limits. These limits include those issues common to clinical settings.
    A. All toys remain in the play therapy room.
    B. The child does not leave the play therapy session until the session is over. Obviously there are exceptions to this limit — if the child were to become ill or need to use the restroom.
    C. When the play session is over, the child must leave the room.
3. Reactionary Limits. These limits are particular to an individual case.

They arise from the child's needs and personality (e.g., a child who sets out to destroy a toy or a part of the playroom). Reactionary limits usually occur as a reaction to the therapist setting one of the clinical or absolute limits. The child does not have the security in the realtionship to accept the clinical or absolute limit, so the child creates an additional behavior in order to give himself more opportunities to gain security with the therapist.

The deliberate destruction of toys is a reactionary limit that is commonly tested by children. Children must not be allowed to break toys intentionally or for the sake of communicating their pain. Obviously, toys will get broken during play therapy. Some children will play with toys in a rough manner while working on an issue of violence seen in their family. If a toy should accidentally get broken during this type of play, the child may be concerned about the reaction of the therapist. Frequently, the child from a violent home will manifest this concern with a quick glance at the therapist. It is almost as if the child enters a state of hypervigilance or displays a startled response because he thinks he's going to get hit for breaking the toy. This is when a therapist should say, "No, that's all right. You were playing, and I know the grill came off the car. It's all right. It was an accident." These children need the therapist to provide security statements because of the fear they are experiencing. A toy broken in this manner is quite different from the child who, in defiance of a limit, breaks another toy and then another.

Case Example of Tyler

Tyler was a five-year-old boy who had been beaten by his father. Although the father was no longer living in the home, the mother was currently neglecting Tyler. One of Tyler's symptoms was impoverished speech.

During a session with Tyler, the therapist set a limit of not breaking toys. At that point, Tyler turned around and walked away, as if to say, "I don't see why you're setting this limit!" He was feeling vulnerable and insecure at that moment. Following are excerpts of this session.

Session	Commentary
1. Child: (Picks up some marbles.) *See these marbles? Will they go all the way up to the sky?* (Begins counting.) *One, two, three, four, six, five. These are five dollars!*	1. Metaphorically, Tyler was counting his anxiety: You set that limit, and my anxieties are all the way up to the sky. Consequently, when the therapist set a limit, Tyler began feeling the emotional pain of past experiences. In addition, when Tyler put a label on the counting (i.e., dollars), he was metaphorically representing security and empowerment. At this point, the

therapist uses the words *powerful* or *safe* in her response to assist Tyler in regaining his empowerment.

2.   C: (Stuffs play money in his pockets.)

   Therapist. *You feel real powerful with all those in your pocket.*

   C: (Stuffs more play money in his pockets.)

   T: *Those are really safe in your pocket.*

2.   The therapist is metaphorically communicating, *You are safe with me.*

3.   C: (Picks up a gun and a knife and tucks them into the waistband of his pants.)

3.   Tyler is communicating his need for protection.

4.   C: (Makes an association with his experience of that moment:) *I had a mouse in my hair.*

4.   Commentary: One night in bed, a mouse ran across Tyler's bed and into his hair. Tyler began to associate his fear of what was going to happen in this session with what was done to the mouse.   In other words, Tyler was communicating his anxiety related to the limit-setting and the violence in his family.

5.   C: (Pretends to cut off the therapist's hand with the toy knife.)

5.   Tyler's goal with this behavior is to make the therapist ineffective and incapable of physically hurting him. It is also an effort to regain his sense of empowerment.

6.   C: (Picks up a block and begins moving toward the therapist with intentions of hurting her.)

   T: *I will not let you get hurt, and I will not allow you to hurt me.*

6.   During the testing stage, the therapist must take the issues emerging from the child and bring them into the immediacy of the relationship.   This statement will zoom right into the relationship with Tyler. A different direction would be taken in a later stage. However, in this stage, Tyler needed to know how the therapist was going to

protect him through the relationship. In other words, she would protect him and provide security if his own emotionality were to get out of control while he was getting in touch with his internal pain. She will help him regain his control.

7.   C: (Throws several toys off the counter. Approaches a bucket containing 300 toy soldiers with the intent of throwing it off the counter also.)

T: *I know you are angry, and that's okay; but we are not going to throw any more toys off the counter.* (Puts an arm on the counter to stop any future devastation.)

7.   Once Tyler threw the second toy, it became repetitive, and the therapist needed to set a limit. This type of behavior will continue until the therapist sets a limit.

The therapist's statement communicates to Tyler that she recognizes and accepts his feelings, but that she will not allow them to get out of control. If the therapist had said, *You want to clear off that whole counter*, it would only serve to set an inappropriate goal. The purpose of that type of response is empathy. In the Testing for Protection Stage, however, this type of statement serves to allow the play to become aggressive. It is, therefore, necessary here to intervene.

8.   C: (Pauses and then puts his arm parallel to the therapist's arm.)

8.   By modeling the therapist's posture, the child is indicating, *I accept your limit.*

9.   Later in the same session:

T: *We have five minutes left to play today.*

C: (Begins stuffing his pockets full of toys.) *I'm going to take these home with me.*

T: (Sets no limit on Tyler's statement that he is going to take the toys with him when he leaves.)

Five minutes later:

C: (Starts out the door with all the toys in his pockets.)

T: *It's time to go, and you will have to take the toys out of your pockets.*

C: *No! I'm going to take them all home. You take these toys from me, and I'm going to run away when I get home!*

T: *I know you would like to take them home with you, but they must stay in the playroom. They'll be here next week when you come.* (Begins to help him put the toys back.)

C: (Puts some toys on the counter where the therapist's arm had previously been when she set the limit. Then, he swipes them onto the floor. He doesn't go beyond that line where her arm had set the limit, however. Makes a run for the door.)

T: (Gets to the door first and pushes against the door to stop him.)

C: (Maneuvers the therapist down to the other end of the room and then makes another run for the door.)

T: (Again, gets to the door first and pushes it closed.) *I know you really want to take those with you, and you're angry with me because I won't let you. It's okay to be angry with me, but it's not okay to take the toys. I'm going to have to check your pockets now to make sure they're all empty.*

C: (Acquiesces)

T: (Searches and finds nothing.) *Now we're ready to leave.*

9. C: *No! No! We can't go home! The gun case is down my leg ... I mean, the knife case. You forgot the knife*

9. Tyler conveys, *I trust you enough now that I can tell you things about me that you don't know.* It was at this

case. It's down my leg! (It had fallen through a hole in his pocket.)

point that Tyler began trusting the therapist to protect him, and she became his therapist. He was then able to enter his play and add content to it through association, fantasy play, and metaphors.

In Tyler's case, he was finally willing to leave the room, having developed a trust in his therapist. What should a therapist do, however, if a child refuses to leave the room in spite of any interventions on the part of the therapist? In this situation, the therapist would need to use a caring tone of voice and say, "I'm going to come over and take your hand and walk you out of the room and back to your parents." If the child fights the therapist leading him out of the room, it may be necessary to say, "I'm going to come over and pick you up and carry you out to the waiting room back to your parents where I will set you down." When this is said, however, it is very important to be on the same eye level as the child, even if the child is sitting on the floor. If the therapist is standing and begins to walk toward the child in an authoritative tone, the child will become very anxious and react to this event in a reversal of the therapist's goal of development of trust.

In most cases, when a therapist walks over to a child after such a statement, the child will run out of the room. The important thing is for the therapist to set a limit and begin to follow through with it. For the child who is being oppositional, it is very frightening when the therapist walks towards him, because the child recognizes that he will not benefit from a combative encounter with the therapist.

On rare occassions, a child will lose control and thrash around. In this case it is necessary to restrain the child by holding him until he is back in control. Then, they can walk out of the room together.

In a situation where the child has refused to leave and has taken perhaps an additional 10 minutes, action should be taken in order for the child to experience respect for time limitations. For instance, if the child went 10 minutes longer than the allotted time, the therapist could walk out to the waiting room at the beginning of the next session and say,

"Joey, it's time for our session. However, we went 10 minutes longer last time, so we will lose 10 minutes of today's session." Then, the therapist would go back into his office and wait 10 minutes. At that point, he would go back out and get the child. This is not done as a punitive action, but rather an action to teach respect.

When children who have been abused come in for therapy, this testing for protection can be a difficult time. The therapist will be able to judge when the testing time is approaching because he knows the length of time the child has been in therapy and is somewhat familiar with the child's style of relating. At that time in the therapy process, telling the child he has 10 minutes left when in fact he has 15 is a good way to give him plenty of transition time. It is necessary to have ample time to respond appropriately to the child's testing. For this reason, it is important to never say to a child who is intense in his play, "Oh, I forgot the time, and our time is up. Let's get the toys on the shelf and get out of here." This would be counterproductive to therapy because of the lack of closure it allows for the child.

Putting the Toys Away Together

There are a number of reasons for the therapist and child to put the toys away together. For instance, after the child has come out of his fantasy play, it is a good time to help the child transition from the immersion in his pain during fantasy play back to reality. This transition from fantasy to reality must be made in the playroom so that the child does not lose his security and so that the child can regain orientation before leaving the playroom. This is also an excellent opportunity for the therapist to empower the child and help him reframe his experience. It is an opportunity to engage in the type of direct therapy which cannot be done while the child is in fantasy play. For example, "You know, you really worked hard today. I can see how much stronger you're getting."

This is a valuable time in which to help the child put closure on the emotionality experienced during fantasy play. The child's process of going in and out of his pain resulting in his feeling stronger and more empowered is part of the process of healing. If the child is left feeling vulnerable, the session is lost. Closure of the session becomes closure on that pain and eventually healing of the child's all-encompassing pain.

Consequently, it is vital to the therapeutic process to put closure on each session.

CHAPTER 7

THE WORKING STAGES OF THERAPY

The Dependency Stage: Confronting the Pain

The third stage of play therapy is called the Dependency Stage. This is the emotionally intense, working stage of the play therapy process. It begins after the establishment of trust that occurred in the Testing for Protection Stage. With this trust, the child now depends on the therapist for her emotional security and protection as the play shifts in style and intensity.

Identifying Characteristics of the Dependency Stage

The major identifying characteristics of this stage are:

1. The child has progressed through the Testing for Protection Stage.

2. The child will usually enter fantasy play to disguise the content of the play.

3. The child's play begins to contain the emotional themes that are personally meaningful. To protect the pacing of disclosure, these themes are created in the form of metaphorical or fantasy play.

4. Because of the trust established previously, the child is now willing to invite the therapist into her fantasy play.

5. The manner in which the child structures her fantasy play is very intense and pressured with the child appearing driven to express her concerns through this play.

6. The child exhibits regression in her play style in that it becomes reminiscent of the style of play that occurred during the developmental,

experiential level in which the child was engaged during the onset of the issue.

A small portion of children will not invite the therapist into their fantasy play because, in the early part of the Dependency Stage, they must maintain a greater level of control over the event before they can allow another person to participate in the play process.

The Healing Journey

Fantasy or metaphorical play during this stage is a way of disguising the painful realities of the child's life. In addition, to the child it is a form of empowerment over these painful or annoying realities. In the reality of the world, the child is victim to the circumstances of her world or immediate environment. In fantasy play, the child can rule the world — especially the events in her emotional world — by controlling the conditions of the play experience. This, then, enables the child to control the direction of the therapeutic process. It is this fantasy play — controlled, created, and directed by the child — which leads the child, together with the therapist, toward a healing process. Amazingly, children have the internal knowledge of the necessary direction for healing, although it is often at an unconscious level (Landreth, 1991; Nickerson & O'Laughlin, 1980).

This self-created play process is called the *healing journey*. Given the resources of toys, children have an internal wisdom that basically knows not only how to create the necessary conditions but also how and where to take their play in order to move through their pain toward the process of healing. The mystery is that all children's journeys are unique to their own experiences. Each child paces her play at the level at which she can integrate the change or healing properties within her play. A therapist cannot move a child's play any faster than the child is willing to play or any faster than the child has the capacity to integrate empowerment over the experience that she created during the play session.

Responsibilities of the Therapist

The importance of listening, observing, and receiving what the child is communicating is vital during the beginning stages of fantasy play. It is during this time that the child will unleash an intense amount of energy while unveiling her pain over event(s) and relationship(s).

Consequently, the goal of the therapist during this stage is to receive the experiential situations and emotional themes the child creates in her metaphorical play and then convey understanding and acceptance of these experiences as valid for the child. The therapist must receive these real events in their metaphorical or disguised form. This occurs as the therapist plays and experiences with the child the fantasy created by the child. This, then, gives the child permission to move her play to the next internal level or sequence of experiences that she needs to gain empowerment over and then to integrate that newly empowered experience. The more the therapist conveys the elements of the honoring process and acceptance of the child's experience through the developmentally matched play[1], the faster the process proceeds, and the greater the movement within the healing process.

For this process to occur, the child becomes *dependent* on the therapist to provide emotional protection and security. Once the therapist is given this trust by the child, the therapist must continue to provide both acceptance of the child's emotional expression and protection from the frightening elements of that experience. With this new protection, the child can now focus her emotional energies, previously used for protection, toward re-creating the emotional experiences that will be confronted in therapy. In addition, the child now realizes that the therapist will, if invited, join the child's play for the purpose of emotional and physical protection, acceptance, and understanding. The therapist's continued responsibilities are to validate these experiences created by the child and to convey through play that she understands the emotional meanings of these experiences in all the emotional tones and intensities associated with the event.

Sometimes children want to play their experiences in front of the therapist without interruption or intrusion. In this case, the therapist's

---

1. The child's play style will be characteristic of the development level of the child at the time of the onset of the incident(s).

responsibility is to witness the experience with observational comments or with silence, if the child indicates this desire, until or unless the child invites the therapist into the play. Reflections, if any, at this point would be to the toys or to the overall experience created by the child. Reflections directly to the child would be kept to a minimum since the disguise and anonymity is to be respected.   Interpretative responses should be avoided. Exposing what the child is disguising through fantasy and metaphor, rather than reflecting into the fantasy play itself, could cause the child to abandon her play focus because she loses her control over the pacing of the play. (See Chapter 8 for a more in-depth discussion of appropriate therapeutic responses during the various stages of therapy.)

At this point, the child has not given permission to the therapist to know that these events are her own experiences. Forcing her to acknowledge their reality violates her need to have control over them and disrupts the therapeutic process. It is important for the therapist to remember that the child is the director of the play, and nothing is known, only experienced, until the child chooses to identify the events. This usually does not occur until the emotional pain is under the child's control. At that point the pain will no longer flood her emotionally. The identity of characters or situations does not occur until the latter phase of the Therapeutic Growth Stage. Indeed, sometimes children never choose to identify traumatic events during the therapeutic process.

At this stage of therapy, the therapist becomes one of the more significant persons in the child's life. The parents do not understand what the child is attempting to communicate about her pain. Although they can and often are supportive, they cannot be as facilitative to the child. As a result, this hour of therapy is the most important hour in the child's week. In fact, if a session is missed, regardless of whether the therapist or the child is the cause, the child may feel a sense of abandonment and disappointment. This may cause her to appear angry when she comes in for her next session, and may further cause her to revert to the Testing for Protection Stage at the beginning of this session for a mini-testing period. Unconsciously, she is expressing a need to have her feelings of abandonment and disappointment acknowledged. Once the child feels as though she has been heard, the relationship with the therapist is usually restored, and the child will enter into fantasy play again.

This need to be heard is universal with all children. Unfortunately, if this need is not met, the next generation will suffer the consequences. If individuals are not attended to as children, when they become adults, they will not have acquired this skill. As a result, intimate relationships will be difficult to maintain. Their own children will seem annoying when they continue to request that their parents attend to them. If this attitude prevails within the parents, it leaves their children at risk for abuse.

The ability to be a good listener is not an innate quality. It must be modeled and taught. It is, therefore, advantageous for the therapist to begin training the parents in this important skill. Many parents have a tendency to belittle the child's feelings by comments such as, "Oh, that's not a big problem. You're just a kid and will get over it. Just never mind." Often, these statements will be followed by quick suggestions as to how the child should handle the situation. Sadly, the child is just longing to have someone hear her pain and give some empathy by reflective statements.

A good example of listening to a child's pain is illustrated in the case of Jamie.

Jamie was 11 years old when she graduated from elementary school to middle school. She had always been a tomboy. Now, however, the boys began to say, "We can't play with you because the other kids will think you're a girlfriend." The girls told her they had nothing in common with her. When Jamie came home, she cried and said, "I'm a geek! Nobody likes me or wants anything to do with me!"

Her mother held her and listened to her pain. Then she gave her some empathic statements such as, "Yeah, it really hurts. It's really hard when you feel like you don't fit anywhere." Several days later, the mother was able to interject, "You know, I remember a time when I was about your age. My friends decided they weren't going to have anything to do with me either. I hurt so bad inside that I cried and felt as though nobody in the world liked me."

Jamie looked at her mother and said, "You mean, that happened to you?" Realizing her mom had had experiences such as these helped Jamie not to feel so isolated.

Several days later, while talking before going to bed, Jamie's mother told her a story about a snail who got cut as she slid past a splinter that had been put in her path by some of her "friends" as a joke. The snail was hurt so much, she decided she was never going to stick her neck out of her shell again. So she stayed in her shell where she felt nice and warm and safe. After a few days, however, she began to notice that she was becoming hungry. She tried to ignore the hunger pains and the loud noises her stomach was making in an effort to get her to stick her neck out for some food.

Inside her shell, the snail could hear other snails sliding about outside, playing games, and eating rich, soft leaves. Soon her hunger became so great that she decided to take just a little peek outside her shell. Maybe there would be a small leaf lying next to her. Alas, however, there was no such leaf. Determinedly, she decided to stick with her decision to stay in her shell. Eventually, she became so weak that she knew if she didn't stick her neck out soon, she would be too weak to stick it out at all. Slowly, her head appeared out of her shell. As her view of the world became greater, she spied a huge leaf within a few minutes' slide away. Unlucky for her, another young girl snail was already lunching on it. She knew she had no choice, though, and slid over to the leaf. Very quietly, she asked the other girl snail, "Do you mind if I share your lunch?"

"I would love to have you share," the other snail replied. "This is much too big for me to eat alone. I was hoping someone would come along and ask to share with me. I'm just too shy to ask anyone."

As they feasted on the leaf together, they began to talk. They soon discovered that they both liked to play Chase the Caterpillar and Toss the Crumb. After that shared lunch, they spent hours together playing their favorite games and inventing new ones. Pretty soon the other snails noticed how much fun they were having and asked to join them. One day upon returning home, tired and dirty, the snail told her family, "I'm sure glad I decided to stick my neck out."

Jamie didn't say much at the time. Several days later, however, as Jamie's mother was putting her to bed, Jamie had a smug look on her face. "You look like the cat that swallowed the canary," her mother remarked.

Jamie then said, "I stuck my neck out today. I asked to join some girls for lunch!"

Many adults tend to give advice rather than listen to children.

There are times during the Therapeutic Growth Stage when it becomes appropriate to be more directive by making suggestions, but doing so during the Dependency Stage is premature. Because the child has reached a point where she feels that the therapist knows her pain, she is able to receive these suggestions. It is almost as though the child is saying, "You have to listen to me before I'll listen to you!" Tragically, if the therapist initiates action by making suggestions without having first listened, the child may be compliant in responding to the suggestions physically, but most likely will not be able to assimilate the desired goal of the suggestions. The child is the one who must initiate fantasy play in order to experience her pain. She will only do this to the extent that she knows she is emotionally prepared to confront her pain and may replay it several times in a number of different contexts before she can begin to feel it as less painful. Initiation of action on the part of the therapist could well contaminate the relationship, hindering further therapy.

Questioning to Identify Perpetrator
Can Hinder Therapy

Forensic questioning in this stage of therapy would be counterproductive to the therapeutic outcomes being created by the child. Direct questioning has the effect of pulling the child out of her protective fantasy play and forcing her into the reality of her experiences. This violates the sanctity of the protection provided by the therapist in her relationship with the child. When this happens, the therapeutic process is hindered, perhaps even permanently. It is very difficult to encourage a child back into the healing journey because the fear of loss of protection now remains a constant possibility. The emotional protection that was so secure in the play therapy process is now only temporary. This would cause the child to redirect her play back into a protective style of play or to stop her play altogether. When a child continues in protective play, unable to create a theme, enter fantasy play, and begin her regression to the developmental stage at the onset of the traumatic event, her play becomes circular.[2]

The Child's Need to Defend for Protection

Some children experience such an intense need to defend themselves from the emotional pain they are experiencing that their play reflects a protective style. This form of play is often characterized by intense aggression and hostility. As the child begins to feel safe in the presence of the therapist, she begins to express her anger and hostility toward the experiences she has endured. Usually, the more aggressive the play in this phase of therapy, the more painful were the events that the child needs to confront and resolve.

This anger and hostility can be expressed in many forms. For instance, the child may set up a scene where soldiers are having a battle in the sand, or floods are drowning the dinosaurs, or a child is either shooting from a fort that is under attack or fencing with swords to fight off the bad guys. Often, the therapist will be directed to join the process and help defend the fort or fight against the attackers. The therapist communicates her understanding of the child's intense need for protection and control when she joins the child in this process. As the child recognizes that the therapist believes in her play and takes the stance of the child in the event, she gains further confidence to direct her play to a deeper level.

This is not a fun type of play but rather an extremely intense form of therapy that confronts painful events and allows the child to experience a release from the pressure of the pain that consumes her. These painful feelings are associated with the anger, shame, guilt, and other emotions the child would rather not have had to experience. Consequently, the therapist would never make a statement at the end of a session during this

---

2. Circular play is also experienced by the child who is currently in an abusive environment. The child will continue in this style of play until the perpetrator is removed from her environment. Even in the event the perpetrator is no longer perpetrating but still in the environment, circular play can continue, hindering therapy.

phase of the Dependency Stage such as, "We had fun today playing." A more appropriate statement would be, "We worked hard today."

Expression of Aggression

It should be noted that a child must have the freedom to express her aggressive tendencies and hostile feelings in order to progress in the therapeutic process. Many children must fight their way back to their traumatic event. This is extremely important during this phase of the Dependency Stage. However, this raises critical issues for both child and therapist. For instance, what is the meaning of this aggression for the child? What is the meaning of this aggression for the therapist? How will the therapist choose to engage or disengage from this expression by the child? In addition, counter-transference issues generated by the child's expression of anger and hostility can elicit uncomfortable feelings from the therapist, especially in this model of experiential play therapy.

Issues for the therapist can effect how the aggressive expressions of the child are viewed and received by the therapist. These perceptions can determine the effectiveness of the course of treatment. The therapist's reaction will define whether play intervention enhances or hinders the child's progress toward healing. The Dependency Stage is the stage in which many errors are made by play therapists-in-training. The therapist can either facilitate the release of the emotional energy motivating the aggressive tendencies, or reinforce aggressive play as a method of dealing with the situation. Expression of aggression is a critical intervention issue. If the therapist reflects the child's external behavior to the child, then aggressive behavior is being reinforced by the therapist. Reinforcing aggressive behavior simply for the sake of aggression is inappropriate. It would also be inappropriate if reinforcement of aggressive behavior were to be maintained by the therapist for any reason other than the initial identification of the intensity of the child's expression.

Aggressive play may appropriately be utilized for resumption of empowerment. To accomplish this, the therapist must assist the child in expressing the motivational intent of the aggressive behavior. The therapist must always strive to change externalized aggression into expression of the internal emotional energy motivating the aggression. For example, when a child hits the bop bag, it would reinforce aggression and not enhance the therapeutic process for the therapist to reflect to the child, "You really hit that hard. You want to hit him harder and harder. You want to hit him over and over again."

More appropriately, the therapist would enhance the facilitation of these feelings by expressing the motivation behind the display. The therapist could say, "You're really angry at that person." Pause. "You want him to know that you don't like the way he has treated you." Pause. "You want to tell her to stop being so mean to you." Pause. "You'd like to tell him to leave you alone and never hurt you again." This form of responding allows the child to be understood without focusing on the style of expression (i.e., the aggressiveness).

When the child realizes the therapist understands her emotional experience of the event, her play will move into more intensified dramatic scenes. In other words, the understanding provided by the therapist has the effect of giving the child permission to continue to express her deeper, more personalized feelings about this relationship or event. For instance, in the child's play scenes, she will begin to place the therapist in the child's role of being the victim. At this point, the therapist will begin to experience what the child felt (or feels) when encountering the event or relationship. The play interactions consist of the child's perceptions of the relationship or event which have created meaning to the child rather than merely being the expression of anger or aggression. The child's angry behavior may be her means of communicating that experience.

This deeper level of play usually requires the therapist to join the play and to experience what the child felt during the events that occurred. One of the first desires of a child is to communicate what it felt like to be the victim. Once the therapist experiences the child's powerlessness and resultant need for empowerment and reflects those feelings back to the child, the child feels understood. At this point, the child can then switch roles and begin playing the part of the victim confronting the painful relationship or event from an empowered stance. This puts the therapist in the role of the perpetrator. These now become the intensely therapeutic moments of growth — the child creating her experience for the therapist to encounter, and the therapist reflecting that experience back to the child. As the child reexperiences her feelings of the past/present pain, she realizes that the therapist truly understands her feelings of the incident/relationship. Through this style of experiential play, the child gains emotional control over her pain. As a result, the need to aggressively express her message is less necessary. In this way, the movement and integrative value of the therapy is enhanced.

Effects of Non-Play,
Verbal Forms of Therapy

An example of an experiential play response on the part of the therapist would be, "This really hurts! You're scaring me! I don't want this to happen!" On the other hand, a non-play, verbal response would be, "You're feeling angry. You're feeling scared." This latter style of responding is an adult, verbal, left brain, therapist, distance-from-experience response. These non-play, verbal forms of responses result in children feeling as though the therapist has not felt their pain. Consequently, a child feels as though she must reenact the event repeatedly (circular play) in order to capture the meaning of her experience and receive the response from the therapist that lets her know her pain is understood and accepted. Each time the child reenacts the event, she uses more aggression in her attempts to express her pain. The aggressive style is then addressed and reinforced rather than addressing the meaning behind the aggression. Non-play or verbal forms of therapy tend to result in children acting more aggressively.

By changing this important dynamic of therapy, the child will express less aggression during the overall therapeutic process, although the aggression that is expressed will be quite intense during a short period of time. Children progress toward resolution of their pain faster by using experiential play responses than when only verbal responses are used. When only verbal responses are used in therapy with children, the therapy is adult therapy reflected into children's play. This is less effective in communicating empathy to the child. On the other hand, when the therapist is invited into the child's play and then plays in the developmental style of the child, the total experience of the moment is conveyed to this child. This enables the child to experience that her world is being understood.

Reframing the Emotionality Attached to the Painful Event or Relationship

This understanding of the child's experience, together with the protection and security she senses from the therapist, allows the child to create a progression of theme play that enables her not only to confront portions of her emotional pain but also to regain her sense of empowerment over those portions. Each time this occurs, the degree of intense emotionality related to that event begins to lessen. This allows the child to slowly regain her internal sense of security, appropriate to her age or stage of development during the onset of the painful event. With this reduction of emotionality related to the painful event comes a lessening of the need to protect herself with behaviors that are inappropriate or with feelings that are rooted in the pain. As the child continues this process, adding new elements of meaning to the play, the total event is slowly reframed emotionally. The emotional intensity that the event once created is replaced with an internal sense of well-being. In other words, the emotionality associated with the original experience is slowly reframed so that, eventually, the memories of the events that once caused intense emotional pain and flooding and, therefore, inappropriate behaviors or attitudes, no longer incapacitate the child. The child's feelings are now in the normal range for present events in her life. She can now change the purpose of her play from confronting that pain to regaining her developmental play in rehearsal for adult life.

Although this may appear to be a similar process to that of desensitization, it is not nearly as formal a procedure. One of the biggest fears most sexually abused victims experience is the fear that their emotions will overwhelm them. Consequently, in play therapy, the object of fear is the emotionality attached to an experience. In desensitization, the object of fear may be a known factor (e.g., a snake or the fear of flying) (Cormier & Cormier, 1991). This is not true in the reframing process of play therapy. For instance, although it may be known that the child was sexually abused, it is not necessarily known who the perpetrator was or the exact details of the abuse. Indeed, this is not even necessary in order for therapy to occur as long as the child is now protected from the perpetrator. During play therapy, the child reframes the emotionality associated with an experience of an event.

In addition, in desensitization, the therapist guides the process by slowly introducing the object of fear to the client over a period of time (Cormier & Cormier, 1991). It is based on the reality of the object of fear. This is not true in play therapy where the process involves fantasy play, and the child is allowed to lead the process. Although the relationship with client/therapist is always important, desensitization is not as dependent upon this relationship in order for therapy to occur as is play therapy.

Case History: Continued
Work With Juan

In Chapter 3, the background and initial session with Juan was discussed. The following excerpt demonstrates the shift from the Dependency Stage into the Therapeutic Growth Stage. During his therapeutic process, it became necessary to introduce Juan to a new therapist. (See *Premature Terminations* in Chapter 9 for discussion of the process of changing therapists.) His new therapist was an Hispanic male. There were a number of advantages to Juan's therapist being an Hispanic male, some of which are obvious. For instance, there was a shared cultural background, race, and gender identity. Another shared similarity was the fact that the therapist came from a financially impoverished family. As a child, he never had any toys. The contrast in the male role model set by the male therapist and Juan's father was also significant. These differences include the fact that the therapist was a very gentle person, whereas Juan's father had been very aggressive. In addition, the therapist was a sensitive, caring individual, whereas Juan's father had been unable to display any caring in a genuine manner.

In this excerpt, it is apparent that Juan's therapy has progressed to the point where he now returns to the ball and bat that he had picked up briefly in his initial session. This time, however, he uses it in a different way. He is now ready to use it for fun. In this session, Juan decides to play baseball. Learning to play catch is a cultural experience. Because the therapist had never had the opportunity to play catch during his childhood, he did not know how to catch a ball. At one point in the following excerpt, this fact causes him to experience counter-transference. Because he begins to feel inept (as Juan has so often felt), the therapist at one point goes along with Juan's statement of being out even though, technically, he was not.

The therapist's goal for the following session was to assist Juan in experiencing feelings of playfulness in a safe atmosphere. This would enable Juan to return to a child-like state. At one point during the game, Juan instructed the therapist to pitch the ball and attempt to tag Juan out at one of the bases. This was difficult, however, because the therapist was unable to catch Juan's hits. The game continued with Juan getting numerous runs.

This is their fourth session together, and their relationship is established. In this session, however, Juan moves into a more child-like state, which causes his trust in the therapist to become even more profound as he allows himself to be vulnerable.

Session	Commentary
1. Juan: (Hits the ball and then runs to the designated first and second bases. Gruffly says:) *Ha, ha. I made it!*	1. Juan gets to second base and displays an attitude of *I got you*, a need for superiority over his opponent (his father, the perpetrator). He knows he's safe, but he still has the competitive attitude of winning since he is in the phase of regaining his internal sense of empowerment.
2. Therapist: *Wow! What a hit!*	2. The therapist acknowledges the power.
3. J: *Ghost runner on second base.* (Goes back up to bat.) T: *Get ready. Here it comes!*	3. *Ghost runner* is a metaphor for past relationships that are too emotionally impacting for Juan but are haunting his memories.
4. J: *Okay.* (Tips the ball:) *Tip. It doesn't count as a strike, but it's a tip. This one is going to go right past the base.*	4. Still, Juan doesn't feel comfortable being vulnerable to the therapist. So, when he gets a strike that would represent vulnerability, he says no. It changes to a tip, and a tip doesn't

count. So he eliminates the vulnerability.

5. J: (Hits a fly ball. The therapist puts his hand up to catch it, and the ball goes right into his hand. When Juan sees this, he swings around and says:) *Ah, I'm out!*

5. Juan makes the assumption that he is out rather than assess the situation for what is happening.

6. T: (The ball bounces off the therapist's hand and down onto the floor. The therapist walks over and picks it up.)

6. Since the therapist knows he will never catch the ball, he decides to accept the assumed out that Juan called. The therapist is experiencing the inferiority that Juan is creating in the play for him. Since the therapist is not skilled in catching the ball, this creates a counter-transference.

7. T: *Man on second.*

7. The therapist called the runner a man rather than *ghost runner*.

8. J: (Hits the ball and runs around the bases, breathing hard as he runs.)

8. Juan is cautiously enjoying his success. He is experiencing empowerment in his current stage of development, especially in the presence of a male father figure, although he has not yet internalized it.

9. T: *Home run!*

9. The therapist validates the experience.

10. J: *One out.*

10. At this point in the game, Juan deals with his vulnerability rather than with his accomplishment.

11. T: *Brought one man in, too.*

11. The therapist uses the term man rather than ghost runner again.

12. J: *Still one out.*

12. Again, Juan deals with his vulnerability rather than his accomplishment.
    Juan is freer and more casual in his body movements than in his previ-

ous batting. He is just beginning to show movement toward the spontaneity and playfulness that has been a therapeutic goal for him. His voice is becoming softer. As he is moving toward playfulness, he is moving away from the competitiveness exhibited earlier. However, he still focuses on the negative (i.e., one man out).

13. T: *You really want to do well on this.*

13. The therapist validates his internal motivation. This allows the empowerment to begin to internalize.

14. J: (Hits the ball and then runs more slowly and relaxed around all the bases.)
    T: *Another hit!*
    J: (Starts falling down, giggling.) *Yeah!*

14. Juan could easily have gone all the way around the bases but didn't. As he moves toward the ground, he is starting to go back into childhood experiences. He's starting to feel safe. He's still watchful of the therapist, but he's feeling safer than he was at the beginning of the play.

15. T: *Another home run!*
    J: (Giggles)

15. This is a reassuring statement. The metaphor for Juan is that he is safe in the presence of a respecting therapist. Juan is still wary of the therapist, however, and doesn't understand why the therapist is always dropping the ball.

16. T: *It feels good to be able to do what you want to do. You feel proud of yourself.* (Pitches the ball.)

16. The therapist validates the feelings of completion. In addition, he enhances Juan's internalization as he affirms the sense of pride Juan is experiencing.

17. J: (Hits the ball and then runs around the bases. Stops at third base:) *Safe!* (Falls down while giggling.)
    T: (Runs around trying to catch up with the ball.)

17. Juan is now expressing his feelings of safety. He could have created a home run but stopped closer to the therapist and states, *Safe.* He leans toward the floor which indicates his

regression to an earlier stage in his development.

18. J: *Safe on third base.*

18. Juan affirms his feelings of safety.

19. T: (Touches Juan with the ball:) *You're safe!*

J: (Gets up, walks to home base, and picks up the bat:) *Ghost runner on third base.*

T: (Drops the ball as he swings his arm to pitch it.)

J: (Laughter)

T: (Pitches the ball.)

19. The therapist touches Juan with the ball for tactile validation — *You're safe.*

20. J: (Hits the ball and goes to first base. Then, in a softer voice:) *Ah, safe! Ghost runner on first base. Ghost runner on first and second.* (Returns to bat again.)

T: *Here comes the ball.* (The ball goes past Juan.)

20. Juan moves to first base only and states in an appropriate tone — *Ah safe!* He is now affirming that he is safe in this experience, which represents earlier experiences in his life.

21. J: *You could have got me, but I'm too fast for you.*

T: (Drops the ball as he swings his arm to pitch it.)

J: (Laughter)

T: (Pitches the ball.)

21. Juan still feels the need to maintain some defenses against the vulnerability he's experiencing from his past.

22. J: (Strikes at the ball but misses:) *It's a tip ... it's a ball. It doesn't count.*

T: *Ball one.* (Pitches the ball again.)

J: (Hits the ball and then runs around the bases slowly and casually.)

22. Juan reaffirms his need for caution in not being too vulnerable too quickly.

23. T: (Picks up the ball and runs up to Juan, who has now slid into home. Takes the ball and stands over Juan:) *You're safe!* (Touches Juan with the ball:) *What a good job you did!*

23. When the therapist stood over Juan after Juan slid into home, it created a father-son or parent-child paradigm, communicating, *You're safe.* Then he touches Juan to kinesthetical-

ly validate the safety. This is important since Juan was physically abused. The therapist confirms with the verbal response, *What a good job you did.*

24. J: (Hits another home run. Runs around the bases.)

T: *You're having a great day at this. The score must be five to zero.*

24. Juan hits a home run to self-validate his empowerment in relation to the *safe at home* experience with the therapist.

25. J: *No, it's 15 to zip!*

25. Juan's change in the score — from five to 15 — is a measure of the level of empowerment he is currently feeling. The *15* is not a running up of the score, but a compliment to the therapist of the gains of empowerment Juan is making internally. The level is three times greater than the therapist's perception of the gain.

26. J: *Can you throw a curve ball?*

T: *You want to show me how well you can do.* (Pitches the ball.)

26. This question is his way of communicating that he feels safe in the relationship, and that they can now experience different variables within their relationship.

27. J: (Hits the ball, runs to first base, reaches with the bat for second base, then stays holding onto both bases as he lowers himself toward the floor, giggling.)

27. Juan does not run the bases but stays closer to the therapist in his play. He feels safer now than at any time in his therapy.

28. J: *Safe on two bases.* (Returns to home base and prepares to bat again:) *Ghost runner on first and second.*

T: (Throws the ball.)

28. Safe on two bases means he feels twice as safe in the experience as he did moments earlier when he was only safe on first base. The experience of safety has now been reestablished back into his experiential repertoire.

One of the therapeutic goals for Juan — indeed for all children in play therapy — is to assist him in regaining appropriate empowerment for his age and stage of development. Children whose empowerment level has been violated by authority figures in their lives will have to compensate in some way, usually by inappropriate behavior in an effort to protect themselves. Juan's compensation has been the inappropriate behavior on the playground — verbal and physical aggression as well as stealing, lying, and cheating. In other cases, it may manifest as fear and withdrawal. When a child regains appropriate empowerment for his age and stage of development, displaying inappropriate behavior in order to compensate for that loss will no longer be necessary. Juan has returned to his childhood, and his right to be a child is being empowered by the therapist. Because of his new sense of empowerment, he doesn't have to intensely guard himself anymore.

Session (cont.)	Commentary (cont.)
29. J: (Hits the ball and then runs around the bases for a home run.) T: (Fumbles around with the ball.)	29. The home run power style hit is done to confirm within himself the new sense of well-being he is experiencing internally.
30. J: (Giggling:) *I made it. All the time.* T: *You like hitting those home runs.* (Pitches the ball.)	30. This is the joy of experiencing internal security again in the total experience of the moment.
31. J: (Hits the ball and then moves casually around the bases, tapping them with the bat and giggling the whole time:) *Made it!* T: *Another home run!*	31. Juan repeats the event to reconfirm the experience as true to him. It is as though he is having trouble believing he is really experiencing what is happening internally.
32. J: (Makes a Tarzan-type yell.)	32. Juan has now validated that the experience of safety and empowerment — appropriate to his childhood stage of development — has been regained. A child cannot use formal

language to describe this experience. Rather, it must be expressed in a primitive, guttural yell of power, using his whole body.

33. T: *You're a strong and powerful hitter.* (Pitches the ball.)

33. The therapist validates Juan's internal experiences by sharing that he experiences Juan's power too.

34. J: (Swings and misses:) *Strike.*
    T: *Strike one.* (Pitches the ball.)

34. At this moment, he is experiencing being a child, appropriate to his age and stage in development. Therefore, he has no need to defend himself against the strike call. He now feels safe enough to experience vulnerability.

35. J: (Hits the ball and then runs casually around the bases. At home base, he collapses in laughter.)

35. Juan is experiencing a sense of joy in this process. Consequently, he doesn't need to maintain the state of hypervigilance he maintained earlier.

36. T: (Bends down and touches Juan with the ball, laughing:) *You keep getting runs. You've had a lot of hits today.*

36. The touch, in conjunction with the verbalization, taps into both processing modalities. The tactile is more primitive than the verbal in conveying the message of safety.

37. J: (Gets down on his hands and knees:) *This time, I'm on the ground.*
    T: *You're so sure of yourself. You know you can do it any way you want to.* (Pitches the ball.)

37. When a child moves to the floor in the playroom, it indicates moving to issues in a previous stage of development. A child's behavioral style will be regressive to indicate this also. Juan feels such safety and empowerment that he now goes to bat for his entire childhood. This is done in order to reframe the traumatic memories of his past.

38. J: (Swings and misses:) *Strike one.* (Rolls the ball back to the therapist on the floor in a primitive style

38. Juan has difficulty hitting the balls since his play has regressed to the skill development level of a two-year-old.

while at the same time making guttural sounds that are indicative of the earlier stage in development.)

T: (Pitches the ball.)

J: (Hits a foul:) *Foul ball. Strike two.*

T: *Let's see what's going to happen here. Runner on first.*

39. J: (Hits the ball, runs to first base, and then stops, giggling, as the therapist approaches him with the ball. He turns around to return to home base with a big smile on his face:) *You gotta' be quick.*

T: *Runners on first and second now.*

39. Once Juan touches first base, he has confirmed his reframe of past emotional memories. He smiles the happiest smile he has expressed since starting play therapy.

40. J: (Backs up behind home base as far as the room will allow.)

T: *Boy, you want to show me that you can hit this ball a long way.*

40. Juan now confirms his experience by putting his empowerment into the swing.

41. J: (Hits the ball and runs to first base where he falls to the floor laughing.)

T: *It feels good to do the things you want to do and have a good time too.*

41. Juan now celebrates his joy by being childlike and falling to the floor in the silly, spontaneous, joyful style of a happy child.

42. T: (While leaving the playroom at the end of the session:) *You really had a good day today.*

J: *A good day? This has been the best day of my life!*

42. Juan confirms that he has regained his empowerment in relation to his emotionality surrounding the perpetrator and the abuse. He is now ready to progress through his developmental stages.

Therapeutic Growth Stage: Experiencing Empowerment

Once a child has confronted her emotional pain and regained her sense of empowerment, she begins to experience a sense of loss. Whereas before the child regained her sense of empowerment, control, and dignity, her play focused on such needs as protecting herself, either from the pain of a traumatic event or from a relationship. Now she begins to unconsciously mourn the loss of her normal developmental play that did not occur because of her overwhelming emotional needs. For instance, if an abuse or traumatic event occurred when the child was four but she did not receive therapeutic intervention until the age of seven, she has lost three years of developmental play. The child begins to wonder, "Who am I?" During this phase, the child's energy level is low, and her play appears uninvolved with little emotionality or intensity. Although she has confronted her pain, she has not regained the developmental stages that were lost due to the painful event or relationship. It is very common during this period of time to see children take something representative of value (e.g., gold coins) and bury them in the sandbox. The child may then smooth over the sand, symbolizing, *"My value isn't seen yet. My value was lost, and nobody knows it's there."* It is also common during this time to see children identify with the brokenness of a toy, wanting to fix it.

Within a few sessions, the child begins to feel a sense of renewal (i.e., "I am me. Isn't it great!") and begins moving through her lost stages of development. Now, however, she reexperiences these stages with the well-being she lacked because of the effects of the painful event or relationship. In addition, she begins integrating the feelings of empowerment and confidence that were gained from facing her pain. Her play will begin to take on the characteristics of a child who feels safe (e.g., joy, silliness, laughter, even goofiness). Because she is discovering her value, she may now want to dig up the valuables that she earlier buried in the sand or have the therapist dig them up.

Dynamic Shifts in the
Child's Behavior

As the child begins to integrate her regained sense of empowerment into her lost developmental stages, her behavior begins to move toward more normalized expressions, appropriate to age and stage of development. From the lowest point of the Dependency Stage to the end of the Therapeutic Growth Stage, there are dynamic shifts in the child's behavior. Before the child faces and overcomes the painful event or relationship, she experiences so much pain that her play is dominated by fantasy. She is totally focused on the intense activity in which she is engaging and appears very self-centered. This style of play contains intense emotional projection. In addition, the child is driven to control her environment through her play and the relationship with her therapist by placing demands on the therapist and often exhibiting manipulative, aggressive, oppositional[3], even resistive behaviors. She appears fearful, cautious, and guarded in her play, reflecting the need for protection. As the child reframes her experiences, she begins to experience feelings of safety, and her play shifts to a rehearsal-for-life style, taking on the characteristics of spontaneity and silliness, including laughter, giggling, and a genuine enjoyment of life style of play. She becomes more cooperative and interactive with her therapist, family, and peers. Whereas her relationship with the therapist was characterized by extreme dependency, she now starts to move toward an interdependency in this relationship.

In addition, when a child experiences a painful event or relationship, her self-esteem, self-worth, self-respect, sense of dignity, and empowerment suffer greatly. She feels isolated and alone. High levels of distrust, caution, and lack of power in her environment are exhibited. Her play may indicate her experience of being disrespected. As these characteristics begin to shift, the child begins to regain her sense of dignity and empowerment (appropriate to age and stage of development). She begins to move toward trusting and respecting others, interactions which are appropriate to her age. Rather than an external locus of control, indicated by her caution and lack of trust, she begins to have an internal locus of

---

3. This opposition is the child's process. This is not to indicate that she would be diagnosed as Oppositional-Defiant Disorder.

control, learning appropriate behaviors and actions. Rather than base her opinion of herself on what others think of her, she gains the ability to assess her self-worth based on her own values.

Moving from reality disorientation to reality orientation occurs slowly over a period of months, sometimes even years. In fact, it is not uncommon, just before termination, for a child to experience a relapse or reminiscences of the aggressive style of the Dependency Stage. For instance, a little boy may wear a gun and holster while playing a game and then, occasionally, take the gun out and shoot at something. This is not the intense, pressured, fantasy-dominated play of the Dependency Stage, but rather flashback memories of his abuse. No longer do these feelings dominate and incapacitate the child.

The following is an example of a child's play during the Therapeutic Growth Stage. Tyrel was referred for therapy because of a lack of social acceptance at his school. He was socially immature and had no friends. The other children teased and made fun of him. In his home neighborhood, he played with children who were two to three years younger. In addition, Tyrel was on medication for hyperactivity.

During this excerpt, Tyrel and his therapist are playing with puppets. Tyrel has the butterfly puppet on his right hand. On his left hand is the crocodile puppet, which growled when he put it on. The therapist has both the hippopotamus and the lion puppets. Tyrel flies the butterfly around the room and then clumsily lands it on the table, like a bird on ice. He then has the butterfly fly again and land in the same clumsy style on the table. At that point, Tyrel comments that he (the butterfly) just can't do things quite right. The butterfly then takes off again and crashes in a patch of flowers. The awkward butterfly regains his composure and takes off again. Once again, he lands on the table. Meanwhile, although the crocodile is present as the play evolves, there is no verbal involvement. (This is Tyrel's style in the family.)

Session	Comments
1. Client: (Flies the butterfly through the air and awkwardly lands it on the table where the hippopotamus and lion	1. The butterfly is coming into this social situation in a clumsy style and meets two more grounded and respected animals.

puppets are located:) *Hi, my name is Butterfly.*

Therapist: *Hi, I'm Hippo.*

C: *Hi, Hippo.*

T: (In a lower tone of voice:) *I'm Lion.*

C: *Yeah, I know.*

2. T: (Working both puppets:) *We sure wish we could fly. It looks like fun.*

2. The therapist gives credit and respect to the competencies of the butterfly. Then she gives the offering that it would be fun to join with the butterfly.

3. C: *Hey! Well, get on my back.*

T: *Could we?* (Puts Hippo on Butterfly's back:) *All right!*

3. Tyrel feels surprised and excited at the strength to give the animals a supportive ride.

4. C: *You can always trust a butterfly.* (Butterfly begins to rise with Hippo on his back.)

T: (As Hippo:) *Wow! I'm going up!*

4. Tyrel indicates the beginning of integration of his belief in himself and the empowerment to give support to others.

5. C: *Do you want to land in a tree or not?*

T: *I can trust this butterfly. Yeah, let's go up in that tree.* (The tree is painted as part of a mural on the wall behind them.)

5. Tyrel feels empowered enough to allow others to make some of the decisions. He can give up some of the control.

6. C: (Singing:) *Get along here.* (Speaking:) *We're gonna' go all the way up to ...*

T: *Okay, it's the first time I've ever been this high. Wow ...*

6. Singing is the joy of the trip and the sense of confidence he is feeling. He wants his sense of confidence to go as high as possible.

7. C: *Oh, no! We've gotta' go. There's a bumble bee!*

T: (As they fly away:) *Oh, no! Not a bumble bee!*

7. Tyrel is still not completely confident, especially when an intruder (perpetrator) is in the area.

8. C: *Oh, no! Let's fly away fast!* (Tyrel quickly waves the butterfly up and down, simulating a butterfly's flight, while he moves it forward. Hippo is still on Butterfly's back.)
C & T: *O-o-o-o!*

8. Tyrel exhibits a high need to escape from the intruder. The flapping of the wings is the nervousness this experience creates for him. It also validates his empowerment to flee when he needs to escape.

9. T: *I'm holding on! It's a little scary up here, being free.*

9. The therapist reflects the tenuousness of his experience in this change process.

10. C: *I got you!*

10. He confirms that while they had to flee, he still has a level of mastery over the situation.

11. T: *I trust you, Butterfly.* (As they land on the table:) *Oh-o-o!* (They rest for a moment on the table.)

11. The therapist confirms Tyrel's ability to handle the situation as they swoop onto the table in a quick landing. Tyrel is starting to believe in himself, although he has not totally affirmed this belief.

12. C: *I'm gonna' go fly away now.*
T: *Thank you, Butterfly.*

12. Tyrel needs to integrate more of the empowerment he is gaining internally before sharing with Hippo.

13. C: (Flies the butterfly away, making noises of flying.)

13. The noises are representative of the internal changes in his being.

14. (Conversation between Hippo and Lion:) *Hippo: I went on a butterfly trip.*
    Lion: *You what?*
    Hippo: *I went on a butterfly trip, and Butterfly took good care of me. We went so high that it was a little scary.*
    Lion: *Oh, I bet!*
    Hippo: *But you can trust Butterfly.*
    Lion: *He took good care of you?*
    Hippo: *I know I can trust Butterfly, 'cause he says I can trust*

14. The conversation between Hippo and Lion reflects the struggle or fears that occur within Tyrel as he experiences his change process. Tyrel stands quietly listening to the conversation as he reverses the butterfly puppet into the caterpillar puppet. The therapist reconfirms that he can trust himself as he proceeds in his process of change and belief in himself as a more empowered person.

him, and he took go-o-od care of me.
That's how I know.

C: (While the conversation was taking place between Hippo and Lion, Tyrel returned the butterfly puppet to the table and turned it inside out to the caterpillar side:) *I need to get ... can you help me get this shut?*

T: *Sure.* (They work on it together:) *Okay, you got it.*

15. C: (Makes a melody of the caterpillar crawling along and sings:) *I make a good way, but I'm getting ready to be pretty nice for friends. When I get to my cocoon, I have to jump in and then turn into a butterfly. I act like a band. When you hear me marching, you think I'm a pile of ants* (as he pulls the caterpillar backwards).

15. The sounds tell the mood of the person (the caterpillar) as he reexperiences what he has been through and the acceptance of his personage as he prepares for changes. *I have to jump in and turn into a butterfly* means he has to risk and make the change. *You think I'm a pile of ants* means the world thinks I'm insignificant and always just going along with things. Remember, change doesn't occur in one shift, but in a sequence of experiential shifts that may be repeated a number of times for confirmation as the change is being integrated.

16. T: (As Hippo:) *You must be a trusting caterpillar.*

16. *You can trust yourself to make the changes that you are struggling to complete.*

17. C: *Who wants to ride on the army?*

T: (As Hippo:) *Oh, can I?*
(As the Lion:) *Can I?*

17. The army is a metaphor for the social/emotional battles he has fought to survive in a world that has not been very accepting of him. In the change process, the child must return to the emotional places he wishes to change in order to shift the experiential meaning from that unpleasant experience to the new sense of being.

18. C: (Raises up the crocodile puppet and says:) *Who is ... raise their ... raise their, uh, hand — if they got one.*
    T: (As Hippo and Lion, together:) *Oh, I don't have a hand.*

18. Tyrel has to be able to make change in the presence of his intruder or perpetrator or the change won't last.

19. C: *Just raise your mouth.*
    T: (Raises mouths of Hippo and Lion.)
    C: *Well, okay, Hippo.*
    T: (As Hippo:) *Oh, boy, I get to go! Whoopee!*

19. To raise their hands (mouths) is to ask, *Who believes I can make this change?* Both Lion and Hippo believe.

20. C: (Singing:) *Dat-dat-dat-dat.* (Hippo gets on the caterpillar's back. The caterpillar crawls along.)

20. He is feeling the support at this point in his transition. He sings as he approaches the time to shift the experience.

21. T: (As Hippo:) *Boy, that train really works.*

21. Another validation that this transformation can occur.

22. C: (As Caterpillar:) *Oops, we gotta' go. Now, you have to get off cause I gotta' do something.*
    T: (As Hippo:) *Well, all right. Thanks Caterpillar.* (Caterpillar crawls under the table. Hippo says to Lion:) *Wow, was that neat!*

22. Now it's time to move to the shift in the transition. He has received the support from Hippo but has to go through the journey alone since the transformation is internal.

23. C: (Crocodile puppet jumps anxiously. Then Tyrel takes the crocodile puppet off his hand. Singing in a high, gruff voice:) *Looking at-at-at.* (He makes primitive sounds like an infant being born.)
    T: (As Hippo to Lion:) *Maybe Caterpillar will come back and see us some time. I can recognize him.*

23. Again, he must make his changes in the presence of his perpetrator (his father who is not very tolerant of him). The change is like being reborn into a new person.

24. C: (In the same high, gruff voice:) *No, you can't recognize me ...* (pulls the butterfly out from under the table)

24. *You won't recognize me because I've transformed into a new self.* Tyrel is very proud of himself; and as he

... *'cause I'm a butterfly now.* (Butterfly flutters his wings and rises in the air.)

rises in the air, he can integrate his new experience of being.

25. T: *O-o-oh, wow, have you changed!*

25. Recognition and validation of the change.

26. C: *I know.*

26. Agreement and confirmation.

27. T: *You're our same friend, and you've changed to a beautiful butterfly.*

27. *You're the person we like, and you have changed into a more beautiful being.*

28. C: *I was ugly once, but now I'm beautiful. Who wants a ride?*

28. *I was unacceptable once, but now I'm acceptable; and I have the empowerment to support that view.*

29. T: *That's true.*

29. The therapist validates the change again. He needs to know that his transformation is recognized by others.

30. C: *Lion* ... (Butterfly is stretching his wings.)

30. Now he can feel the internalization as he is validated by Hippo and Lion, his friends.

31. T: *You know, it's kind of like you were always beautiful, but we just couldn't tell.* (Lion gets on Butterfly's back, and Butterfly rises. Then, Hippo says to Lion:) *You can trust Butterfly. Don't be afraid.*

31. The therapist is metaphorically saying that she has always liked him and knew he had potential that was not recognized. Again, this is validation that he can trust his change.

32. C: (As Butterfly, and as they approach the opposite corner of the room:) *Oh, no! I can't turn around.*

32. Now that the transformation has occurred, he knows that he can't revert back to his past style or beliefs about himself.

33. T: (As Lion:) *I trust you. I know you'll find a way.* (They turn and begin flying back toward the table.)

33. She again tells him he can trust and believe in himself that he is capable of making the changes he is experiencing, and that he will be all right.

34. C: (Humming)
    T: *You have to trust your friends.*

34. The humming is the process of internalizing the belief in himself.

35. C: (As Butterfly:) *We gotta' land.* (Butterfly and Lion land on the table with a little jolt:) *Whoops! You can stay, Butterfly. Yeah. Pretty soft landing.*
    T: (As Lion:) *Thank you, thank you. That was wonderful!*

35. Tyrel lands to complete this validation trip and says to himself (through the Butterfly) that he can stay with his changes. The soft landing is the acceptance of a softer, more gentle side of himself that is acceptable.

36. C: (Butterfly rises again and flies away:) *Ah, I gotta' go get my little brother.*
    T: *All right.*
    C: *Yeah, he needs to change into a butterfly today, too.*

36. He has now accepted the transformation into his present self and must regress to an earlier stage in his development and make the transformation in that part of his being also. Tyrel does not have a younger brother. Younger brother means a younger part of himself. He repeats a similar play pattern at a younger stage in his development. The same process of validation and recognition occurs in this play as he validates the experience in this stage of his development.

CHAPTER 8

ENRICHMENT OF THE
"PLAY AS METAPHOR" PROCESS

Therapeutic Responses

For many people in society today, communication with children consists of directives, questions, or responses to the immediate superficial behavior of the child or to a stereotypical view of children. Even people who are trained in educating children often respond primarily to the academic functioning of the child. Indeed, for many people within the mental health profession, children are an enigma to be allowed to cross the threshold of the hallowed halls of psychotherapy only as one member of the system called family. For many therapists, therapeutic communication with children is a contradiction in terms and, in point of fact, strikes fear in the hearts of many capable adults or adolescent therapists.

Literature, while not extensive, is available on methods of treatment for children. Most of what is written is fraught with techniques for treating the symptoms children present. However, few of these authors address the issue of relating to the child in a personal manner, giving respect to the individual nature of each child's being and responding to the child's issues within that context. Certainly the child-centered theorists and therapists espouse the communication of warmth, acceptance, and empathy with children (e.g., Axline, 1947b; Landreth, 1991; Moustakas, 1959/1992).

In addition, certain theorists emphasize how interpretation can be helpful in assisting the child to go beyond the content of the child's play and/or verbalizations. These therapists attempt to explain or shed light upon events in the child's life as they have occurred (Lewis, 1974; O'Connor, 1991).

Other theories on therapy with children are grounded in behavioral manipulations or the use of therapists' verbal responses to children's verbalizations. However, the credibility of children's verbalizations is questioned repeatedly, not only in the child's customary environments (e.g., home, school), but especially in the courtroom. (See, Ceci & Bruck, 1993, for a review.) If a child is not capable of accurate verbalizations due to the child's lack of an extensive vocabulary or of formal operational thought, then how can this child be expected to communicate to a therapist about such abstract concepts as feelings and their derivations? In addition, it is unreasonable to expect a young child to understand a therapist making connections among previous occurrences, their resulting feelings, and how these relate to current behavior.

Through play, a child expresses his view of the world and creates his own metaphor for understanding and for resolution. In that way, children use play as their modality for communication. Then the question becomes, how is it possible to use a child's play to facilitate change for the child? Exactly what is the element that moves the process from simply play to therapeutic play? Certainly the first and probably most critical element lies within a relationship where the child is accepted and understood (Landreth, 1991; Moustakas, 1959/1992, 1973). This type of relationship, however, does not occur serendipitously. Rather, it is a slow, evolutionary process, nurtured by appropriate responses on the part of the therapist. These responses enable the child to experience feelings of safety, security, and acceptance by the therapist. However, even though a therapist gives appropriate responses, out of necessity, before the child can trust, he will still test this level of acceptance on the part of the therapist.

Dimensions to Consider When Giving Appropriate Responses to Facilitate Change

Responding in such a manner as to facilitate change in children varies according to certain dimensions. These dimensions include the stage in the play therapy process, the depth level of the relationship between the therapist and child, and the modality of the response.

Stage of the Play Therapy Process

Exploratory Stage. In the initial stage of the therapeutic process, or the *Exploratory Stage*, the child is new to the situation and involved in exploring the room as well as getting to know the therapist and the expectations of himself in this new setting. Responses made to the child at this time are acknowledging of his activities and presence. The purpose of these responses is to communicate to the child that the therapist is present with him, tracking him, accepting whatever he is doing, and allowing the child to be the leader in what occurs in the room. The Exploratory Stage generally takes one to two sessions. An example of a response during this stage is, "I notice you're looking at everything in the playroom so you'll know what there is to do in here."

The following is an excerpt of a session which occurred during a training seminar. It is a good illustration of both the type of responses to be given during this stage and the effect of an empathy statement introduced too early in the relationship. It is taken from the first session with five-year-old Scotty. Approximately three years earlier, Scotty's parents divorced. While living with his mother, he began seeing a therapist who suspected he was being sexually abused in the home. Eventually, Child Protective Services investigated the situation and confirmed that, indeed, Scotty was being abused by his mother's boyfriend. After being removed from the home, Scotty went to live with his father. His stepmother, however, soon began to experience problems with him. At that point, it was decided to have Scotty participate in therapy. The day before this first session was Scotty's first day in kindergarten. This excerpt is taken from the first minutes in the playroom.

Scotty:	(Looks around the room and sees a toy garage. Kneels down and begins to play with it.)
Therapist:	(Pulls up a chair and sits down in back of Scotty.) *I notice you are just kind of checking around and seeing what we have here.*
Scotty:	(Laughs) *Guess so.* (Looks across the room.) *Man!* (Walks over and looks in a fairly large toy house.) *What's in there?*

Therapist:	*You're checking that out. It looks kind of interesting in there.*
Scotty:	(Looks inside. Tries to pick it up.) *That's a big one, isn't it?* (Moves it a little more and then looks to the side and begins to check out another one.)
Therapist:	*You're looking at all those places and seeing what's in there, tucked away.*
Scotty:	(Picks up the house and moves it to the floor.)
Therapist:	*It's heavy.*
Scotty:	*Yeah.* (Goes back and gets the other house.) *There.*
Therapist:	*Two of them.*
Scotty:	*There.*
Therapist:	*You set them just right.*
Scotty:	(Looks inside. Picks up a box of marbles. Snickers and looks at the therapist.)
Therapist:	*I hear that.*
Scotty:	*Ummm. I got a marble — a big marble.*
Therapist:	*A big marble.*
Scotty:	*Uh-huh.* (Gets up. Lifts the bop bag and moves it. Looks at a toy on the shelf.)
Therapist:	*You're checking out all the things on the shelf there.*
Scotty:	(Shoots a toy gun. Puts it down and keeps looking.) *I used to have one of these.*
Therapist:	*It's nice to see things in here that you recognize.*
Scotty:	*Yeah. I used to have one of these.*
Therapist:	*I didn't recognize it.*
Scotty:	*It used to have a little ball, but I lost my stuff to it.*
Therapist:	*You lost your stuff to it?*
Scotty:	*Uh-huh.*
Therapist:	*That must have made you sad.*
Scotty:	*I don't think so!*
Therapist:	*Oh, you don't think so.*

This therapist did a good job of tracking what Scotty was doing. At one point, however, she gave an empathy statement: "That must have made you sad." Because he was not ready for this level of response, he denied it by saying, "I don't think so!" Essentially, he just wanted tracking-types of responses, almost giving the appearance of a running narrative of observations during the session: "You're checking that out. You're wanting to see everything that you can see. You want to make sure you get it just right."

Testing for Protection Stage. Once a child understands the setting and feels socially comfortable, and before he can move into personally meaningful material, it is necessary to assess the level of commitment on the part of the therapist toward the child. This is accomplished through testing: on one level, of the situational settings, and on another level, of the acceptance of the child's not-so-socially acceptable material by the therapist. The goal of this stage is the establishment of trust in the relationship. In the process of setting the limits, the therapist accepts the child's feelings and protects the child by not allowing those feelings to become overwhelming. In so doing, the child realizes he can trust the therapist and is, therefore, ready to move into communicating, through play, his unresolved issues. Verbal communications to the child during the Testing for Protection Stage first recognize the feeling underlying the testing, and then set the limit. For example, "I know you are angry at me right now, and that's all right; and I won't allow you to destroy the toys." At this time, it is important to keep responses in the "I-Thou" modality, because of the interpersonal nature of this time. Establishing trust through testing for protection usually takes one to two sessions.

The following excerpt is from a session with three-year-old Lindy, who loves to test limits. In fact, this is the reason her mother brought her in for therapy.

| Therapist: | *In one minute, Lindy, it will be time for us to go.* |
| Lindy: | *No. No. No.* (Lindy then walks over to the toy shelf, picks up a baby bottle, and walks to the sandbox. She puts the bottle into the sand and begins scooping. She then tries to get the lid off the bottle but can't.) *Can* |

	you get the lid off? (Starts to scoop sand again.)
Therapist:	*If we get the lid off, then maybe you can fill it up with sand.*
Lindy:	*Yeah.* (Brushes sand off the bottle.)
Therapist:	(Reaches for the bottle.) *I can get the lid off for you tomorrow when it's time to come back, because our time is up for now.*
Lindy:	(Points and shakes finger at therapist.) *No, you do it right now!* (Begins stomping her feet.)
Therapist:	*And now ... when we're in here, Lindy, it's your turn to be in charge, and you can play whatever you want in here; but when our minute is up, I'm in charge, and it's time to go.*
Lindy:	(Grabs bottle.) *Well, you open it!*
Therapist:	*And I will. That will be here for us to open tomorrow.*
Lindy:	*Open it right now!* (Kicks her feet against the floor.)
Therapist:	(Gets up and picks up Lindy's shoes from the floor.)
Lindy:	*No!*
Therapist:	(In a calm and gentle but firm voice:) *I said it's time to go and our minute is up. And I'm going to think about you tonight and be waiting to see you tomorrow.*
Lindy:	(Runs over to the toy shelf and grabs a toy.)
Therapist:	(Reaches to get the toy.)
Lindy:	(Runs away.)
Therapist:	*And now we're going to walk out and see your mom ...*
Lindy:	(Keeps running away from therapist.)
Therapist:	(Gently takes hold of Lindy.) *... and not have a chasing game, Lindy.*
Lindy:	*No!*

Therapist:	(Picks Lindy up and walks toward door.) *Today, we're going to go out ... we're going to walk out ... because our time is up ...*
Lindy:	*No! No!*
Therapist:	(Opens the door.) *And we'll be back tomorrow.*

This excerpt is a fairly mild example of testing. However, notice the responses are warm and supportive, recognizing the feelings behind the testing. During this stage, it is appropriate to begin talking about feelings. For instance, "I know you have a good time and like being here, and I like being here with you, too. But our time is up for now; and when our time is up, we have to go." By setting these limits, the therapist communicates that he will protect the child. This is very important because children need to know they will be protected before they will work on the issues they have come to address.

Working Stages: Dependency and Therapeutic Growth. By the time the therapist and child have reached the Working Stages (Dependency and Therapeutic Growth), all avenues of communication are open between the two of them. These stages are the longest of the play therapy process, the duration depending upon the severity and chronicity of the issues necessary for the child to address. The responding styles are the same for both stages. At this point, examples of responses are: "The dolphin gets nervous when the shark starts drinking," or during play, "I can't find the wand; I guess all my magic is gone."

The following is another excerpt with five-year-old Scotty. Before the video was turned on during this session, Scotty had spent a great deal of time setting up a scene in which two dinosaurs were facing a red car. Other animals were in the area, but all had their backs to the car. During this excerpt, Scotty is playing out his sexual abuse for the therapist. The therapist, however, did not recognize the metaphor. The two dinosaurs facing the car represent the two people who knew about the abuse. All the other animals represent those who ignored his dilemma. During his play, one of the dinosaurs begins eating the front and back of the red car.

It is interesting to note that this car is the toy with which Scotty chose to identify. He noticed it on his first day of therapy. In fact, the way in which Scotty tested the therapist was by wanting to take the red car home

with him. At the beginning of each session, Scotty would look for this
red car and then keep it beside him — whether he was actually playing
with it or not.

Scotty: (Pushes the car across an area of the floor
                     toward the animals.)

Therapist: *... and he's keeping on going. He's making a
                     mess of things. Sometimes, he gets angry
                     when he sees ... in order ...*

Scotty: *But this car didn't like ... he's looking for
                     something.*

Therapist: *He's looking for something.*

Scotty: (Pushes car into a stack of foam blocks.) *He
                     knows they live in there.*

Therapist: *He knows they live in there, and so he's
                     going in on purpose. He's showing them
                     he's angry with them.*

Scotty: *He ... they're pretending they're ... so they'll
                     think they're not alike, but he knows. He's a
                     little minder* [reminder].

Therapist: *He knows ... there's a little minder in there.*

Scotty: (Begins to attack one of the dinosaurs with
                     the red car.)

Therapist: *He's attacking them and showing them he's
                     angry with them.*

Scotty: (Takes the red car and goes back while the
                     dinosaur eats — first the rear of the car, and
                     then the front of the car.)

Therapist: *... and he's going back, and he's biting him.
                     He* [the car] *wants to let him* [the dinosaur]
                     know how much he [the dinosaur] *hurt him*
                     [the car].

Scotty: *Yep.   That's the way it was, but he did
                     some ...*

Therapist: *Sometimes people hurt our feelings, and we
                     get angry.*

Scotty: (The red car falls over on its back.)

Even though the therapist had not recognized that Scotty was playing out his sexual abuse, she was able to facilitate his process by recognizing the feelings that were being displayed in his play (i.e., "He's attacking them and showing them he's angry with them."). It is this type of response to a child that is important, whether or not a therapist understands the significance of the play. Notice Scotty's response, "Yep. That's the way it was ..."

Termination Stage. Once play moves into a rehearsal-for-life theme, where the child is mimicking acceptable adult behaviors and the intensity of the play is dramatically decreased, termination is appropriate. Termination is not accomplished in one session, however. It is necessary to maintain the therapeutic alliance to assist the child in accepting the severance of the relationship (Thompson & Rudolph, 1983). This may take up to six weeks, with the general formula being one terminating session for every month in therapy. It is important to communicate with the child about the impending loss of the relationship for both the child and the therapist. For example, "We only have two more weeks to play together. I'll miss you when you don't come here anymore, but I'll feel good knowing you're happy and having fun."

Following is an excerpt of a very special terminating session. Not all terminations will be like this. In this case, the therapist and child, Andy, had very special feelings for each other. At some point during the beginning of the session, Andy discovered some transitional gifts that the therapist had prepared for him. One of them was the *Lump of Love* doll, which is a small unisex figurine of a small child sitting with his/her knees hugged up and head down.

Andy:	(Practicing swinging a play bat.) *Okay.*
Therapist:	*That was practice. Now, here we go.* (Throws the ball.)
Andy:	(Hits ball and runs around the bases.)
Therapist:	*Okay. That's good. You hit it. I'm trying to get it. Where did it go? Where did it go? I'll get you. I'll get you. Gee whiz! You got all around. You got to every base. Got home safe. You have learned how to take care of yourself and get around all the bases.*

Andy:	(Laughs.) *How did you know I liked sculptures?* (Holding bat, ready to hit the ball again.) *How did you know I liked them?*
Therapist:	*You like sculptures? Well, I thought maybe you would, because I've thought of you a lot and you know ... I got that Lump of Love. You know, some people get a lump in their throat when they're kind of sad, and they feel like crying.*
Andy:	(Andy puts the bat behind his neck and begins moving around. Then, he puts his neck back on the bat and looks around.)
Therapist:	*You ever get a lump in your throat about leaving somebody or something? Well, that's kind of the way I feel about us not being able to be together anymore.*
Andy:	(Touches the Lump of Love doll on the toy shelf where the therapist had placed it before the session.) *You got that?*
Therapist:	*I got this because there's a lump in my throat because I love you so much, and I thought, "Well, I'll give you this little sculpture."*
Andy:	(Swings Nerf bat. Hits himself in the head. Puts bill of hat up.) *My baseball hat. Just in case it hits me in the head.*
Therapist:	*You got protection. You don't want anything to hit you in the head.*

Notice the therapist's response, "You have learned how to take care of yourself and get around all the bases." On the surface, this means that the child knows how to play a ball game. Andy, however, knew that it meant more than that and said, "How did you know I like sculptures?" The therapist is tying loose ends together and is, in essence, reprocessing their journey together. Then Andy refers to his baseball hat. "My baseball hat. Just in case it hits me in the head." In other words, "I've got my baseball hat on for protection." Terminating for Andy was like hitting him in the head. He actually wanted some protection from this termination. At the same time, however, he now feels more capable of protecting himself.

Before his relationship with the therapist, Andy had not experienced a positive male role model in his life. In fact, his mother had been involved in a destructive relationship. Andy's relationship with the therapist was the most positive one he had ever experienced with a man. Consequently, terminating was very difficult for both of them.

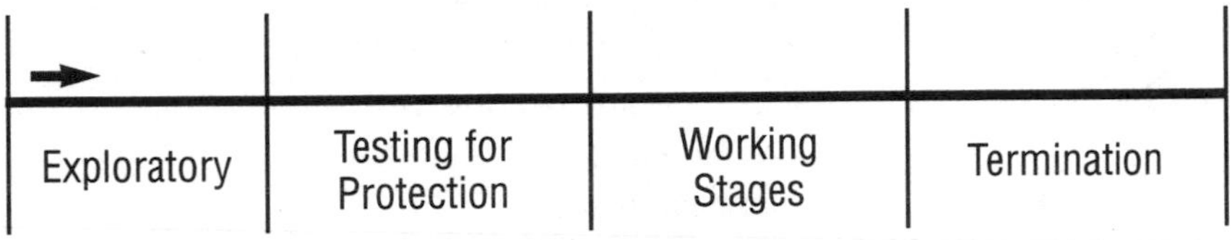

Exploratory	Testing for Protection	Working Stages	Termination

Illustration 8-1

Depth Level of the Response

A second dimension to consider when facilitating change in children is that of the *depth level* of the response given by the therapist. Just as in therapeutic work with adults, it is overwhelming for a child to receive a deeper level (i.e., interpretative, confrontive, connective, insightful, etc.) response (acknowledgment) before a rapport has been established. Once rapport (trust) has been established, the client recognizes the caring behind the deeper level response.

Observational Responses. More appropriate initial responses are called observational responses (i.e., a description of the child's observable behaviors or a running narrative of what the child is doing) such as, "You're just looking around to see everything that is in this room."

An example of this type of response is taken from another excerpt of a session with five-year-old Scotty.

Scotty:	(Points a toy gun toward the therapist and shoots it.)
Therapist:	*You're going to shoot me.*
Scotty:	(Continues shooting.)
Therapist:	*You got me.*
Scotty:	(Turns toward window and shoots at some thing outside.)
Therapist:	*... out the window ...*
Scotty:	(Turns to his left, points the gun and shoots. Then he points the gun at the bop bag and shoots.)
Therapist:	*Ah, right in the heart.*
Scotty:	(Shoots at the bop bag again.)
Therapist:	*Ah, right between the eyes.*
Scotty:	(Points gun at the top of the head on the bop bag.)
Therapist:	*... on the top of the head.*
Scotty:	(Turns back to his left and points the gun in the sandbox and shoots. Then he looks in the sandbox, touches the sand with his hand, and gives a startle response.) *That's sand!* (Laughs.)
Therapist:	*Yes, it is.* (Laughs with Scotty.)
Scotty:	(Puts the gun down.) *It looks like it's quick sand.* (Picks up his leg and scratches it and then puts his leg down and looks back at the sand.)
Therapist:	*It looks like it's quicksand.*
Scotty:	*Uh-huh.*
Therapist:	*And then you tested it and found out it was just sand.*

| Scotty: | (Goes back to the sandbox, puts his hand in the sand, takes it out, looks under the sandbox and walks away, making a guttural sound. Turns toward therapist and then looks over at the toy shelf. Goes back to the toys he was playing with on the floor.) |
| Therapist: | *There's so many toys in here. It's hard to figure out which ones you want to play with.* |

Scotty's play contained a wealth of information for the therapist. He took the gun and wanted to shoot her, communicating, "I'm not sure I can trust you, and I'm not going to give you a chance to hurt me." Then he took the gun and began shooting the bop bag — again, wanting to protect himself and/or hurt someone who has hurt him. Because the relationship had not been established to the point that the therapist could go beyond observational responses, she very appropriately responded, "You're shooting him there. Ah, right between the eyes."

Also, notice his experience at the sandbox. After looking at the sand and touching it with his gun, he had a startle response. When he said, "It looks like it's quicksand," he was communicating, "I'm afraid that if I start experiencing my feelings, I'm going to get caught and pulled down into them and get lost." In essence, since sand is representative of a child's emotionality, he was communicating that he was afraid of his feelings, thinking they would overwhelm him. His startle response confirmed this interpretation. Again, the therapist gave observational responses rather than deeper level responses because of the lack of a relationship at this point in the therapeutic process.

Notice that when Scotty shot the therapist, she did not drop dead on the spot. She was not exactly sure what he wanted her to do, thus the response, "You're shooting me." If Scotty had then replied, "Okay, die. You're supposed to die!", then it would have been appropriate to do so. At this point in the therapeutic process, if the therapist had died when Scotty shot at her, the realization that he had so much power over someone so quickly may have overwhelmed him.

Communicating Through Toys. One aspect that differentiates psychotherapy with children from psychotherapy with adults is the availability of toys as a medium of communication (Sweeney & Landreth, 1993).

If play is the language of the child, then toys are the words. Just as a child will use toys as his words, so a therapist can respond to and through those same toys. For instance, as a child plays that a truck is sinking into the mud, the therapist can respond: "The truck feels scared because something is happening that is out of his control; and he doesn't know what will happen to him." While the response is given to the toy, the message is to the child.

Notice in another excerpt of this session with Scotty how the therapist communicates to Scotty about his feelings through the red car.

Scotty:	(Pushes a car forcefully across the tile floor toward the play gas station on the carpet.)
Therapist:	*All the cars are in here.*
Scotty:	(Pushes the car toward the gas station again.) *Didn't get it.*
Therapist:	*He didn't get it. He's aimed at that gas station. He won't quit until he gets it.*
Scotty:	(Keeps pushing the car toward the gas station and then around it.)
Therapist:	*He's mad at something. He keeps going after it.*
Scotty:	*I guess so. I'm going to get him some gas.*
Therapist:	*He needs to get more power.*
Scotty:	(Continues to play with car.)

Scotty used the car to represent himself. All children go through a stage when they attribute human characteristics to inanimate objects. In essence, it is less risky and overwhelming for a child to hear that the car is feeling hurt than it is to hear that he's feeling hurt. The toy provides the child with the safety of distance and anonymity.

Also, notice how the therapist responded when Scotty ran the car into the gas station: "He needs to get more power." In fact, that is exactly what this child is doing by coming in for therapy — he is regaining his empowerment so that he can keep going. The therapist reflects to Scotty that when he gets mad, he keeps on going. It is very empowering for a child to hear that it's okay to keep on going, to persevere until he reaches some resolution.

Addressing Relationship Issues.   Occasionally, a child will be concerned with the immediacy of his relationship with the therapist or another significant adult. This may be verbalized by the child directly to the therapist or played out metaphorically. When this is the case, it is important for the therapist to recognize what is occurring and to respond about the relationship. For example, the child directs the therapist in their preparations for a dangerous trip into the jungle. Finally, as they depart, the therapist says, "If we move slowly and stay together, we'll be safe."

Following is a good illustration of a session where the child is addressing her relationship with her mother, although this is never specifically articulated during the session. Carrie is five years old and lives with both parents and a nine-year-old brother. The brother is the identified troublemaker in the family. Carrie's mother is controlling and critical.

Carrie and the therapist are playing with the walkie-talkies and are at opposite ends of the room.

Carrie:	*... blocked ears ...*
Therapist:	*No, I don't actually. I heard you that time. And I was really glad.*
Carrie:	(Loudly.) *I can't hear you!* (Giggles.)
Therapist:	*Ah, I can hear you.*
Carrie:	(Giggles.) *Hello?*
Therapist:	*Hello.*
Carrie:	*I can't hear you.*
Therapist:	*That's too bad because I can hear you, and I'd really like to talk with you.*
Carrie:	*Get in here!*
Therapist:	*I'm here.*
Carrie:	*No, you're not. Get in here!*
Therapist:	*Where should I be? Where should I be?*
Carrie:	*You should be by me.*
Therapist:	*Oh, okay, here I come.*
Carrie:	(As soon as the therapist moves towards her, she runs across the room.)
Therapist:	*Oh, no!* (Turns around and faces Carrie.) *Every time I start to get close to you, you run away!*

Carrie:	(Giggles and then yells:) *Get over here!*
Therapist:	*I'm afraid to. I'm afraid you'll run away.*
Carrie:	*I won't run away.*
Therapist:	(Walks over to Carrie.)
Carrie:	(Runs to the other side of the room.)
Therapist:	*Oh, you tricked me again!*
Carrie:	(Giggles and then says:) *Get over here!*
Therapist:	(Starts to walk toward Carrie.)
Carrie:	(Runs to other side of room.)
Therapist:	*Ooooh.*
Carrie:	(Runs across the room again and then says:) *Get over here!!*
Therapist:	(Stands up.) *But, if I go over there, you're going to run away ...*
Carrie:	(Runs back across the room and giggles.)
Therapist:	*... and if I run over here, you're going to run away. And we're never going to get close; and I'm feeling so discouraged.* (Hangs her head.)

Carrie is disclosing her feelings of futility in her attempts to gain nurturing and emotional intimacy from her mother. Note how this communication is accomplished entirely in the context of play.

Empathy Responses. Just as it is appropriate with adults[1], it is significant to give empathy responses when establishing and maintaining the relationship with a child. It is necessary, however, to determine not only that the child is capable of understanding a verbal response, but also that a verbal response at that particular time in the session will not detract from the child's work. Some children function best through metaphorical creations in their play, and a direct verbal response would tend to take them out of the affective state and into a cognitive state. Children change through experiencing a new affective response to associations with previously painful material. If a child is in the midst of that experience, a

---

1. For more information on therapeutically effective responses with adults, see Bergantino, 1981; Carkhuff, 1969; and Gazda, 1975.

verbal response directed to the child may distract the child from his experience.

For the same reason, questions are generally inappropriate with children. There is, however, one exception. As the director of the play, the child may assign the therapist a role. If the therapist is unsure how the child wants the role played, it is better to ask for direction (e.g., "What does the daddy doll do?" or "Am I an angry tiger, or a happy one?"). Even then, it is important to keep these questions at a minimum. This is one of the most difficult areas for therapists, especially if they have developed the habit of finishing statements with questions: "Boy, you really want to make sure everything's the way you want it, don't you?" Rather, therapists need to risk making wrong responses. The child will let them know if it's a wrong response. For instance, if, during the session, the child says to the therapist, "I'm going to visit my mom this weekend," an appropriate verbal response directly to the child would be, "You're uncertain about what to expect this time, because last time she got angry and yelled at you. That hurt your feelings, and you didn't know what to say to her."

The next excerpt is taken from a therapist's work with a four-year-old boy. His mother is very strict with him. He is learning disabled and has profound articulation difficulties.

Caleb:	(Patting the sand.) *You have sand in your room?*
Therapist:	*Yes, we have sand in here to play with.*
Caleb:	(Pats the sand in his hands as if he were making a snowball. Looks at the therapist and at the [one-way] mirror in front of him.) *Can me (th)row it on here?*
Therapist:	*You can throw it if you want.*
Caleb:	(Throws the sand at the mirror. Most of it lies on the ledge around the mirror. However, some of it falls into the waste basket. Looks wide-eyed at the therapist.) *Some of it went in there.*
Therapist:	*It's fun to see it go all over!*
Caleb:	*Mom not (l)ets me at home.*

Therapist:	*Your mom doesn't let you throw sand at home ...*
Caleb:	*Noooo!*
Therapist:	*... and you wish she did.*
Caleb:	(Continues throwing sand at the window.)

Caleb loved the freedom he was allowed in the playroom. After the initial thrill of the lack of rigid strictures on his behavior, he moved into his therapeutic work.

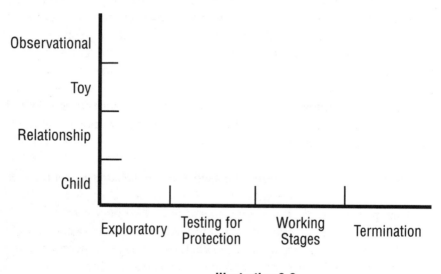

Illustration 8-2

Modalities of Responses

Since children are not verbally communicative about their struggles, fears, confusions, hurts, pains, doubts, or frustrations, it becomes necessary for them to utilize other modalities. In fact, the interactive style of retrieval and reintegration may be foreign and very anxiety provoking for many children (Donovan & McIntyre, 1990). In order to help the child, an essential skill for the therapist to develop is the ability to communicate through the use of the child's modalities.

Play. Play is the natural medium in which a child can experience his hurtful feelings and gain some resolution or sense of mastery over them (Landreth, 1993a). Consequently, in the beginning stages of the play therapy process, a child will create a context for examination of his uncomfortable feelings. As he gains some resolution or sense of mastery over those feelings, his aggressive and intrusive themes will abate, and his play will turn to more socially sanctioned behaviors. Through this play, the child will experience a new and more positive affective response to previously hurtful material. For example, in the initial stages of therapeutic work with a sexually abused child, his play may show the wolf being hit, beaten, and annihilated by the herder. In the latter stages of play therapy, his play may show the herder moving sheep to safety.

Metaphors. Occasionally, during the process of treatment, a child will reach a point where he is predominantly exhibiting repetitious play. The impression of the therapist is that of movement being stopped or the child being stuck in his emotional growth. In this case, a useful tool will be the creation of a therapeutic metaphor (story). This is also useful when limited time is available for therapy. The works of Joyce Mills, Ph.D., Richard Crowley, Ph.D. (Crowley & Mills, 1986); Steve Lankton, M.S.W., and Carol Lankton, M.S.W. (Lankton & Lankton, 1986) are excellent resources on the creation of therapeutic metaphors.

Of course play itself is the child's creation of his own metaphor. Metaphors, then, may be the child's creation (i.e., play), or the therapist's creation (i.e., a verbal metaphor [story]). (See Page 258-268 for an example of a verbal metaphor used with a young client, Sara.)

Following is an example of a child's creation of a metaphor in play.

Antonio is a five-year-old boy whose dad was killed in a crop dusting accident two years prior to his being seen in therapy. After the father's plane hit a pole, he pulled the plane up to avoid hitting the house behind the pole. As a result, the plane came straight down, killing the father instantly.

Six months prior to Antonio beginning therapy, his mother's best friend's husband was killed in a snowmobile accident. Then, during the course of Antonio's therapy, another of his mother's male friends was killed in a car accident. As a result, Antonio had developed an internal script that being male meant he would grow up, marry, have children, and then die tragically. An important therapeutic goal was to break that script for Antonio.

On this particular day, Antonio came in and drew a picture of a tree on the whiteboard. (This whiteboard covered one wall of the playroom.) It was a brown tree. On the left side, it had brown branches which were protruding from the tree in a perpendicular fashion. On the right side of the tree, however, although he drew the same style of branches, they had small green leaves on them. Utilizing projective drawing where the tree represents a father figure, the brown branches on the left side represent Antonio's father. Antonio's mother had recently entered into a relationship with another man, bringing a new father figure into Antonio's life. This new relationship is represented by the small green leaves on the branches on the right side of the tree.

Antonio:	(Puts an airplane in the sandbox. Then he puts sand in the tail end of the plane and begins to fly the plane around the room. On the wall of the playroom is a mural of a forest. He flies there first. Although he bumps into the trees, he manages to keep flying. The airplane moves on around the room until it hits the tree he drew on the white board. At that point, it crashes onto the floor. Antonio picks up the airplane, carries it back to the sand box, and says:) *I have to get more fuel and start over.* (He puts sand in the tail end of the plane and begins to fly the plane around the room again. He turns to the therapist and says:) *Come on!* [He wants to know he will have her support as he delves into his exploration of his father's death and the course of his own life.]
Therapist:	(Takes her airplane, puts fuel in it, and follows him.)

Antonio:	(Bumps his plane into the forest but keeps flying. Again, Antonio's airplane hits the tree but manages to limp onto the sand landing strip for repair and refueling.)
Therapist:	*We only have one minute left. This will have to be our last trip.*
Antonio:	*No, wait!* (He flies the plane. This time, however, he flies past the forest without bumping into it, then over to the tree which he passes, and then lands safely on the sand landing strip.) *I'll be back tomorrow.*

Verbal. In the course of the play therapy process, there will be much verbalization. Most of it will be embedded in the play such as the child who says, "Quick, hide! The monster is coming!" The therapist responds, "I'm hiding, but I'm scared he will find me." These are considered play rather than verbal responses. However, there will be times when the child is playing quietly, and the therapist will verbalize an empathy statement to him. To illustrate, consider the child who has just finished a magnificent creation with the clay and says, "That was hard to make." A therapist might respond, "You're proud of yourself that you were able to keep working at it until you got it just the way you wanted it."

The following excerpt was taken from one of Andy's sessions during his Dependency Stage. He had been playing with the bop bag extensively during the session. At one point, he tried to get on top of it. However, because it was unstable, he fell off the bop bag onto the floor. He was chagrined at the sudden turn of events.

Andy:	(Sets the bop bag against the wall and starts throwing a ball at it.) *I'll get you!*
Therapist:	*He hurt you a while ago, and you want him to know what that felt like.*
Andy:	*Yeah! I'll show him.*
Therapist:	*You want him to know you don't like it when he hurts you.*

The verbal response is a response that is constructed and delivered verbally to the child in a direct, conscious manner.

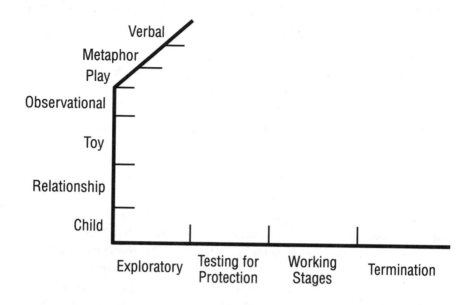

Illustration 8-3

Interaction of the Dimensions

Having considered the dimensions independently, it has probably become apparent that it is difficult to isolate them as there is definitely an interactive effect. The prototypical response of the *Exploratory Stage* tends to be at an *observational* level using a *verbal* modality. Likewise, a *child*-level response would be appropriate in the *Therapeutic Growth Stage*, where it is not appropriate in the *Exploratory Stage* and could be communicated in either the *play* or *verbal* modality. All dimensions considered, there are four (stages[2]) times four (depths) times three (modalities) possibilities. (See Illustration 8-4.) However, since a *child*-level response is not appropriate in the *Exploratory Stage*, that eliminates the *Exploratory-child-play*, the *Exploratory-child-metaphor*, and the *Exploratory-child-verbal* responses. In like fashion, since observational

---

2. Four stages assumes the combining of the Dependency and Therapeutic Growth stages since responses in these two stages are similar.

level responses are not appropriate[3] in the *Working Stages* or *Termination Stage*, *Working Stages-observational-play*, *Working Stages-observational-metaphor*, *Working Stages-observational-verbal*, *Termination-observational-play*, *Termination-observational-metaphor*, and *Termination-observational-verbal* responses are eliminated. With those nine possible responses eliminated, 39 types of responses remain. This illustrates the breadth of the repertoire of possible therapeutic responses and relieves the novice therapist from searching for the *one right* response.

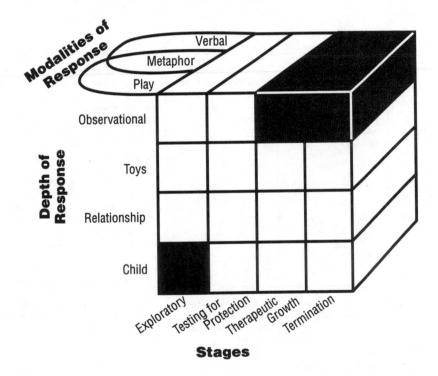

Stages

3. Occasionally a child who has been in the Working Stages for some time may one day come in for a session and revert to the Exploratory Stage or Testing for Protection Stage. Obviously, something has occurred since he was last seen, although at this point the actual events may be unknown to the therapist. When a child has been abused again or there has been a major, unsettling change in the child's life, the child will revert to previous stages of his treatment. It may be necessary to return to a few observational level responses until the child once again feels safe enough to return to the growth work.

To further illuminate the differences and similarities among all the types of responses, examples are given in the following tables of responses that might be utilized in the case presented. To facilitate recognition, each stage is considered individually.

		Exploration Stage		
M O D A L I T Y	**V e r b a l**	"It seems like you want to touch everything in the room today."	"If those binoculars could talk, they'd say, 'I have a lot of power and I like it that way.'"	As the child looks through first one side of the binoculars then the other, "You can bring me up close or send me back far with these."
	M e t a p h o r	Playing with the marbles, "Those marbles are just rolling around seeing where they can go and what there is to see."	The child drives a truck all around the room. It goes to every corner and cubby.	Once a little bear and his mom had to move to a new forest because their old one had been burned by a fire. As they approached the forest, the little bear looked around and wondered, "Will you be a good forest to me? Can I trust you to have the food that I need and a nice warm place for me to sleep? Will I be safe here?" At that moment, the sun rose over the mountains throwing streams of color through the sky and caused the dew on the leaves to sparkle. The little bear's eyes moved across the fresh looking trees and rocks. Suddenly, his eyes widened as they fell on a bush with ripe berries--his favorite kind.
	P l a y	The child picks up the binoculars and looks at the therapist. The therapist picks up the binoculars, looks at the child, and says, "Ah-ha, I can see you too."	The doll goes shopping, looking everywhere for just the right thing to buy.	The child picks up the binoculars and looks at the therapist. The therapist picks up the binoculars, looks at the child, and says, "I can see you up close too."
	Observational		**Toys**	**Relationship**
	DEPTH OF RESPONSE			

Table 8-1
Examples of Therapeutic Responses in
the Exploration Stage

Testing For Protection

MODALITY		Observational	Toys	Relationship	Child
	Verbal	"I know you want to throw everything on the floor, but I'm not going to let you."	The doll says, "Ouch, I want you to stop pulling my legs and tearing my clothes."	"You wonder if I care about you when I say it's time to go."	"I know you want to let me know you are angry at me by hitting me. It's okay to be angry, but it's not okay to hit me. Here, you can hit the pillow to show me just how angry you are."
	Metaphor	"You are hitting that car as hard as you can just like the bulldozer who didn't want the world to know that he felt hurt by all the dents he had on his fenders and his body. So, he went around hitting others with his play. Soon, everyone else was dented and hurt too. They learned when they saw the bulldozer coming to stay out of his way. But, when the bulldozer didn't have anyone else around to hit, he became lonely. This hurt even more. One day, one of the cars fell into a hole he could not climb out of. The bulldozer recognized that he could move the dirt and made a smooth ramp so that the car could just drive out. After he did this, the cars cheered him and mentioned how he was the only one of all of them who could have done this. From that day on, the cars and the bulldozer became friends and played happily. The cars loved the ramps that the bulldozer made because they could race over them and jump over their friends and invent games that kept them happy for hours."	"Those soldiers want to shoot everything they see, but the people build a wall to stop them. Then, the soldiers figure out they can go through the gate if they put their guns down and play with the people instead of shooting them."	There once was a mommy sheep who had two baby lambs at the same time. One lamb was white like the mommy. The other lamb was black. As they played, ate, grew bigger, and learned a lot about life, the black sheep began to wonder why she didn't look like her mommy and sister. She decided her mommy loved her sister more because they looked alike. She was angry about looking different and thought her black wool was ugly. So, every time her mommy would ask her to do something, she would say, "NO!" When her mommy tried to play with her, she kicked rocks in Mommy's face. Whenever she did this, Mommy made her sit by the fence post while her sister played for the afternoon. You see, she thought it was her mommy's fault that she was so ugly. One day, a person came to visit the sheep family and all their neighbors. He explained that he needed the most special sheep wool around to make a blanket for the new princess. Mommy sheep stepped forward and explained that her lamb daughter had the best wool around because it was soft and free of tangles. Also, it was different from everyone else's which made it one-of-a-kind for a one-of-a-kind baby. Thinking her mommy was talking about her sister, the black lamb turned to walk away. Then, she heard her mommy say, "See my daughter with the beautiful black wool?" The person was delighted and took the special wool for the special baby. The black lamb was so proud and knew then that her mommy did love her, and that she was beautiful.	"I know you want to take the teddy bear home with you. It feels all warm and soft when you hug it just like a caterpillar wrapped in its cocoon. The caterpillar thinks nothing can feel as cozy and warm. But, when the caterpillar turns into a butterfly and flies away from the cocoon, it learns that other things can feel just as warm. The sunshine warms its wings in the day and at night the leaves of a tree protect it from the cold rain. It loves to be free to feel all these different things."
	Play	In the middle of a play scene, the child stops and says, "Let's go look in the other office for another gun." The therapist responds, "We don't have time! They're catching up with us. We'll have to make do with what we've got."	The shark is knocking all the toys off the shelf. When it comes to the alligator, the alligator says, "I'm not going to let you knock off any more toys."	In a game of Candyland, when the therapist is within five spaces of winning, while the child is only halfway up the path, the child says, "Let's start moving backwards and see who can get back to *Start* first." The therapist turns the mover around and plays in the opposite direction.	In playing out a violent scene, the child picks up a knife and wants to actually stab the therapist. They struggle, then as the therapist lies down, she says, "I'm dead now. You don't have to stab me anymore."

STYLES

Table 8-2
Examples of Therapeutic Responses in
the Testing for Protection Stage

		Working Stages: Dependency/Therapeutic Growth Stage		
M O D A L I T Y	**V e r b a l**	"When the dolphin gets eaten by the shark, she feels really scared and helpless."	"It's important that we work hard and use teamwork to make sure we get to the new planet."	"When Mommy hits you, you feel scared and helpless."
	M e t a p h o r	"You can feel the sand running through your fingers now just like you know it's okay to feel your feelings now. The sand will not hurt you or make you dirty."	In a game of base-ball, the therapist attempts to tag the runner (child) out; but the child is safe. "It feels good to know you're safe. You knew I wouldn't get you out."	"Sometimes, you get hurt by Daddy's words just as the snail is so tender without the shell and can easily be hurt by the grains of sand that blow in the wind. He cannot stop the wind from blowing the sand, but can slowly grow another shell. As the shell becomes harder and harder, the sand hurts less and less, until finally, the snail can draw its entire body in for protection when he needs it. When the snail knows it is safe, he can stick his head out again."
	P l a y	In playing with the doll family, the therapist, as the baby doll, says to the Mommy doll, "Why are we moving away from Daddy? I don't want to."	Child and therapist are constructing a spaceship to journey to a new planet to live. The therapist and child work together intensely planning for the scheduled blast-off. They gather food, fuel, and check equipment as the launch grows closer. They are partners in this special journey into the new future.	The hunters (child and therapist) fight a brave battle with the bear and feel exhausted and safe as the bear runs away into the forest and disappears.
		Toys	Relationship	Child
		STYLES		

Table 8-3
Examples of Therapeutic Responses in
the Working Stages

Termination			
M O D A L I T Y	**V e r b a l**	The horse is playing in the pasture now. He feels happy and knows he doesn't have to stay in the stable to be safe.	"I really like you and have so much fun playing with you. Even though you won't be coming here anymore, we'll still be friends."	"I'll miss you when you're not coming here every week, but I'll feel good when I think about how happy you are."
	M e t a p h o r	"The doll used to fall over when she tried to stand up. Now she can stand tall on her own and know that if she falls down, she is strong enough to get right back up again."	The magic wand used to not have any power, but a star said, "Here, take some of my sparkle. It'll give you the magical glow." Even though the wand never saw the star again, it always had the warmth and happiness it received from the star.	"At this point, you are like the beautiful butterfly who has just come out of her cocoon and is ready to fly off on her own. She's strong and free and looking forward to what she can see on her flights."
	P l a y	Instructions from the child: "Drive the ambulance back home to stay now." As she drives the ambulance, the therapist responds, "It's not needed anymore."	"The child is building with the blocks. In the past the child has usually asked the therapist to help with building. Today, however, she builds alone and with confidence. The therapist responds, "You can build a strong house by yourself now."	In play, when the parent (therapist) hands the baby bottle to the baby (child), the child puts it down and says, "I don't want this now. I want pizza."
		Toys	Relationship	Child
		STYLES		

Table 8-4
Examples of Therapeutic Responses in
the Termination Stage

Tracking the Impact
of Therapeutic Responses

Creating and delivering therapeutic responses is not the extent of the therapist's responsibility in working with children. It is also necessary for the therapist to gauge the child's reaction to the response. Since so much of the child's communication is in metaphor, it is not surprising that much of the child's reaction to responses will also be in metaphor. When responses are accurate, the child will respond in one of several styles.

(1) He may make an additive play response. For example, if he has been playing a family scene, he may move from general home activities to a scene of the parents becoming angry and yelling or hitting the child.

(2) The child may intensify his play activity to indicate appropriate responding (e.g. the anger, yelling, and hitting may lead to the child doll crying and pleading for them to stop, or even standing up and telling them to stop).

(3) The child may exhibit an *instant pause response* (i.e., he may pause in his play briefly as if thinking about what he has just heard).[4]

(4) On a more immediate level, the child may reduce the physical distance between himself and the therapist, feeling more comfortable with the empathy and acceptance that the therapist has displayed.

(5) The child may invite the therapist into the play. The involvement of the therapist in the play at the moment, however, depends not only on appropriate responding but also on the scene being played, its meaning to the child, and the therapist's capacity to participate.

---

4. A *pause response* differs from a *dissociative response* in the time and context in which it occurs. A *pause response* most often occurs during the latter phase of the Dependency Stage when the child is gaining new awarenesses. The child is present in the moment and is crystallizing new perceptions into understanding. A *dissociative response* generally occurs in the initial phases of the Dependency Stage when the child begins moving into his experiences. It is an avoidant response in an effort to protect himself from the pain associated with the experience.

While the child may not have a visible reaction, the absence of an indication that the response is inaccurate would lead to the conclusion that the response is accurate. The absence of a positive reaction could also indicate that although the response was not an additive response, the response did not detract from the child's play either.

Indicators of the inaccuracy of responses may include the following:

(1) The child changes his play focus to another activity of a different theme. For instance, if a child who is playing with the trucks hitting each other hears, "You like playing with trucks," he may change to a solitary game of basketball.

(2) The child diffuses from his play focus (i.e., he loses his concentration, and his play becomes intermingled with tangential play bits).

(3) The child physically distances himself from the therapist or excludes the therapist from the play activity. In fact, the child may even turn his back and block the view of his play from the therapist.

(4) If inappropriate responses continue, the child stops his play completely.

While it is not necessary to search for the one correct therapeutic response to a child's communication in his play, it is, nonetheless, possible to be so inaccurate in the understanding of the child's metaphor that any response reflects the inaccuracy and discourages the child. Therefore, it is important to use cues from the child's reaction to therapeutic responses to guide the therapist toward a more accurate understanding of the child's message. With a more precise understanding, it then becomes possible to create responses with increased effectiveness.

Facilitating Play Through the Use of Metaphorical Stories

During therapeutic play, the child creates his own metaphors in order to reach a resolution to an internal struggle. Because it is the child's own resolution, it will ultimately be more effective than one that is created externally. There are times, however, when a child becomes repetitious in his fantasy play, or the therapist has a very limited amount of time in which to spend with the child due to agency regulations. In these situations, metaphorical stories make a nice adjunct to play therapy in order to gently direct the session.

What is a Metaphorical Story?

A metaphor is a form of symbolic language that is used to convey an idea in an indirect and yet paradoxically more meaningful manner (Mills & Crowley, 1986). Metaphors have been around a long time, although they are generally known by other names such as parables in the Old and New Testaments of the Bible, allegories in literature, or images in poetry and fairy tales. Therapeutic metaphors in play therapy are utilized in order to both convey a message of hope and to empower the child to know that he can help himself in some way to bring resolution to his pain.

The beauty of a metaphor in a poem or story is that it can say different things to different individuals, depending upon what it is that an individual needs to hear or is psychologically examining at the time. Often, many details of the story will go by the wayside because the listener has a need to hear something that is subtly being conveyed. For instance, a viewer may completely dismiss the amount of the violence in a movie because he is internally focusing on one specific aspect of the story. Because metaphors represent or suggest something beyond the immediate appearance, it is easy to see just how much individual experiences influence their perception.

The Relationship Between Cerebral Hemispheric Activity and Symbolic or Metaphorical Language

In the mid-1960s, it was discovered that the two hemispheres of the brain processed information in two fundamentally different ways (Mills & Crowley, 1986). Each hemisphere of the brain specializes in processing information. In addition, both hemispheres integrate in a cooperative manner. During the past 30 years, research unveiled the knowledge that both hemispheres interact synergistically in language production and comprehension. The left brain processes language sequentially, logical-ly, and literally, while the right brain processes it in a simultaneous, holis-tic, and implicative fashion (Joseph, 1992). At this point, one may be thinking that although this is interesting, how does it tie in with the use of metaphors?

> Erickson and Rossie (1979) theorized that since "symptoms are expressions in the language of the right hemisphere, our use of mythopoetic language may thus be a means of communicating directly with the right hemisphere in its own language" ... and ... suggested that this right-hemispheric mediation of both sympto-matology and metaphorical meaning would explain why metaphorical approaches to therapy were less time-consuming than psychoanalytically-oriented approaches....   Metaphor ... goes straight for the target area — the right-brain processes (Mills & Crowley, 1986, p. 17).

In essence, when using metaphorical stories, the therapist is going right to the seed of the emotional processes rather than talking cognitive-ly to the left brain, having it decoded, encoding it, transferring it to the other side of the brain, and then going through the entire process again. Metaphorical stories hit with a quietly diffused impact without an aware-ness that one is being influenced by the message of the story until a later response indicates a new reaction to a familiar situation.[5]

Necessary Components in Constructing a Therapeutic Story

In order to create a metaphorical story during therapy, it is necessary to know how this particular child experiences the world (i.e., some of the events that have occurred in his life, some of his likes and dislikes, and positive as well as negative experiences). In addition, it is also helpful to

---

5. Recommended reading: *Therapeutic Metaphors for Children and the Child Within*, by Joyce Mills and Richard Crowley (1986).

know the child's style of processing information (Crowley & Mills, 1985-86). The knowledge of neuro-linguistic programming (Bandler & Grinder, 1975, 1979, 1982; Dilts, Grinder, Bandler, DeLozier, & Cameron-Bandler, 1979) provides valuable information into how individuals process information and what they remember best (something heard, seen, or done by manipulation) (Crowley & Mills, 1985-86; Mills & Crowley, 1986). Children tend to be more tactile than adults (Bandler & Grinder, 1975, 1979, 1982; Dilts, et al., 1979). This is not to imply that individuals use only one style. Generally, however, one style is primarily used with another secondary style also being exhibited.

In creating a metaphorical story around the type of *environment* that the child experiences in his world, it is important that it not be a direct identification. The result should not be, "Oh, that sounds just like my house." Rather, the identification should be so subtle that, in essence, it builds a *transformational bridge* (Mills & Crowley, 1986). The story should allow the child to experience the metaphor, access the strengths built into it, and then bring those strengths back with the child into his reality, into the *here and now*. By creating an identification with the character in the story, the child begins to lose his sense of isolation. Generally speaking, people in our society have a very low tolerance for being different. It is especially difficult for children to think they are different. They become ashamed of their differences. Realizing a sense of identification helps alleviate these negative feelings because it is now a shared experience.

Once the therapist has created an environment that subtly pertains to the child's world, the next step is to add a *metaphorical conflict*. The story of *The Lion King* (Hahn, Allers, & Minkoff, 1994) by The Disney Studios is a good illustration of these steps. This story of emotional abuse and banishment provides a shared experience of feeling shame, guilt, and inadequacy as it helps to supplant the child's feelings of isolation. The *metaphorical conflict* is created with the birth of the lion cub who will someday become king, displacing his power-seeking uncle.

The next step in creating a metaphorical story is to personify some of the child's *unconscious processes* in the form of heroes or helpers. In other words, the therapist should take the child's abilities and resources and create helpers or heroes out of them. In addition, the child's fears or negative beliefs are utilized in personifying the villains and obstructions.

In this story, the unconscious processes and potentials are first addressed when the king, the lion cub's father, takes him to view his kingdom.

> *"Look, Simba. Everything the light touches is our kingdom. A king's time as ruler rises and falls like the sun. One day, Simba, the sun will set on my time here and will rise with you as the new king."*

Mufasa, the king, then proceeds to explain a king's responsibilities to his son. The child struggles to understand the power of being king and how that becomes congruent with respect for the circle of life.

The hyenas represent Simba's fears of his lack of bravery, lack of intelligence, and the disdain of the other members of the kingdom.

Next a *metaphorical crisis* is introduced which provides a learning experience for the child. Simba's uncle, Scar, forces a paradox on him by telling him only brave lions can go to the elephant graveyard. Simba now feels he must go in order to prove his bravery. Simba's false bravado, however, is challenged by his friend, Nala. She is his helper in learning about true bravery and developing his own identity apart from that of his father. His view of the characteristics of a king include power and bravery only. He has yet to learn about the tender, vulnerable traits of all individuals. Here, in the elephant graveyard, he encounters his first crisis: The graveyard is the home of hyenas who feel no allegiance to him as he will not be their king. In their efforts to escape the danger from the hyenas, Simba fights to protect his friend, Nala, and his mentor, Zazu. His father ultimately comes to their rescue. Nala praises Simba's bravery. Simba, however, can only feel the shame of disappointing his father. Mufasa then teaches Simba about fear and bravery and creates a therapeutic metaphor about the stars being past great kings who will always be there to guide him when he is in need of encouragement. In this experience, Simba learns that even kings face fears and are brave only when they have to be.

The next *metaphorical crisis* for Simba occurs when his uncle, Scar, sets up the stampede that results in the death of his father, Mufasa. Until this point, Simba had always believed his father was all powerful (as he assumed he would be one day). Now Simba must struggle with his father's mortality as well as the belief, implanted and fostered by Scar, that Mufasa's death was his fault. Scar further abuses him by implying that his mother will never forgive him. Simba runs away.

At this point, Simba is offered the opportunity for *parallel learning experiences* as he must learn to survive without his family. Once again, the hyenas attempt to kill him. After escaping this, the vultures attempt to eat him. Then his new friends, Timon and Pumbaa, teach him, "You can't change the past. Put it behind you." They help him to adapt his expectations of himself and of life, to accept himself with his vulnerabilities, and to take a lighter view of life. They also give him acceptance and teach him about shared responsibilities and caring. However, his grief and shame never completely leave him.

Unexpectedly, Nala comes back into his life and reminds him that he is king. She recognizes his potential as king to save the kingdom. His shame will not allow him to accept this position, however. He struggles with the decision but feels unworthy. Rafiki, the medicine baboon, shows Simba his image in the pond and points out that his father, Mufasa, lives on in him.

Simba faces his *metaphorical crisis* in assuming the responsibilities of being his father's son, the true king. Simba's response of "It's only me," reflects his feelings of shame and inadequacy in leading the kingdom because he perceives himself as being flawed and unable to measure up to his father's image. His memory is that he must have no vulnerabilities while at the same time being brave and intelligent.

After being encouraged by Rafiki, the medicine baboon, Simba's statement, "The winds are changing," metaphorically speaks to his budding change in attitude about returning. Yet, he fears facing his past.

Rafiki reminds him the past "... doesn't matter. It's in the past."

Simba replies, "Yeah, but it still hurts."

Rather than running from his past, Rafiki invites Simba to learn from it. Simba begins to recognize that, in fact, he has learned from the past.

As he approaches his kingdom, Simba becomes aware that his Uncle Scar's reign has all but destroyed the kingdom as a result of Scar's lack of respect for others and the environment. As Simba observes Scar physically abusing Simba's mother, it gives him the courage to confront his uncle. It also gives him the awareness that the well-being of others surpasses his own need to psychologically protect himself. Scar's mistaking him for his father, Mufasa, further empowers Simba. As Scar admits his responsibility for Mufasa's death, Simba becomes enraged and leads the others in a battle against Scar and his cohorts, the hyenas. Once again, Scar lies and blames others (the hyenas) and, in fact, attempts to again shame Simba. This time, however, Simba does not assume the shame and overpowers Scar (symbolizing the scar of Simba's own shame from the past). In doing so, Simba assumes the traits he was striving to achieve in his maturity — bravery, the appropriate use of power, and caring for the well-being of others.

At this point, the next important step of a *new identification* occurs for Simba as he assumes both his role as the king and the responsibilities that role entails. He realizes that he can put the past behind him, and that he has the power and the knowledge to utilize that power appropriately. The other animals also recognize his accomplishments and bow down in their respect for him. A *celebration* is held in honor of the return of their king and of their prosperity as the circle of life continues.

Summary of Components of the Metaphorical Story

The following components have been adapted from the work of Mills & Crowley (1986).

1. Similar Environment. Develop the main character(s) within an environment that subtly relates to the child's perceptions of his world.

2. Metaphorical Conflict. Establish the difficulties in relation to the main character and the difficulties with which the child can identify. This provides a shared experience of feelings that help to displace the child's own feelings of isolation. (The lion cub must mature while struggling with the emotional abuse from his power-seeking uncle.)

3. Unconscious Processes. Personify some of the child's strengths and resources in the form of heroes or helpers. Add some of the child's fears or negative beliefs in the form of villains and obstructions. (Nala cites Simba's examples of bravery. Rafiki reminds Simba of his strength of character. The hyenas, however, represent an obstacle to Simba's realizing his potential as a brave, wise, and caring leader.)

4. Parallel Learning Experience. Provide learning experiences where the character expands the skills necessary for overcoming the forthcoming crisis. (Simba learns how to be a friend, how to share the responsibilities of protecting and providing for his friend and himself, and how to put the past behind him. He also learns that he is acceptable and desirable as a friend simply as the individual that he is.)

5. Metaphorical Crisis. Introduce a crisis, or several crises, each one providing additional learning experiences for the child and preparing him to face the ultimate crisis. (When Simba's father is killed, Simba runs away to escape facing his shame and guilt. In his escape, however, he loses his identity, while still carrying his shame and guilt.)

6. Unconscious Potential. Provide a glimpse of the main character's potential. (Rafiki shows Simba his image in the pond and reminds him that his father lives on in him.)

7. Identification. Define the new identification or sense of empowerment that the character feels as a result of successfully moving beyond the crisis. (Simba assumes his leadership role and recognizes the traits of appropriate respect for others and utilization of his power.)

8. Celebration. Celebrate the character's newfound worth as a result of his successful journey. (The other animals bow to him and demonstrate their respect for him.)

This is the story of an individual seeking his self-worth and understanding concerning his role in life. Once having survived the crises, he gains a new sense of identification, realizing his potential is no longer simply potential — it has actually become empowerment. It was after Simba completed the hero's journey that he realized he had a new identity, just as people who have survived a severe illness or major catastrophe say, "I have a lot more strength than I ever realized I had!" They feel a sense of pride in their accomplishment and a new sense of confidence.

Example of Metaphoric Story Used in Therapy

Children will not always just sit and listen to the therapist tell a story. The therapist may introduce the story with statements such as, "You know, this reminds me of ..." or "This reminds me of a raccoon that I heard about one time ..." and then move into the story. If the child changes the context of his play and moves over to another part of the playroom, the therapist can move with the child and do what he asks and then say, "And as I was saying," finishing the story.

Sara was three years old when her mother brought her in for therapy. Sara's dad had come home drunk one evening, loaded his shotgun, and said to his wife, "One of these is for you and the other is for me." Greatly frightened, the mother struggled to gain control of the gun. Suddenly, Sara woke up and came into their room crying. Since Sara's dad cared a great deal for his daughter, he said to his wife, "You'd better stop and take care of Sara." At that moment, the mother had the presence of mind to say, "If you want her taken care of, you do it." Consequently, the father stopped and went over to comfort his daughter. The mother quickly grabbed the gun, ran out of the house, went to a neighbor's house, and called the police. Shortly thereafter, the police arrived and retrieved Sara. Sara was a very sensitive child. This traumatic event was difficult for her to understand.

Since this was not the first time Sara's dad had tried to hurt her mother, the mother finally decided to move to an apartment and obtain an unlisted phone number. She also obtained a restraining order. Sara soon began to feel confused: "Why are we living in this new place?" "Why doesn't Dad come around anymore?" "What has Mom done?" She began to act her confusion out by getting angry at her mother. This is very common with children whose parents have separated, especially when one of the parents is/was an abuser. All these children know is that something is different. In addition, most children have a difficult time with major changes in their lives. Consequently, they take their anger and frustration out on the parent with whom they feel the most secure, which is generally the custodial parent. This is the parent who gets all the anger when, in actuality, it may have been the other parent who precipitated the problems. It is at this point that many single parents seek professional assistance.

This is exactly what happened to Sara. One weekend, about three months into therapy, her mother called Sara's therapist several times saying, "Sara won't let me get close to her. She kicks and scratches and spits on me. I'm not sure how much longer I can take this." Because the therapist was unsure whether or not the mother was capable of physical abuse, she decided to construct a therapeutic metaphor to help Sara understand that it's okay to be angry, but it is important what one does with that anger. One can be constructive or destructive with anger. The therapist wanted to help Sara learn the importance of doing something constructive with that anger.

In this particular case, the court had given the therapist the responsibility of determining visitation privileges. The philosophy of the therapist was a gradual increase in visitation in a situation of this nature. Therefore, she suggested a telephone call to begin the resumption of their relationship. After three minutes of talking with her father, Sara hung up the phone, went into her bedroom, and soiled her pants. This was a most unusual occurrence for Sara.

In the following excerpt from the session in which the therapist introduced a metaphor, Sara is in the Dependency Stage of her therapeutic process. It is apparent in this session that Sara does not like to play with the sand because it is wet. She says it smells and feels bad. It becomes even more obvious that soiling her pants after talking with her father was out of character for this child and demonstrates the high degree of emotionality surrounding her relationship with her father. The wet sand reminds her of the soiling incident and of her anguish over the situation with her father.

Therapist:	(Moves over to the sandbox and begins to build in the sand.) *I would like to tell you about this mountain that stood near this village one time.*
Sara:	*Hey ...* (Walks over to the sandbox and looks around.) *I don't want to play with mud.*
Therapist:	*You don't want to play in the mud. Yeah, the sand's all wet, and it feels like mud.* (Keeps building in the sandbox.) *This mountain here* (points to a mound she has created in the sand) *has all kinds of angry, hot, boiling lava inside it. It just goes ...* (makes a rumbling sound).
Sara:	(Walks away.) *No!*
Therapist:	*It smells bad. It feels bad. Yeah, it seems pretty yukky when it's all wet.*

Sara: *Yeah. I got some in my fingernails.* (Holds her hands out to the therapist for her finger nails to be cleaned.)

Therapist: *You did get some in your fingernails. It's nice to have someone here to take care of the yukky stuff for you.*

Sara: (Walks to the end of the playroom.)

Therapist: *This is a special kind of mountain. It's called a volcano, and it's feeling inside kind of like you were feeling on the outside a minute ago — all hot, bubbly, boiling, and rumbly.*

Comment: On this particular day, it was very cold outside. Because it was warm in the playroom, when Sara came in for her session, she took off her jacket and shoes and anything else she could to be more comfortable. The therapist used this connection of Sara's being hot when telling of the volcano being hot inside. When telling a metaphor and creating an environment, it is helpful to associate it with something that is in the immediate environment.

Sara: (Walks over to the toy counter and picks up a small bulldozer.) *Hey, this picks up dirt!*

Therapist: *It does pick up dirt. It will move the yukky stuff that you don't like to touch.*

Sara: *Yeah, like this.* (Walks over to the sandbox with the bulldozer.)

Therapist: (Continues building the mountain.) *And all around the mountain there are living things. There's a village over here, and fields over here* (points to a different area of the sand box) *and a river running down here where the fish live.*

Sara: (Uses bulldozer to pick up sand.) *I got some in here. Can you get it out?*

Therapist: *Yeah, I can do it. If I get it out for you, then you can play with it without having to get yourself yukky.*

Sara:	*It feels yukky!*
Therapist:	*And you don't like feeling yukky.*

Comment: "Yukky" is Sara's metaphor for the feelings she experiences as a result of the aggression and anger in her family.

Sara:	*It smells!* (Sara walks to the toy counter. She stands there for awhile and then picks up the Nerf bat.) *Somebody bite it. Somebody bite it.*
Therapist:	*Somebody bit a great big chunk out of it.*
Sara:	*It's soft* (vulnerable).
Therapist:	*Yes, it's soft.*
Sara:	*I got soft fingers, huh.* (I am vulnerable.)
Therapist:	*Yes, you do have soft fingers. You wish everything could be nice and soft, and that nothing would hurt it. There are villages around this mountain where people live. Here's a village. Here's a village. Here's a village. And over here, they are working on building a new village* (incorporating her bulldozer). *And all the people are running around ... they work real hard. They plant their crops, and they fish in the river.*
Sara:	(Looks in the sandbox as the therapist tells the story. Moves the bulldozer across the sand.) *I did it!*
Therapist:	*Boy, you're helping ...*
Sara:	*I don't want to touch it.*
Therapist:	*I know you don't want to touch that wet stuff, and you don't have to.*
Sara:	(While holding her hand, Sara walks toward the counter.) *I like dry ... I like dry sand.*
Therapist:	*Yeah, you like the dry sand.*

Comment: Sara wants to join in the activity in the sandbox, but the resistance to the wet sand is greater, at this point, than her desire to join.

Sara:	*Hey, I found the wand!*
Therapist:	*Oh, you found it. Well, good.*

Comment: Sara picks up a baton that has sparkles inside it. This type of toy allows a child to look inside it while being introspective.

Therapist:	(Continues the story:) *All of the hot, bubbly stuff inside this mountain finally, one day, went* (makes a sound like an explosion and throws the sand and her arms up in the air).
Sara:	*Uh, oh!*
Therapist:	*It just exploded and went* (makes explosion sound again while throwing sand up in the air).
Sara:	*Uh, oh!* (Looks at the volcano. Taps the side of the sandbox with the baton as she watches the volcano.)

Comment: Tapping the baton on the side of the sandbox illustrates the anxiety Sara is experiencing while examining, unconsciously, her own anger.

Therapist:	*The lava went everywhere. It hit the village over here, it flowed through the fields, and it filled up the river.*
Sara:	(Falls on the floor.)
Therapist:	*Oh, the poor people. They fell down because they didn't know what to do.*
Sara:	(Lies on the floor in the front of the sandbox.) *I don't want the ...*
Therapist:	*You don't want the volcano to explode.*

Comment: Even though the child is feeling anxious, the therapist persists in the story toward the resolution. When a child begins to be overwhelmed, her behavior will get out of control, or she will withdraw. The therapist is the one who protects the child by not allowing the child to be overwhelmed. Sara was effected by her anxiety, but not overwhelmed.

The playroom is a safe place to allow a child to feel a tolerable level of anxiety. It allows the child to make gains by taking risks.

Therapist:	*But, this mountain has so much of that hot stuff inside, it just doesn't know what to do. It thinks it has to hurt the things around it so that it can get rid of some of its hot, bubbly stuff.*
Sara:	*Where is it? I don't want it.*
Therapist:	*You don't want it in here. You don't want it to hurt anybody.*
Sara:	(Stands in front of the sandbox.) *I want it down.*
Therapist:	*You want it down just like the village people wanted it to stop hurting them. Well, the people came to the mountain and said, "Please don't let that hot stuff come on our village anymore because it kills our fish, and it knocks down our houses, and it hurts our people."*
	And the mountain said, "Well, I have rumbles and grumbles and hot stuff inside of me, and I have to get rid of it."
	So, the people said, "We need to find a way that you can get rid of it that won't hurt us."
Sara:	*Hey, get some more wet stuff.*
Therapist:	*Maybe, if we put some wet stuff in there, it will cool it off so it won't have to explode anymore.*
	The mountain said, "I know what I can do. I'll make a little ditch right here. Then, when I get all rumbly and grumbly and hot and burning inside, all that stuff will come out and just go running down the ditch and running through the field where ..."
Sara:	*I'm making a field, too.*

Therapist:	*Yeah, we're both making fields. Now, they're all wet, and they're all plowed; and now, they have all of this hot stuff that is down there, too.*
Sara:	*That's hot stuff.*
Therapist:	*That's hot stuff, yeah. It's flowing through the fields.*
Sara:	*Yep.*
Therapist:	*Yeah. But, the nice thing about the hot stuff is that when it goes down here to the field, it gets cool, and it makes real ... rich, rich, rich soil; and the plants grow to be big ... big ... big ....* (Makes hand motions up to the ceiling.)
Sara:	*Up to there.* (Points to the ceiling).
Therapist:	*All the way up to there, yeah.* (Looks up at the ceiling and points). *And, the people can't believe it. They say, "Wow! Look at how tall our plants are! Thank you, Volcano, for helping us make our plants grow nice and tall."*
Sara:	(Walks to the sandbox and picks up a toy shovel.) *Hey, I got this!*
Therapist:	*You have one, too. Now we both have one.*
Sara:	*I'm going to make a mountain, too.* (Begins playing in the sand.)
Therapist:	*Yeah, we're going to have two mountains now, with lots of hot stuff inside; and we're going to make sure that the hot stuff goes down the ditch and into the field where the plants can grow nice and tall. And now, the people in the village ...*
Sara:	*I planted too.*
Therapist:	*You planted a field, too. You sure did. You want to make sure your mountain throws that hot stuff to the field so that the plants will grow real tall.*
Sara:	*I need to make another ... another one ...*

| Therapist: | *You want to have plenty of fields for the hot stuff so there will be lots of good crops. And the people in the village go to the mountain and say, "Thank you, Mountain, for making our plants grow. Now we can eat all winter." And they have a big party and say, "We're so happy that we have the mountain, and that now the mountain knows what it can ..."* |
| Sara: | (Looks at Therapist and holds up her hands while holding the shovel.) *We can't do it anymore.* |

Comment: Sara wants to think that there will be no more explosive volcanos to deal with (i.e., no more angry outbursts). However, it is important that she realize that there will be other angry times, and they will have to be handled in a constructive manner.

| Therapist: | *And we can't do it anymore until we plant our next crop. And then, when we plant our next crop, all this hot stuff that went down here will make good plants.* |
| Sara: | *I make some plants.* |

Note: It is possible that Sara's resistance to the wet sand was an indicator of sexual abuse. This was certainly considered in her therapy. However, by necessity, the focus of this session was on Sara's anger and aggressive behavior.

After this session containing the metaphoric story, Sara's aggressive behavior began to subside. A good illustration of its effect is taken from the last five minutes of a session that occurred a few weeks later. When Sara first walked into the playroom and saw that the sand was dry, she said, "Let's go get some water." Numerous trips were made to get water. Sara and the therapist spent the entire session building castles in the sand. First, Sara built a castle. Then the therapist built a castle. Then Sara said, "Let's tear these down and build just one castle for both of us." As she pulled the sand toward the side of the box directly in front of her, some of the sand spilled over the edge and onto the floor. She looked at the therapist and said, "Uh, oh." Then Sara added, "That's okay. Our mommies won't be mad."

During this excerpt, Sara is standing near the therapist, and the two of them have cups in their hands. They are scooping up sand and pouring it over their hands.

Sara:	*Pour this over your hands.*
Therapist:	*We're going to see how this feels on our hands.* (Continues to scoop.) *We know now that it's okay to feel.*
Sara:	*And our mommies might not be mad if we get our hands dirty.*
Therapist:	*Sometimes, we just have to get our hands dirty to do what we have to do.*
Sara:	(Laughs while pouring sand over her hand.) *Our mommies are in our houses. My mommy is in my house, and your mommy is at your house. Yeah.*
Therapist:	*Yeah, our mommies are in the house. We're just going to play with each other.* (Pause) *We have five more minutes to play, and then our time is up for today, Sara.*
Sara:	*Then I go. Then, we'll go find Mom.*
Therapist:	*Yeah. Then, we'll go find Mom.*
Sara:	*We'll take one more bite out of our sand-wich.*
Therapist:	*Yeah, one more bite. I've just enjoyed this so much. I just want to have one more bite to remember it by.*
Sara:	(Begins to make up a song:) *De-de-de-de.* (Scoops and pours sand several times. Tosses the sand in the air.)
Therapist:	*De-de-de-de.* (Scoops and tosses sand in the air.)
Together:	(Sara and Therapist sing together:) *Da-de-de. Da-de-de.*

Sara:	*See, this is what I'm doing.* (Begins to sing louder and louder.) *Sing louder.*
Therapist:	(Begins to sing louder.)
Together:	(Sara and Therapist both sing louder and laugh and scoop sand. Some of the sand gets out of the box.)
Sara:	*That's okay.*
Therapist:	*Yes, that's okay.*
Together:	(Sara and Therapist both continue to scoop and sing and laugh and look at each other for a long time. Then, they start to scoop and toss the sand in the air and laugh and sing again. This repeats several times. Then, Sara falls on the floor.)
Sara:	*Let's do it again.*
Therapist:	*Do it one more time, and we're going to have to go.*
Sara:	*No.*
Therapist:	*I know. This is so much fun, I don't want to go.*
Sara:	(Scoops and tosses the sand and giggles and then falls down.)
Therapist:	(Does the same thing. Then, both Sara and Therapist fall down to the floor giggling again.)

Available Metaphoric Stories

If devising therapeutic metaphors seems overwhelming initially, there are currently on the market a number of books containing metaphorical stories. One such book is entitled *Annie Stories* (1988), written by Doris Brett, an Australian psychologist. This compilation of stories occurred when the author designed a story for her own daughter, Amantha, before her first day at nursery school. Over the years, as Amantha approached a point in her life that was difficult, she asked her mom to tell her an "Annie Story." Ms. Brett finally put this collection of stories into a book to share with others.

Also available is a book entitled *Sammy the Elephant and Mr. Camel* (1988) by Joyce Mills, Ph.D., and Richard Crowley, Ph.D. This is the story of an elephant that works in a circus. It's his job to carry the water, but the water keeps leaking out. Also by Joyce Mills is *Gentle Willow* (1993), a child's story about death.

Stories for the Third Ear (1985) and *Stories That Heal* (1991), by Lee Wallas, are actually written for adults but may be helpful for some children as well. *Tales of Enchantment* (1989), by Steve and Carol Lankton, is also written for adults, although there is a section for children. This book, in particular, has a table of contents that allows a therapist to look up a therapeutic goal for a particular client, and then refers the therapist to the story that is appropriate for that goal.

There are numerous other therapeutic story books available but the titles are too numerous to list. In reviewing any for use with one's clientele, it is recommended that the book be scanned to make sure it includes the necessary components for a therapeutically effective metaphorical story.

CHAPTER 9

TERMINATION

Introduction

The final stage of therapy is the Termination Stage. As this stage approaches, the child's play returns to the normalized rehearsal-for-life style of play. The therapist may notice the child exhibiting less motivation in coming to play therapy, wanting, rather, to play with her friends or meet other commitments. The child is changing from being dependent on the therapist to engaging in other social relationships (Landreth, 1991). Before these signs fully appear, it is time to prepare the child for termination. During each session of therapy, the child has dealt with her painful issues and created an aspect of empowerment and closure to the traumatic event, therefore creating the healing process. Consequently, it is important to bring the therapy, itself, to closure. If done correctly, the child will leave with the same sense of healing she created throughout the play process. If not properly accomplished, the child will leave play therapy not only without a thorough sense of closure to her healing process, but also with new issues related to loss and abandonment. The more the child is prepared for termination of her therapy, the smoother the transition process out of play therapy becomes.

At best, termination is still a delicate process. During the initial stages of therapy, the child came to trust and depend upon the therapist. These are the very attributes that enabled her to face her most difficult issues. Consequently, the following hypothetical question could be asked: *What child would want to terminate a relationship with someone who valued and accepted her, experienced her pain with her, and brought her a sense of security and protection?* When would even an adult individual wish to terminate under these circumstances. Probably never.

Over the course of therapy, the child and therapist developed a deep sense of attachment with each other. Then, during the Therapeutic Growth Stage, the child began to let go of her need for the therapist to provide both emotional security and protection. This could occur because the child internalized her sense of well-being throughout the therapeutic play process. Now the play process has shifted to play that is more representative of the stage of development expected for a child of this age to be mastering. These changes signal the end of the therapy process and the end of the relationship that was created in order for change to occur. Indeed, the therapist herself will need to address her own feelings of the loss of the relationship.

Appropriate Terminations:
Planting Seeds of Ensuing Termination

The concept of termination is introduced in the Therapeutic Growth Stage when the child's play begins to lessen in intensity and the focus changes from the child's internal pain to interactive play that is developmentally appropriate in content and style. The child will begin to interact freely with the therapist. Her play will become more spontaneous and creative with a presence of enjoyment rather than the pressured play observed earlier. The first introduction to termination can be executed with a general statement such as, "You know, we won't always be playing together like this." In essence, a seed is being planted within the child that communicates, "There will be a time when you won't be coming into the play therapy room anymore." While this is not the formal introduction of the termination process, it marks the beginning of preparing the child to leave a process that has honored her being and allowed the confrontation of self that could not have been created in her previous encounters.

Allowing the Therapist to Introduce Termination

Once the therapist believes that termination of the play therapy is approaching, the parents or guardians should be consulted to determine their perspectives on the child's changes and present style of interactions in regard to the presenting issues. When it has been determined that the child is ready for termination, it is very important that the therapist be the one to introduce this to the child — not the parents or the agency responsible for the child's therapy. This must be clearly communicated. If the parent or responsible party introduces termination, a conflict develops. The child feels betrayed by the therapist, and the trust that was earlier developed may be shattered. This may result in a loss of some of the gains made by the child in treatment and can effect the child's transition from therapy, contaminating the child's willingness to trust others in the future.

When to Introduce Termination to the Child[1]

In sessions prior to the actual initiation of termination, there were times when the idea of an eventual termination was mentioned. Then, during the session in which termination is introduced, it should be initiated in the first minutes of the session once the child is comfortable in the playroom. Providing the information in the first 10 to 15 minutes of the session allows time for the child to experience the meaning of the information and then react to it. The therapist must remember that the event that brought the child to play therapy caused him to experience feelings of life being out of his control. Therefore, when termination is introduced, similar feelings may surface. By determining the best time to terminate, the therapist is essentially directing the final phase of the child's therapy. However, the child is now capable of interacting with the world in a different manner than when she first entered therapy. It would be appropriate during the introduction of termination to disclose to the child some of the reasons for deciding on termination. These reasons may appropriately include a list of gains made by the child (e.g., the child's motivation to be with friends, the child's freedom of expression in opinions and feel-

---

1. In determining the best time to introduce termination, the therapist should take into consideration the child's birthday. Generally, children do not want to work in therapy during a session that happens to fall on their birthday. They tend to want the session to be self-validating (e.g., "I'm a neat person.") and focus on themselves. Consequently, if a therapist notices that the child's birthday is falling near the termination date, it would be better, if possible, to go beyond the birthday.

ings, her success in school endeavors, or her enhanced belief in her own self-worth).

Termination may take as few as two sessions and as many as six, depending on the length of therapy. When a child has been seen for a year or more, termination appropriately would take up to six sessions. The format of the termination process may differ depending upon the clinical judgment of the play therapist. Sometimes, a therapist will introduce termination, have two consecutive sessions, and then change to every-other-week sessions with the child, or once a month for two months. These various formats allow for a child's individual needs within the termination process.

Phases of Termination

Saying Goodbye to the Child's Play. When terminating with an adult, the client will often review his therapy (e.g., "Remember when I struggled with ..."). This review is done verbally and cognitively. Since children operate experientially, however, their review of therapy will often occur through their play (O'Connor, 1991). For instance, they may appear to regress to behavior observed during the first stages of therapy (Landreth, 1991).

> During the termination phase of Jimmy's therapy, his play regressed to the original content of play that he exhibited during the Exploratory Stage of therapy before he initiated his testing for protection. Then his play changed to the first phase of the Dependency Stage of therapy. After noticing the child moving through a number of phases, the therapist said, "I notice that the play you are doing is play that you've done here before."
>
> Jimmy turned to the therapist and said, "Well, yeah! I'm saying goodbye to all the parts of my therapy!" Remembering their experience when they first entered therapy, most children will only play the final phase of the Exploratory Stage when trust was initiated by the child as the Testing for Protection Stage began.

This is the first phase of termination — saying goodbye to one's play and the safe environment in which the child was allowed to experience this play. It was here that the meaning of the child's play was accepted and understood. Indeed, the play that was difficult for the child became very purposeful to the child within the context of the meaningful relationship.

Saying Goodbye to the Therapist. The final phase of termination revolves around the feelings concerning the relationship that developed between the child and the therapist. During the initial stages of therapy, the therapist honored the child in such a way as to encourage feelings of self-worth, safety, and security. During termination, trust and the relationship once again become issues in the child's questioning of the reasons for termination, how it will be accomplished, and the loss of the relationship. The significance of this relationship is now the focus, with the meaning that these two individuals have developed for this unique relationship. They now come together one last time to give encouragement and support to each other. This is an opportunity for the therapist to self-disclose with regard to how meaningful the child has become to the therapist. It is important to communicate these feelings to the child. It is also appropriate to make empowering statements such as, "You're going to be a person who has a lot of influence in the world," or, "You're a very, very creative person, and creative people like you have important messages to say." In addition, it is important to let the child know that the success she has experienced in play therapy will continue for her as she continues in life. (See Chapter 8 for further discussion of supportive communication.)

When termination does occur, it should be complete and clear. It is not recommended that therapists make promises into the future such as, "In January, I'll send you a birthday card." If this promise is forgotten, it creates a contamination of the relationship. The initial stages of therapy revolved around being present with the child in her current experience. The relationship was founded on the principle, "What we have is the present. I'm here with you now." Termination continues the principle of being present in the moment with no expectations outside the experience of the moment. "Should we meet again, we'll have our relationship. I will miss seeing you every week, and yet I'll feel good knowing your life is going well."

As the child separates from the therapist, it is important that the child feel no indebtedness to the therapist. The goal of every therapist is for the child to function in a healthy style, independent of the therapist. Keeping the child dependent does not allow the child to successfully complete her therapy. However, termination in many respects is more difficult for the therapist than the child. After being allowed to experience together the difficulties in this child's life, and even being allowed to play in her "moccasins," the therapist is now hearing from this child that she no longer needs the therapist or the therapist's presence to pursue life's challenges. While there is satisfaction in this process, there is an experience of loss that the therapist must acknowledge each time a unique child enters and separates from her life.

Sometimes, a therapist will want to give the child a gift. In this event, it is a good idea to combine something that will both empower the child and represent the internal process the child has experienced. For instance, this might include a toy that was particularly symbolic to the child's play and to the importance of that play. One therapist, who enjoyed writing metaphorical stories, reviewed each child's chart and then wrote a story with built-in empowerments that had occurred throughout the child's healing process. During a child's final session, she presented the child with the story.

Taking a picture of the child and therapist together is another way of enhancing the termination process. Children love this. Almost without exception, they jump at the chance. Many of them lean on their therapist or put their arms around her. It is a good idea to take two pictures — one for the child and one for the child's file.

After children say goodbye to the playroom and their play process, if there are remaining sessions, it is very common for them to want to have those sessions outside the playroom.

> *During one child's last two sessions, the child brought a bat and ball to the session. He asked his therapist if they could go outside to play ball. The two of them went out into the parking lot. For the entire session, the therapist threw the ball, with the child hitting the ball back to the therapist. Then, during his last session, the child wanted to do the same thing. After hitting the ball three times similar to the week before, the child hit the ball so hard it went way beyond the parking area. Metaphorically, he was saying, "See how much power I have?"*
>
> *The next hit, the child did the same thing. Again, he was communicating, "See how much power I have. I'm under my*

own power now." He repeated this for the rest of the session. In addition, while the therapist was chasing the ball, the child was metaphorically separating from the therapist and, in fact, was experiencing separation while at the same time maintaining his empowerment.

Premature Terminations

Most termination processes progress smoothly when each stage of therapy preceding termination has been allowed to reach culmination. When a child's therapy is terminated appropriately, the child maintains the sense of accomplishment in the integration of herself that was gained during the therapeutic process. Unfortunately, the right to therapy is not controlled by the child. The decision lies with parents or guardians, social service agencies, courts, or situations out of the control of the child who may not understand the meaning and complexities of the child's therapy. As a result, therapy may be interrupted or ended at times that are inappropriate for the child. When this occurs, special considerations should be made for the child. Any form of termination takes a minimum of two sessions to allow the child some sense of closure on her therapeutic experience — one session to say goodbye to her play process, and one session to say goodbye to the therapist. Because the process of becoming a child's therapist takes a minimum of two sessions for trust to be established, the child needs the same minimal transition time to disengage from this significant relationship. In addition, the child must be informed that nothing she said or did in the playroom had any bearing on the decision to end therapy. Children have the tendency to incorporate false assumptions if conditions are not adequately explained. Consequently, the therapist must be sensitive to the presenting issues and how these issues may re-emerge in the premature termination. The therapist may wish to identify and, therefore, alleviate any false conclusions and resultant feelings that a premature termination might create for the child (i.e., abandonment or loss issues, rejection, or unacceptableness). By identifying and presenting these possibilities, the child can be relieved of carrying unnecessary issues because of the therapy loss. This also aids the therapeutic process if the child were ever to reenter therapy in the future.

One type of premature termination is when someone decides to terminate therapy without consulting the therapist. When this occurs, there is usually no time allowed for the child to her goodbyes. If this is the case, it is appropriate to attempt to make arrangements for the two final sessions. Sometimes, the therapist must inform the parent, "I need at least two sessions with your child to ensure her well-being through this termination process." If the parent is still reluctant to make these arrangements, the therapist may need to become more assertive: "This is a violation to your child and to the progress she has made in her therapy. She will be hurt and angry and may become cautious in trusting people in the future. She needs this time to express her anger and disappointment with me." Sometimes a therapist may need to make quick arrangements for one session so the child can say goodbye to her play in the room, and then use the telephone to do the final session, enabling the child to say her goodbye to the therapist. In any event, it is important to creatively find a means of closing the therapy process. Otherwise, the child's therapy process is denied closure. This lack of closure is especially detrimental if the child has just revealed her pain and agony through play. In this case, the child may think that revealing her pain through metaphorical play caused the therapist to abandon her. It is very important for the therapist to communicate, "Nothing you played or did caused this to happen between you and me. It is for some other reason." It may even be necessary for the therapist to say, "I do not want our time together to end. This time, things just aren't happening the way I would like for them to."

> *After working with Jeremy for 13 months, his parents abruptly decided to terminate therapy. The therapist said to the child during their last session, "I don't understand why this is ending. I would like more time with you. But I don't own your therapy. Your mom and dad do. They are the ones who have made this decision, and it's sad for me, too. I know it's sad for you." Then they hugged and spoke of how much they cared for one another.*

Again, it is extremely important during premature terminations to communicate to the child that nothing the child has shared during therapy is the reason for the termination. In addition, if the child has an issue with abandonment, it is very important that the therapist clearly communicate to the child that this is not the therapist's desire. She is not abandoning the child. Someone else made the decision.

Sometimes, premature terminations are unavoidable. For instance, for school counselors, it may be the end of the school year. For graduate students, it may be the end of a program or internship, with the therapist moving on to another location.

> *At the end of an internship experience, a therapist by the name of Bruce had to introduce premature termination to six-year-old Ryan. Realizing he would be leaving the state, the therapist spoke with Ryan's adoptive mother, explaining the situation. He then made arrangements to transfer the child to another therapist.*
>
> *As Ryan and his mother were driving to the session at which the therapist was going to introduce termination, Ryan said, "Bruce and I are friends who are going to play together forever." The mother immediately communicated this to the therapist. The session was very delicate and emotional for both Ryan and Bruce.*
>
> *For several sessions, the therapist processed the termination and transfer to another therapist with Ryan. He allowed time for Ryan to say goodbye to the therapy that occurred with Bruce, while introducing the prospect of a new therapist. Then both therapists met with Ryan so that he would have some time to transition and adjust to the new therapist, Sol. After two sessions together, the new therapist disengaged from therapy in order for Bruce to respond to Ryan's feelings. In addition to saying goodbye to Bruce, Ryan also had to confront the new relationship with Sol. During their last session, Ryan turned to Bruce and said, "Bruce, I hate you; and I love Sol." He then turned and ran out the playroom door to his parents in the waiting room. Bruce realized that Ryan was speaking metaphorically, saying, "I hate it that you are leaving me because I love you." Yet it was very painful to hear Ryan's struggle with the separation and the feelings of abandonment that this experience evoked.*
>
> *In the next session, Sol met with Ryan and talked about how painful it was to say goodbye to Bruce. In addition, he emphasized how much Bruce cared about Ryan.*

While everything possible was done to facilitate Ryan's adjustment to the new therapist, the pain of the loss was extremely intense and overwhelming for Ryan. It is important to keep in mind that the play expressions of children have emotionality which is usually much greater than the play will convey. This is especially true for the expression of the child toward the therapist, whether that be positive or negative.

Case Example of Miguel

Miguel was a nine-year-old child who was referred to play therapy by a community support program because of aggressive behavior in the home. He was from a large, impoverished family. Miguel was envious of any attention paid to other siblings. He enjoyed working in the fields with his father because it was the only time he had with his father without his siblings. During treatment, he was able to establish a very close relationship with the therapist even though he was initially hesitant. The parents initiated a premature termination of the therapy process against the recommendations of the supervisors and the agency that had recommended this counseling referral.

In the following excerpt from his final terminating session, Miguel and his therapist had been drawing on the whiteboard. First, they each wrote their complete names in large, bold letters; then, together, they drew a sailboat with the name "Miguel" on its side. The boat is on the ocean with birds, clouds, a moon, and several stars above. Miguel has also drawn a human figure.

Session	Commentary
1. Miguel: *Erase any letter of your name.* (Erases the "o" from the end of his name.) T: *Okay. Erase any letter of my name.*	1. The metaphor is, *I have shared myself with you, and now I will be leaving you and the playroom.* Miguel starts with the "o" because it is the end of his name, and the end of his involvement in this experience.
2. M: *You can erase it in the middle, too.* (Takes his hands and rubs over his hair as he speaks.)	2. *There are also many feelings I have about ending that I am not verbalizing.* One is anxiety (apparent by

the way in which he rubs his hair as he speaks).

3. T: *Okay. I can erase it in the middle, too.* (She erases the "o" from her name and then hands the eraser to Miguel, saying:) *It isn't easy deciding which important letter to take.*

3. The therapist wants to communicate to Miguel that she, too, has feelings about the termination, and that he is significant to her.

4. M: (Erases another "o" from his name and then returns the eraser to the therapist. They continue in this fashion for three more letters each. Then, Miguel erases one of the birds.)

4. Again, a metaphor for the strong feelings he has about their relationship and the meaning of his therapy process. Miguel now moves to a bird drawn above his name which resembles the birds on the mural on the playroom wall, probably a symbol of the playroom experience. This would also represent the freedom he has experienced in the play sessions from a new vantage point.

5. T: *Oh, I can erase something from the picture, too. It doesn't have to be just parts of my name.* (She erases a bird while saying:) *I remember so many important times we've had together in the playroom.* (Returns the eraser to Miguel.)

5. Erasing parts of the picture is moving into memory of the experiences of the play therapy process. This validates each person's importance to one another as the experience becomes memories.

6. M: (Erases the moon.)

6. The moon is the largest symbol at the top of the drawing. Miguel is communicating that he is now beginning to lose the person whose presence has respected and guided him.

7. T: *Oh, there goes the moon. I'm sad that the moon is going away, even though some of the bright stars are left.* (She erases a letter of her name.)
    M: (Erases a letter of his name.)

7. The therapist acknowledges Miguel's sadness that this relationship is ending and the brightness (the presence) of this experience is dimming into memory. The metaphor is that Miguel's therapist and his therapy were bright spots in his life.

8. T: (Erases a cloud.) *I think I'll take away the puffy cloud.*
M: (Erases a star.)

8. Since the therapist drew these symbols, the clouds represent the sadness she is experiencing in ending these sessions with Miguel.

9. T: *Oh, there goes one of the shinning stars. This is getting harder. I'm kind of sad about erasing the picture we made together. I guess I'll take away one of the red birds.* (She erases a bird.)

9. The therapist acknowledges the loss of the guiding star and how their experience together (the picture) causes emotions for her also. The therapist then erases one of the red birds. The red bird represents her intense feelings about the therapy experience — either the brightness of the experience or the anger of losing this experience. The therapist might have better chosen to erase a letter of her name rather than a symbol.

10. M: (Erases the head of the human figure.)

10. Miguel is now beginning to say goodbye to his therapist and his involvement in the play therapy process.

11. T: *The head's gone, and the person is beginning to go away.* (She erases a letter of her name.)
M: (Erases a letter of his name.)

11. The therapist acknowledges the therapeutic relationship moving toward the ending phase. Note how important the closure of this relationship is to Miguel, and that he must move slowly to allow himself a sense of control and security over this loss.

12. T: *Oh, me. It's kind of sad to see the picture go away. I think I'll take the clouds away.*

12. The therapist removes the second and last cloud which represents her sadness of ending this experience that has had so many bright aspects to it for her also.

13. M: (Erases a letter of his name.)
T: (Erases a letter of her name.)
M: (Erases a letter of his name.)

13. Miguel focuses on his name rather than the symbols as it becomes more evident that the picture is fading.

14. T: *Your name is nearly gone. Your short name* (his nickname), *and I'll remember it.* (She erases a letter of her own name.)

14. Miguel leaves his nickname to say that they are friends who have gotten to know each other in a deeper, more meaningful manner. She acknowledges that the memories will be of this close, meaningful relationship.

15. M: (Erases a letter of his name.)

15. He is now moving toward the final phase of saying goodbye.

16. T: *Oh, I guess now I have to take away some of my happy stars.* (She erases a star.)

16. The therapist knows that the end is coming, and she can't change the inevitable — that this meaningful time together is ending.

17. M: (Erases another star.)

17. Miguel confirms the reflection that he feels the same way about ending their time together.

18. T: *Even though the head is missing on the person you drew, I'm going to remember your face.*

18. The therapist moves the focus to the main symbol and concentrates on the feelings of separating and remembering each other.

19. M: *I just drew it there. But, you're not the person.* (He erases the legs of the person.)

19. Since this is a more interpretative response, it shifts too close, and he has to ground himself by saying that she is not the person (he is the person). He then erases the legs which would represent the support and grounding that is ending.

20. T: *And now the legs are gone. It just has the body left. He can't stand where he wants without legs.* (She erases a star.) *I hate to see the bright stars fading away.*

20. The therapist acknowledges Miguel's desire to remain in play therapy, and that it is not his choice to have to leave his stance (i.e., wanting to remain in play therapy).

21. M: (Erases an arm of the person.)

21. The contact Miguel has made with the therapist is now ending. He begins the emotional disengaging that he

knows is happening with the ending of play therapy.

22. T: *Pretty soon, I won't be able to see that person any more. But you know, even though I won't be seeing you, I'm going to remember you.*
     T: (Erases a star.)

22. The therapist changes the loss of contact to the memories that she will have of him.

23. M: (Erases the other arm.) *Now, it just has clothes left.*
     T: *Now, it's just clothes left.*
     M: (Erases a letter of his name.)
     T: (Erases a star.)

23. The metaphor is, *We don't have our same contact anymore, but I still have my feelings about separating which I need to keep covered.* One can sense how difficult this process is for each person.

24. (Erases a small part of the shirt of the person.) *Someone bit that part off.*

24. Miguel now gives the deeper feeling that separating is painful for him with the metaphor, *Someone took a bit out of me, and a part of me is gone.* He lets her know how painful this separation is for him.

25. T: *Someone bit that part off. Oh, that hurts. That hurts to see the person go.* (She erases a letter of her name.)

25. The therapist reflects the hurt he is experiencing as the two confront their separation.

26. M: (Erases the shirt.) *He threw the shirt away.*

26. The separation feels like he has been thrown away or discarded. This has a similar theme to his presenting issues of feelings of exclusion and lack of validation of his unique and special qualities.

27. T: *And there ... threw the shirt away? Oh, I'm sad the shirt got thrown away.* (Erases a star.) *I guess I'm going to leave my short* [a shortened version of her first name] *name up there awhile.*
     M: (Erases a letter of his name.)

27. The therapist expresses empathy for the loss he is experiencing as the separation and closing of therapy continues. Leaving her short name is symbolic of the fact that she is having difficulty ending this relationship also.

28. T: *Well, there goes all of your short name, but I'm going to remember that name.* (Erases another star.)

M: (Erases a letter of his name.)

28. Miguel erases the last letter that gives recognition of his name as it would be read, the metaphor being that only the meaning of our relationship remains, which only we can recognize.

29. M: (Erases the last remnants of the person.)

29. The relationship is now becoming a memory since it is ending in the present experience.

30. T: *There goes the special person ... and a bright star* (erases a star); *but I'm still going to remember knowing you and the special times we had together.*

M: (Erases another star.)

30. The therapist acknowledges the loss again and gives meaning to the special experience that is part of their relationship.

31. T: *There are still some shining stars left.* (Erases part of the water under the boat.) *Let's remove this part of the water because Miguel and the boat are going to sail on ... on the water.*

M: (Erases a star.)

31. The therapist states that there are still some bright spots in this experience. She then conveys that Miguel will continue on sailing with the support he experienced in their relationship in play therapy.

32. T: (Erases the sail on the boat.) *You know, I believe you can sail even if your sail gets kind of blown around, 'cause that sailboat can still go.*

M: (Erases another star.)

32. The therapist wants to let Miguel know that he has potential on his own, and that he can accomplish his own goals as he moves on in his life.

33. T: *Well, I think I'm going to have to take off my name.* (Erases a letter of her name.)

M: (Erases a star.)

T: *Three shining stars left.* (Erases another letter of her name.)

M: (Erases a star.)

33. The therapist experiences the realization that there is no choice but to remove herself from the picture. She erases the last letter that would give her name recognition.

34. T: (Erases the last letter of her name.) *Oh, and my name is all gone.*

34. Now, the person of the therapist is out of the picture, except for memories.

35. T: *I don't want to see the sailboat go. Uh, this is kind of sad to do.* (Erases most of the water from under the boat.)

35. The support the therapist has given Miguel directly in the form of therapy is ending as the boat sails on into the future.

36. M: *Now, we can erase two letters.*
   T: *Okay.*
   M: (Erases two letters of his name.)

36. Now, Miguel increases the pacing of the closure process because he knows that the end is near.

37. T: *You have more letters left, and mine are all gone. I like having the two shining stars left up there.* (Erases the rest of the water from under the boat:) *Okay. The water is gone.*
   M: (Erases a star.)

37. The therapist gives the metaphor of the two shining stars which would be the memory of the two of them in their relationship. The realization of the end of the supportive relationship is near as the water is erased.

38. T: *Only one bright star left. Ooo, what can I do now? Oh, I'm going to miss this sailboat.*
   M: (Erases two more letters of his name.)

38. The therapist is reluctant to erase the symbol that represents Miguel's movement in play therapy.

39. T: (Erases the rest of the sailboat.) *Well, even if the sailboat is gone, Miguel is still in my heart.*
   M: (Erases the last star.)

39. The therapist communicates the end of the relationship and the importance of the meaning of their relationship to her.

40. T: *The last shining star.* (Erases part of the inscription "Miguel" that had been on the sailboat.)
   M: (Erases more letters of his name.)

40. A metaphor for, *The end is near, and you will be going away.*

41. T: (Erases more of the inscription.) *I am erasing your name, and I am remembering you.*
   M: (Erases more letters of his name.)
   T: (Erases the last letter of the inscription.) *Well, the name on our sailboat is all gone.*

41. The therapist repeats the comments that the end of the relationship is approaching, and that this has been an important relationship to her.

42. M: (Erases one more letter of his name.) *Want to erase with me?*

T: *Okay. There's only two letters left.* (Erases one letter.)

42. The symbols of him in the relationship are now being erased. Miguel asks her to join him in erasing the remainder of the drawing.

43. M: (Erases the last letter.)

T: *Even though our play time has ended, I'm still going to remember you and all the time we spent here together. I have a little something for you to remember this time.*

43. Miguel completes the ending of the drawing and the closure of the time in play therapy. Both now know the play therapy process is over, and the relationship is changing to memory. The therapist gives him a gift as a symbol of the meaning of their relationship in play therapy.

The therapist presented Miguel with a blue car similar to the one he had played with in the playroom. She reminded him of the special magic to change and heal hurts that he had assigned the car during his play. She told him that he would always have that special magic within him, and that the car would remind him of that special quality within himself.

Termination is the culminating stage of therapy and is the point in which all the efforts of therapy merge for closure of the process. How well termination occurs determines how well the experience of therapy is integrated, especially in the future of the child.

APPENDIX A

List of Basic Toys of the Playroom

Airplane

Animals (Domestic)

Balls

Animals (Wild)

Cars

Clay

Doctor's Kit

Dolls

Doll House

Family Figurines:

    Adult Male

    Adult Female

    Boy

    Girl

    Baby

Guns

Knife

Money/Gold Coins

Musical Instruments

Paints

Puppets

Teddy Bear

Telephone

Knife

Musical Instruments

APPENDIX B

List of Symbolic Meanings of Toys

Airplane: escape, distance, speed, search, freedom, safety, protection, etc.

Animals (Wild): aggression, fear, survival, power, strength, etc.

Animals (Domestic): protection, family, relations, vulnerability, compliance, dependency, etc.

Baby Bottle: regression, nurturing, orality, coping issues, dependency, babies, siblings, urinating, etc.

Ball: interaction, relationships, trust, reevaluation, competition, reassurance, etc.

Binoculars: perspective, relationship (close/distance), surveillance, hunting, finding, searching, intimacy, hypervigilance, self-examination, etc.

Blanket: regression, security, protection, boundaries, etc.

Blocks: defenses, boundaries, construction, limits, rigidity, closure, structure, protection, barriers, vulnerability, etc.

Boats: support, unconscious, stable/unstable, emotionality, balance, vulnerability, security, etc.

Books: bibliotherapy, secrets, past, future, present, identity, knowledge, escape, metaphors, etc.

Box: secret, known/unknown, non-content existence, hidden, control, containment, boundaries, belief, confirmation, gift, self, dignity, internal, etc.

Broken Toys: issue, self, identity, defeat, change, compensation, ineffectual, struggle wound, loss, adjustment, etc.

Camera: proof, validation, conformation, past, truth, evidence, change, memory, knowledge, etc.

Cars: mobility, power, escape, conflict, safety, protection, travel, parent, defenses, family issues, etc.

Chalk/Dry Board: environment, world, creation, emotional expression, integration, creativity, etc.

Clay: aggression, manipulation, creation, self-esteem, change, expression, contact, pressure, nurture, etc.

Costumes: relationships, communication, anonymity, fantasy, impulses, disguise, perpetrator, etc.

   Gloves: avoiding, distant, safety, control over content, etc.

   Hats: identity, roles, expectations, fantasy, power, denial, etc.

   Masks: relationships, communication, anonymity, fantasy, impulses, perpetrator, disguise, etc.

   Sunglasses: hiding, avoiding, distant, safety, etc.

   Wigs: relationships, communication, anonymity, fantasy, impulses, disguise, person, etc.

Doctor's Kit: healing, repair, respect, power, life/death, pain, body image, crisis, changing, intrusion, internal, etc.

Blood Pressure Bulb: internal issues, anger, calm, state of mind, internalized feelings, need for change, etc.

Operation: crisis, intervention, intrusion, action, risk, resolution, control, pain, vulnerability, healing, etc.

Stethoscope: internal feelings, unknown, undisclosed, validation, relationship, etc.

Syringe: intrusion, violation, pain, healing, fear, impact, contact, penetration, etc.

Thermometer: internal feelings, sick/okay-ness, need for help, crisis, need for change, mood, etc.

Dishes/Cooking: nurturing, celebration, security, orality, attention, neglect, demands, etc.

Dolls: self-identity, regression, sibling, anatomy, competition, closeness, friendship, nurturing, relationships, etc.

Doll House: family, family interaction/attitude, environment, security, etc.

Family Figurines: authority, power, nurturing, perpetrator, protection, dependency, interaction, competition, relationship, security, acceptance, rejection, etc.

Male: above issues with father, male figures, modeling, brothers, uncles, teachers, sitters, etc.

Female: above issues with mother, female figures, modeling, sisters, aunts, teachers, sitters, etc.

Girl: self, sister, sitter, identity, image, friend, peer relationship, social, etc.

Boy: self, brother, sitter, identity, image, friend, peer relationship, social, etc.

Baby: nurturing, sibling, competition, regression, needs, history, past, etc.

Finger Paints: contact, involvement, impact, grounding, regression, security, etc.

Flashlight: control, secrecy, fear, searching, leadership, dependency, observing, scanning, etc.

Games: control of life, competition, success/failure, compliance, empowerment, structure, resistance, change, competency, cooperation, environment, family, etc.

Grooming Utensils: self-image, self-concept, change, thoughts, validation, caring nurturing, etc.

Guns: aggression, control, anger, hostility, power, death, pain, intrusion, impact, protection, boundaries, etc.

Keys: secret, control, unknown, containment, protected, boundaries, security, etc.

Kitchen Set: home, nurturing, care, neglect, sibling conflict, relationship, family, respect, family process, emotional support, etc.

Knife: utensil, aggression, penetration, power, defense, protection, intrusion, sexual pain, etc.

Lights: control, power, secret, escape, hiding, denial, change, miserable, etc.

Magic Wand/Crystal Ball
fantasy, wishes, goals, change, desire, future, need for resources, etc.

Marbles: relationship, grouping, family, peers, interaction, social, (see *Games*), etc.

Mirror: self-image, self-concept, memories, past, change, thoughts, validation, etc.

Models: consistency, completion, motivation, focus, persistence, goal, validation, etc.

Money/Gold Coins: security, power, control, loss, cheated, self-esteem, worth, value, etc.

Monster Figure: fear, mysterious, frightening, unknown, friendly, secretive, power, ambivalent, fantasy, aggression, conflict, perpetrator, relationship, revenge, attack, etc.

Musical Instruments: self-expression, internal, communication, creativity, contact, mood, etc.

Paints: distance, expression, inaccessible needs, environment, attitude, resource, creativity, view of world, etc.

Pillow: bed, safety, territory, throne, parent, monster, aggression, relaxation, burden, etc.

Playing Cards: money, control, power, secrets, spontaneity, (see *Games*), etc.

Puppets: relationships, family, perpetrator, victim, communication, anonymity, fantasy, impulses, attitude, disguise, etc.

Puzzles: problem solving, decisions, completion, accomplishment, integration, solving, getting-the-picture, getting-it-together, etc.

Sand: construction, destruction, environment, community, feelings, change, emotional world, creativity, etc.

Sand-Bottom Bop Bag: aggression, conflict, perpetrator, power, relationship, revenge, family, etc.

Soldiers: conflict, attack, aggression, force, life-death, struggling, people, survival, grouping, etc.

Space (Box, Tent, House): hidden, be and not be, shame/respect, distance/contact, acceptance, trust, boundaries, etc.

Sword: aggression, distance, conflict, defense, protection, intrusion, relationship, power, etc.

Tape Recorder: self, relationship, evidence, existence, validation, reassurance, consistency, control, observation, confirmation, etc.

Targets: self-confidence, goal setting, appropriateness, need for success, expectations, fear of failure, competition, adjusting, adaptability, etc.

Teddy Bear: warmth, nurturing, security, companionship, self, protection, etc.

Telephone: communication, distance, safety, control, power, disconnect, etc.

Tinker Toys/Legos: structure, construction, completion, closure, goal attainment, etc.

Tools: resources, change, impact, construction, security, authority, confidence, problem solving, decisions, etc.

NOTE: Toys can symbolize a need for or lack of some feeling, emotional state, or competency.

APPENDIX C

Symbolic Meanings of Environments

Bank: worth, value, security, loss, dignity, secret, family, etc.

Beach: safe, free, playful, tactile, secure, child-like, etc.

Body: self, pain, intrusion, violation, power, source, life, etc.

Bridge: transition, change, crossing, boundary, connection, path, above it all, etc.

Buried: death, hidden, avoiding, pending, unrevealed, covert, depression, etc.

Camping: basics, family, survival, current/active, escape, retreat, relief, change, refuge, calm, primitive, etc.

Castle: home, authority, protection, impenetrable, boundaries, past, family, cold, rigidity, power, safety, body boundary, etc.

Cave: protection, guarded, hidden, secret, unknown, refuge, ambivalence, encapsulated, grave, trapped, contained, etc.

Cemetery: past, death, loss, memories, fear, history, unknown, curious, etc.

Church: family, values, death, protection, fears, morals, strength, guilt, salvation, etc.

Circus: excitement, control, overwhelming, magical, attention, confusion, etc.

City: community, friends, neighborhood, crowds, activity, grouping, etc.

Cliff: dangerous, fearful, cautious, boundary, life/death, fear of loss of control, approaching the line, etc.

Desert: void, anger, alone, non-nurturing, emotionally empty, neglect, survival, defenseless, wanderer, vulnerable, exposed, etc.

Dinosaurs: past, history, death, power, extinction, fear, conflict, loss, environment, etc.

Dungeon: torture, unconscious, prison, capture, suffering, pain, jail, crime scene, intense past, etc.

Farm: nurturing, civil, protection, home, society, controllable, grounding, etc.

Fire: rage, intense, pain, destroy, excitement, heat, anger, annihilate, out-of-control, controlling the out-of-control, etc.

Foggy: unclear, doubt, less control, unsure, hidden, surrounded, everywhere, consumed, encapsulating, etc.

Forest: foreboding, exploring, encapsulated, shelter, hidden, rescued, lost, etc.

Fort: home, authority, protection, impenetrable, boundaries, family, power, safety, body boundary, etc.

Frozen: stop, control, suspend (time), stunned, unavailable, immobile, helpless, dead, gone, etc.

Garden: growth, development, nurturing, family, caring, beauty, appearance, internal self, peaceful, etc.

Ghost: person, fear, memories, revenge, pain, loss without loss, pending, perpetrator, guilt, etc.

Haunted House: secrets, unconscious, home, family, past, fearful, extended family, unresolved, scary, etc.

Hospital: crisis, repair, pain, intrusion, healing, violation, risk, life/death, etc.

House: home, security, internal, protection, conflict, marriage, parents, family, etc.

  Attic: history, past, family, old, memories, storage, etc.

  Bedroom: isolation, self, protection, violation, secrets, validation, identity, etc.

  Bathroom: internal, toilet training, body control, clean, etc.

  Basement: hidden, unresolved, deep, fear, etc. (See *Cave.*)

  Kitchen: nurturing, family, needs, (see *Dishes*), etc.

Invisible: victim, devalued, hypervigilant, pain, avoidant, secret, powerful, etc.

Island: alone, isolation, abandoned, survival, refuge, lost, hostage, etc.

Jail: containment, punishment, guilty, avoided, judged, control, restraint, boundary, protection, etc.

Jungle: fear, tumultuous, survival, dangerous, hypervigilance, disempowered, violence, anxiety, confusing, loss of control, lack of security, etc.

Lightening: intrusion, rage, shock, hypervigilance, striking, physical abuse, unexpected, unforseen, etc.

Map: search, seek, path, journey, quest, treasure, plan, strategy, problem solving, etc.

Maze: confused, unknown, unsure, searching, endurance, path, lost, overwhelming, challenge, obstacle, defeated/conquering, etc.

Mountain: expectations, attainments, overwhelming, impasse, obstacle, power conflict, challenge, etc.

Night (Dark): scary, vigilant, sneaky, hidden, dependent, alone, invisible, loss of control, etc.

Ocean: overwhelming, fear, survival, change, depth, internal, pervasive, loss of control, etc.

Operating Room: crisis, pain, intense, intrusion, internal, care, change, etc.

Outer Space: isolated, abandoned, lonely, void, survival, dependent, future, peaceful, etc.

Picnic: family, nurturing, safe, playful, celebration, etc.

Puppet Show: enactment, metaphor, family, relationships, disguise, disclosure, etc.

Race: competition, relationships, challenge, win/lose, conflict, power, etc.

Rain: depression, sadness, crying, disappointment, stained, cleansed, renewed, etc.

Rainbow: hope, change, improvement, different, new perspective, safe, etc.

Restaurant: nurturing, celebration, neglect, hunger, etc.

River: power, journey, boundary, conflict, energy, struggle, resource, force, need for direction, separation, etc.

Sailing: force, escape, support, emotionality, stable/unstable, etc.

School: control, authority, power, change, social, peers, relationships, grouping, acceptance/rejection, etc.

Snow(ing): cold, hidden anger, lack of nurturing, needy, etc.

Storm: turmoil, anger, confusion, pain, impending, anxiety, internal, etc.

Sunshine: healing, warmth, well-being, change, hope, caring, self, etc.

Swamp: burden, struggle, sadness, bogged down, etc.

Thunder: anger, power, fear, hypervigilance, agitated, verbal abuse, force,   energy, etc.

Tornado: rage, destruction, uncontrollable, fear, anxiety, force, emotional, misuse of energy, etc.

Treasure: valuable, hidden, worth, security, power, protected, loss, search, etc.

Underground: hidden, avoidant, pending, unrevealed, covert, etc.

Underwater: unconscious, overwhelmed, deep fear, unknown, etc.

War: aggression, conflict, rage, destruction, annihilation, violation, perpetrator, attack, revenge, death, relationships, etc.

Water: emotionality, flexibility, freedom, enuresis, anxiety, womb, orality, sadness, depth, internal, regression, primitive, unconscious, aggressive impulses, approachability for the cautious child, freedom for the inhibited child, calming for the more explosive child, etc.

Zoo: control, view, jail, capture, containment, protected, fear, obser-
    vation, etc.

APPENDIX D

Symbolic Meanings of Animals

Alligator/Crocodile: aggressive, frightening, oral aggression, lurking, impulsive, violating, vulnerable, hungry, seeking, controlling, etc.

Bear: strength, power, aggression, intimidation, masculine, father, withdrawal, independent, contact, fighting, confrontive, fearless, loner, wanderer, internalized, moody, etc.

Beaver: stability, persistent, workaholic, eager, structure, compulsive, organized, etc.

Birds: escape, freedom, perspective, alone, on-top-of-things, distance, searching, gliding, etc.

Bull: aggressive, mean, strong, territorial, intrusive, masculine, angry, tumultuous, rageful, forceful, etc.

Butterfly: searching, freedom, beauty, transformation, renewal, exploring flighty, etc.

Cat: gentle, independent, warm, agile, lazy, moody, calculating, curious, aloof, etc.

Cheetah: swift, fast, escape, agile, loner, etc.

Cow: nurturance, food, docile, gentle, conforming, non-assertive, mother, etc.

Dolphin: friendly, social, helpful, likeable, rescuer, etc.

Deer: swift, feminine, graceful, surefooted, withdrawal, vulnerable, flight, gentle, etc.

Dinosaurs: past, history, death, power, extinction, fear, conflict, survival, environmental, etc.

Dog: protection, aggression, friend, pet, nurturance, companion, loyalty, etc.

Dragon: powerful, unknown, fear, misunderstood, unexpected, wise, mysterious, fight, anger, rage, fantasy, etc.

Eagle: freedom, respect, escape, hunter, distant, admired, surveillance, independent, autonomous, etc.

Elephant: slow, powerful, gentle, constricted, stable, awkward, etc.

Fish: vulnerable, primitive, regressive, swift, slippery, escape, etc.

Fox: manipulative, cunning, observant, alert, business, task-oriented, sneaky, distrustful, etc.

Goat: stability, distant, aloof, surefooted, well-grounded, etc.

Gorilla: power, strength, father, masculine, fearful, mobile, primitive, human, instinct, etc.

Giraffe: avoidance, naive, perspective, aspirations, hypervigilant, non-aggressive, etc.

Guinea Pig: defenseless, cute, dependent, docile, trusting, vulnerable, victim, etc.

Horse: power, speed, flight, beauty, stable, escape, endurance, contact, support, internal, respect, etc.

Kangaroo: security, mother, nurturing, protection, mobility, birth/baby, pregnancy, bonding, attachment, close, etc.

Kitten: vulnerable, playful, naive, soft, innocent, etc.

Koala: loveable, cuddling, huggable, non-aggressive, clinging, etc.

Lamb: vulnerability, nurturing, protection, innocent, baby, rescue, etc.

Lion: power, dangerous, control, speed, majestic, regal, proud, stalk, predator, wanderer, father, authority, nobility, prowler, intimidation, aggressor, etc.

Mouse: quiet, fearful, meek, afraid, hiding, frantic, observant, vigilant, secretive, anxious, etc.

Monkey: playful, anxious, social, territorial, happy, silly, fearful, mobile, clinging, child-like, aggressive, etc.

Owl: wise, knowing, alert, nocturnal, observant, witness, quiet, internal, aloof, uninvolved, distant, etc.

Parrot: identity, expectations, conformity, imitation, reflection, routine, structure, validation, etc.

Pig: earthy, dirty, hungry, rejection, scavenger, docile, lazy, undesirable, etc.

Rabbit: vulnerability, nurturing, protection, alert, quick, curious, surveillance, etc.

Rat: dirty, untrustworthy, calculating, adaptable, survival, undesirable, etc.

Rhinoceros: defensive, tough, protected, belligerent, reclusive, unknown, powerful, loner, etc.

Shark: aggression, fear, perpetrator, powerful, cunning, unpredictable, persistent, perseverance, etc.

Sheep: friendly, member, warm, belonging, insulated, docile, follower, etc.

Snake: sneaky, phallic, cunning, evil, dangerous, lonely, mysterious, unattached, aloof, etc.

Squirrel: nervous, quick, hypervigilant, hoarding, security, etc.

Swan: elegant, beauty, admiration, grace, respect, etc.

Tiger: swift, fighting, power, alone, stalk, dangerous, control, speed, predator, wanderer, prowler, self-sufficient, etc.

Turtle: shy, quiet, defended, passive, slow, persistent, patient, etc.

Unicorn: magical, fantasy, wishes, unknown, beauty, alone, etc.

Wolf: aggressor, perpetrator, distrustful, selfish, hungry, cunning, loner, etc.

Zebra: contrast, clear, unique, black/white, decisive, limited power, etc.

NOTES:
1. Symbolic meaning of animals will basically be the same whether used as a puppet, plastic figure, acting, drawing, or talking.
2. Also note the setting of the play — forest, air, swamp, jungle, desert, home, city, farm, underwater, outer space, day/night, etc.
3. Animals and the meanings of animals can and will change during the course of therapy.
4. Selection of animals can be helpful in metaphorical use.

APPENDIX E

Assessment Tools and Rating Scales of Child Psychopathology

The ADD-H: Comprehensive Teacher's Rating Scale (ACTeRS) (Ullmann, Sleator, & Sprague, 1984).

The Attention Deficit Disorders Evaluation Scale (ADDES) (McCarney, 1989).

The Bellevue Index of Depression (BID) (Petti, 1978).

The Burks' Behavior Rating Scale (Burks, 1977).

The California Preschool Social Competence Scale (Levine, Olzey, & Lewis, 1969).

The Child Behavior Checklist (CBCL) and the Revised Child Behavior Profile (Achenbach & Edelbrock, 1983).

The Childhood Autism Rating Scale (CARS) (Schopler, Reichler, & Renner, 1986).

The Children's Apperception Test (CAT) (Bellak & Bellak, 1976).

The Children's Assessment Schedule (CAS) (Hodges, Kline, Stern, Cytryn, & McKnew, 1982).

The Children's Depression Inventory (CDI) (Kovacs, 1981).

The Children's Depression Rating Scale-Revised (CDRS-R) (Poznanski, Grossman, Buchsbaum, Banegas, Freeman, & Gibbons, 1984).

The Children's Eating Attitude Test (ChEAT) (Maloney, McGuire, & Daniels, 1988).

The Children's Eating Behavior Inventory (CEBI) (Archer, Rosenbaum, & Streiner, 1991).

The Connors' Parent Rating Scale-Revised (Goyette, Conners, & Ulrich, 1978).

The Connors' Teacher Rating Scale-Revised (Goyette, et al., 1978).

The Depressive Self-Rating Scale (DSRS) (Birleson, 1981).

The Eyberg Child Behavior Inventory (ECBI) (Robinson, Eyberg, & Ross, 1980).

The Gordon Diagnostic System (GDS) (Gordon, 1983).

The Hand Test (Wagner, 1983).

The Hopelessness Scale for Children (Kazdin, Rodgers, & Colbus, 1986).

The House-Tree-Person Technique (H-T-P Technique) (Buck, 1966).

The Kiddie Schedule for Affective Disorders and Schizophrenia (K-SADS) (Puig-Antich, Chambers, & Tambrizi, 1983).

The Leyton Obsessional Inventory-Child Version (LOI-CV) (Berg, Rapoport, & Flament, 1986).

The Louisville Behavior Checklist (LBCL) (Miller, 1984).

The Martin Temperament Assessment Battery (Martin, 1984).

The Parent Symptom Questionnaire (PSQ) (Conners, 1970).

The Personality Inventory for Children-Revised (PIC-R) (Wirt, Lachar, Klinedinst, Seat, & Broen, 1984).

The Piers-Harris Children's Self-Concept Scale (Piers & Harris, 1969).

The Preschool Behavior Questionnaire (Behar & Springfield, 1974).

The Revised Behavior Problem Checklist (Quay & Peterson, 1987).

The Revised Children's Manifest Anxiety Scale (RCMAS) (Reynolds & Richmond, 1985).

The School Behavior Checklist (Miller, 1977).

The Teacher Questionnaire (TQ) (Conners, 1969).

Insert Table E-1

Measure:	ACTeRS	Connors' Parent Rating Scale-R	Connors' Teacher Rating Scale-R	GDS
Ages Assessed:	5-12	3-17	3-17	3-16
Factors Assessed:				
Aggression		X		
Attention Deficits	X	X	X	X
Anxiety		X		
Autism				
Conduct Problems		X	X	
Depression				
Distractibility				
Eating Problems				
Emotional Intensity				
Fears/Phobias				
Hopelessness				
Hyperactivity	X	X	X	
Immaturity				
Impulsivity		X		X
Learning Problems		X		
Obsessive/Compulsive				
Oppositional Behavior	X			
Personality Disturbances				
Psychosis/Psychotic Behavior				
Psychosomatic Problems		X		
School Adjustment		X		
Social Competence				
Social Problems	X			
Informant:				
Parent		X		
Teacher	X		X	
Child				X
Clinician				

Table E-1
Assessment Tools and Rating Scales of Psychopathology:
ACTeRS, Connors' Parent Rating Scale-R, Connors' Teacher Rating Scale-R, GDS

Insert Table E-2

Measure:	CARS	Eyberg Behavior Inventory	Child Behavior Checklist	Louisville Checklist
Ages Assessed:	0-10	2-17	3-16	4-17
Factors Assessed:				
Aggression			X	X
Attention Deficits			X	
Anxiety			X	
Autism	X			
Conduct Problems		X	X	X
Depression			X	
Distractibility				
Eating Problems				
Emotional Intensity				
Fears/Phobias			X	X
Hopelessness				
Hyperactivity			X	X
Immaturity				X
Impulsivity				
Learning Problems				X
Obsessive/Compulsive				X
Oppositional Behavior		X		
Personality Disturbances				
Psychosis/Psychotic Behavior				X
Psychosomatic Problems			X	X
School Adjustment				X
Social Adjustment			X	X
Informant:				
Parent		X	X	X
Teacher			X	
Child			X	
Clinician	X		X	

Table E-2
Assessment Tools and Rating Scales of Child Psychopathology:
CARS, Eyberg Behavior Inventory, Child Behavior Checklist, Louisville Checklist

Insert Table E-3

Measure:	PIC-R	California Preschool Scale	Martin Temperament Battery	Burks' Behavior Scale
Ages Assessed:	3-16	3-5	3-7	3-6
Factors Assessed:				
Aggression	X			X
Attention Deficits				X
Anxiety	X			X
Autism				
Conduct Problems	X			
Depression	X			
Distractibility			X	
Eating Problems				
Emotional Intensity			X	
Fears/Phobias				
Hopelessness				
Hyperactivity	X		X	
Immaturity				
Impulsivity				X
Learning Problems				
Obsessive/Compulsive				
Oppositional Behavior				
Personality Disturbances	X			X
Psychosis/Psychotic Behavior	X			
Psychosomatic Problems	X			
School Adjustment				
Self-Esteem				
Social Adjustment	X	X		X
Informant:				
Parent			X	X
Teacher		X	X	X
Child	X			
Clinician			X	

Table E-3
Assessment Tools and Rating Scales of Child Psychopathology:
PIC-R, California Preschool Scale, Martin Temperament Battery, Burk's Behavior Scale

Insert Table E-4

Measure:	CAT	Preschool Behavior Questionnaire	House-Tree-Person Technique	The Hand Test
Ages Assessed:	3-10	3-6	3 and Older	5 and Older
Factors Assessed:				
Aggression		X		
Attention Deficits		X		
Anxiety				X
Autism				
Conduct Problems				X
Depression				
Distractibility		X		
Eating Problems				
Emotional Intensity				
Fears/Phobias				
Hopelessness				
Hyperactivity		X		
Immaturity				
Impulsivity				X
Learning Problems				
Obsessive/Compulsive				
Oppositional Behavior				
Personality Disturbances	X		X	X
Psychosis/Psychotic Behavior				
Psychosomatic Problems				
School Adjustment				
Self-Esteem				X
Social Adjustment				
Informant:				
Parent				
Teacher		X		
Child	X		X	X
Clinician				

Table E-4
Assessment Tools and Rating Scales of Child Psychopathology:
CAT, Preschool Behavior Questionnaire, House-Tree-Person Technique, The Hand Test

Insert Table E-5

Measure:	CDI	Hopelessness Scale for Children	Piers-Harris Self-Concept Scale	CDRS-R
Ages Assessed:	8-13	7-17	5-12	6-12
Factors Assessed:				
Aggression				
Attention Deficits				
Anxiety			X	
Autism				
Conduct Problems				
Depression	X	X		X
Distractibility				
Eating Problems				
Emotional Intensity				
Fears/Phobias				
Hopelessness		X		
Hyperactivity				
Immaturity				
Impulsivity				
Learning Problems				
Obsessive/Compulsive				
Oppositional Behavior				
Personality Disturbances				
Psychosis/Psychotic Behavior				
Psychosomatic Problems				
School Adjustment				
Self-Esteem			X	
Social Adjustment				
Informant:				
Parent				X
Teacher				X
Child	X	X	X	X
Clinician				X

Table E-5
Assessment Tools and Rating Scales of Child Psychopathology:
CDI, Hopelessness Scale for Children, Piers-Harris Self-Concept Scale, CDRS-R

Insert Table E-6

Measure:	ChEAT	CEBI	Kiddie SADS	RCMAS
Ages Assessed:	8-13	2-12	6-17	6-17
Factors Assessed:				
Aggression				
Attention Deficits				
Anxiety				X
Autism				
Conduct Problems				
Depression			X	
Distractibility				
Eating Problems	X	X		
Emotional Intensity				
Fears/Phobias				
Hopelessness				
Hyperactivity				
Immaturity				
Impulsivity				
Learning Problems				
Obsessive/Compulsive				
Oppositional Behavior				
Personality Disturbances				
Psychosis/Psychotic Behavior			X	
Psychosomatic Problems				
School Adjustment				
Self-Esteem				
Social Adjustment				
Informant:				
Parent		X	X	
Teacher				
Child	X		X	X
Clinician				

Table E-6
Assessment Tools and Rating Scales of Child Psychopathology:
ChEAT, CEBI, Kiddie SADS, RCMAS

Insert Table E-7

Measure:	LOI-CV	Children's Assessment Schedule	Parent Symptom Questionnaire	DSRS
Ages Assessed:	8-18	7-16	3-17	7-13
Factors Assessed:				
Aggression				
Attention Deficits			X	
Anxiety			X	
Autism				
Conduct Problems			X	
Depression				X
Distractibility				
Eating Problems				
Emotional Intensity				
Fears/Phobias		X		
Hopelessness				
Hyperactivity			X	
Immaturity				
Impulsivity			X	
Learning Problems			X	
Obsessive/Compulsive	X			
Oppositional Behavior				
Personality Disturbances				
Psychosis/Psychotic Behavior		X		
Psychosomatic Problems		X	X	
School Adjustment				
Self-Esteem		X		
Social Adjustment				
Informant:				
Parent			X	
Teacher				
Child	X	X		X
Clinician		X		

Table E-7
Assessment Tools and Rating Scales of Child Psychopathology:
LOI-CV, Children's Assessment Schedule, Parent Symptom Questionnaire, DSRS

Insert Table E-8

Measure:	BID	School Behavior Checklist	Revised Behavior Problem Checklist	TQ
Ages Assessed:	6-12	3-13	5-16	3-17
Factors Assessed:				
Aggression		X	X	
Attention Deficits			X	X
Anxiety			X	X
Autism				
Conduct Problems			X	X
Depression	X			
Distractibility				
Eating Problems				
Emotional Intensity				
Fears/Phobias				
Hopelessness				
Hyperactivity			X	X
Immaturity				
Impulsivity				
Learning Problems				
Obsessive/Compulsive				
Oppositional Behavior		X		
Personality Disturbances				
Psychosis/Psychotic Behavior			X	
Psychosomatic Problems				
School Adjustment		X		
Self-Esteem				
Social Adjustment		X		
Informant:				
Parent			X	
Teacher		X	X	X
Child	X			
Clinician			X	

Table E-8
Assessment Tools and Rating Scales of Child Psychopathology:
BID, School Behavior Checklist, Revised Behavior Problem Checklist, TQ

Those interested in purchasing these instruments may contact the following:*

        American Guidance Service
        4201 Woodland Road
        Post Office Box 99
        Circle Pines, MN 55014-1796
        1-800-328-2560

        Multi-Health Systems, Inc.
        908 Niagra Falls Boulevard
        North Tonawand, NY 14120-2060
        1-800-456-3003

        Pro-Ed
        8700 Shoal Creek Boulevard
        Austin, TX 78757-6897
        1-512-451-3246
        (FAX)1-800-397-7633

        The Psychological Corporation Order Service Center
        555 Academic Court
        Post Office Box 839954
        San Antonio, TX 78204-2498
        1-800-228-0752

        Psychological Assessment Resources, Inc.
        Post Office Box 998
        Odessa, FL 33556-9901
        1-800-331-8378

* Purchase and use of these instruments may be restricted based on qualification guidelines outlined in the Standards for Educational and Psychological Testing (American Psychological Association, 1985).

Bibliography

Achenbach, T. M., & Edelbrock, C. S. (1983). *Manual for the child behavior checklist and revised behavior profile.* Burlington, VT: Author.

American Psychiatric Association. (1987). *Diagnostic and statistical manual of mental disorders: DSM-III-R* (3rd ed. rev.). Washington, DC: Author.

American Psychiatric Association. (1994). *Diagnostic and statistical manual of mental disorders: DSM-IV* (4th ed.). Washington, DC: Author.

American Psychological Association, American Educational Research Association, & National Council on Measurement in Education. (1985) *Standards for educational and psychological testing.* Washington, DC: American Psychological Association.

Archer, L. A., Rosenbaum, P. L., & Streiner, D. L. (1991). The children's eating behavior inventory: Reliability and validity results. *Journal of Pediatric Psychology,* 16(5), 629-642.

Axline, V. M. (1947b). *Play therapy.* Cambridge, MA: Houghton Mifflin.

Axline, V. M. (1950). Entering the child's world via play experiences. *Progressive Education,* 27, 68-75.

Axline, V. M. (1964). *Dibs in search of self: Personality in play therapy.* Boston: Houghton Mifflin.

Axline, V. M. (1969). *Play therapy (revised edition).* New York: Ballantine Books.

Bandler, R., & Grinder, J. (1975). *The patterns of the hypnotic techniques of Milton H. Erickson* (Vol 1). Palo Alto, CA: Behavior & Science Books.

Bandler, R., & Grinder, J. (1979). *Frogs into princes.* Moab, UT: Real People Press.

Bandler, R., & Grinder, J. (1982). *Reframing: Neuro-linguistic programming and the transformation of meaning.* Moab, UT: Real People Press.

Barlow, K., Strother, J., & Landreth, G. (1985). Child- centered play therapy: Nancy from baldness to curls. *The School Counselor,* 33, 347-356.

Behar, L., & Springfield, S. (1974). A behavior rating scale for the preschool child. *Developmental Psychology,* 10, 601-610.

Bellak, L., & Bellak, S. S. (1976). *Children's apperception test.* Larchmont, NY: C.P.S.

Bemporad, J. R., Smith, H. F., Hanson, G., & Cicchetti, D. (1982). Borderline syndromes in childhood: Criteria for diagnosis. *American Journal of Psychiatry,* 139(5), 596-602.

Berg, C. J., Rapoport, J. L., & Flament, M. (1986). The Leyton obsessional inventory — child version. *Journal of the American Academy of Child Psychiatry,* 25(1), 84-91.

Bergantino, L. (1981). *Psychotherapy, insight and style: The existential moment.* Boston: Allyn & Bacon, Inc.

Birleson, P. (1981). The validity of depressive disorder in childhood and the development of a self-rating scale: A research report. *Journal of Child Psychology and Psychiatry,* 22, 73-88.

Bolig, R., Fernie, D. E., & Klein, E. L. (1986). Unstructured play in hospital settings. *Children's Health Care: Journal of the Association for the Care of Children's Health,* 15(2), 101-107.

Bow, J. N. (1988). Treating resistant children. *Child and Adolescent Social Work,* 5(1), 3-15.

Bow, J. N. (1993). Overcoming resistance. In C. E. Schaefer (Ed.), *The therapeutic powers of play* (pp. 17-40). Northvale, NJ: Jason Aronson, Inc.

Brett, D. (1988). *Annie stories.* New York: Workman Publishing Co.

Bromfield, R. (1989). Psychodynamic play therapy with a high functioning autistic child. *Psychoanalytic Psychology,* 6(4), 439-453.

Bromfield, R. (1992). *Playing for real: The world of a child therapist.* New York: Penguin Books.

Buck, J. N. (1966). *House-tree-person (H-T-P technique) revised manual.* Los Angeles: Western Psychological Services.

Budd, L. (1990). *Living with the active alert child.* New York: Prentice Hall.

Burks, H. F. (1977). *Burks' preschool and kindergarten behavior rating scales.* Los Angeles: Western Psychological Services.

Burris, A. M. (1994). Somatization as a response to trauma. In A. Sugarman (Ed.), *Victims of abuse: The emotional impact of child and adult trauma* (pp. 131-137). Madison, CT.

Butler, A. (1978). *Play as development.* Columbus, OH: Merrill.

Carkhuff, R. R. (1969). *Helping and human relations: A primer for lay and professional helpers.* New York: Holt, Rinehart, & Winston.

Cattanach, A. (1992). *Play therapy with abused children.* London: Jessica Kingsley Publishers Ltd.

Ceci, S. J., & Bruck, M. (1993). Suggestibility of the child witness: A historical review and synthesis. *Psychological Bulletin,* 113(3), 403-439.

Conners, C. K. (1969). A teacher rating scale for use in drug studies with children. *American Journal of Psychiatry,* 126, 152-156, 884-888.

Conners, C. K. (1970). Symptom patterns in hyperkinetic, neurotic, and normal children. *Child Development,* 41, 667-682.

Cormier, W. H., & Cormier, L. S. (1991). *Interviewing strategies for helpers: Fundamental skills and cognitive behavioral interventions (3rd ed.).* Pacific Grove, CA: Brooks/Cole Publishing Company.

Courtois, C. (1988). *Healing the incest wound.* New York: Norton Publishers.

Covington, S. (1988). *Leaving the enchanted forest: The path from relationship addiction to intimacy.* San Francisco: Harper and Row.

Crowley, R. J., & Mills, J. C. (1985-86). The nature and construction of therapeutic metaphors for children. *British Journal of Experimental and Clinical Hypnosis,* 3(2), 69-76.

Danielson, A. (1986). *Att bygga sin varld: Handbok Ericametoden.* Stockholm, Sweden: Psykologiforlaget.

Delaney, R. (1991). *Fostering changes: Treating attachment disordered foster children.* Fort Collins, CO: Corbett Publishing.

Delpo, E. G., & Frick, S. B. (1988). Directed and non-directed play as therapeutic modalities. Children's health care: *Journal of the association for the care of children's health,* 16(4), 261-267.

Despert, J. L. (1946). Psychosomatic study of 50 stuttering children. Roundtable: Social, physical, and psychiatric findings. *American Journal of Orthopsychiatry, 16,* 100-113.

Dilts, R., Grinder, J., Bandler, R., DeLozier, J., & Cameron-Bandler, L. (1979). *Neuro-linguistic programming (Vol 1).* Cupertino, CA: Meta Publications.

Donovan, D. M., & McIntyre, D. (1990). Child psychotherapy. In J. G. Simeon & H. B. Ferguson (Eds.), *Treatment strategies in child and adolescent psychiatry* (pp. 177-197). New York: Plenum Press.

Dulcan, M., & Popper, C. (1991). *Child and adolescent psychiatry.* Washington, DC: American Psychiatric Press.

Einbender, A. (1991). Treatment in the absence of maternal support. In W. N. Friedrich (Ed.), *Casebook of sexual abuse treatment* (pp. 112-136). New York: W. W. Norton & Co.

Erickson, M., & Rossi, E. (1979). *Hypnotherapy: An exploratory case book.* New York: Irvington.

Esman, A. H. (1983). Psychoanalytic play therapy. In C. E. Schaefer & K. J. O'Connor (Eds.), *Handbook of play therapy* (pp. 11-20). New York: John Wiley and Sons.

Fagan, J., & McMahon, P. P. (1984). Incipient multiple personality in children: Four cases. *The Journal of Nervous and Mental Disease, 172*(1), 26-36.

Fossen, A., Knibbs, J., Bryant-Waugh, R., & Lask, B. (1987). Early onset anorexia nervosa. *Archives of Disease in Childhood, 62,* 114-118.

Garmezy, N. (1986). Developmental aspects of children's responses to the stress of separation and loss. In M. Rutter, C. Izard, & P. Read (Eds.), *Depression in young people* (pp. 297-324). New York: Guilford.

Garvey, C. (1977). *Play.* Cambridge, MA: Harvard University Press.

Gazda, G. M. (1975). *Human relations development: A manual for health sciences.* Boston, MA: Allyn & Bacon.

Gelinas, D. (1983). The persisting negative effects of abuse. *Psychiatry, 46,* 313-332.

Gil, E. (1991). *The healing power of play: Working with abused children.* New York: Guilford Press.

Gil, E. (1993a). Individual therapy. In E. Gil & T. C. Johnson (Eds.), *Sexualized children: Assessment and treatment of sexualized children and children who molest* (pp. 179-210). Rockville, MD: Launch Press.

Gil, E. (1993b). Sexualized children. In E. Gil & T. C. Johnson (Eds.), *Sexualized children: Assessment and treatment of sexualized children and children who molest* (pp. 91-100). Rockville, MD: Launch Press.

Ginott, H. G. (1960). A rationale for selecting toys in play therapy. *Journal of Consulting Psychology*, 24(3), 243-246.

Gordon, D. (1978). *Therapeutic metaphors.* Cupertino, CA: META Communications.

Gordon, M. (1983). *The Gordon diagnostic system.* DeWitt, NY: Gordon Systems Inc.

Goyette, C. H., Conners, C. K., & Ulrich, R. F. (1978). Normative data on revised Conners' parent and teacher rating scales. *Journal of Abnormal Child Psychology*, 6, 221-236.

Guerney, L. F. (1983). Client-centered (nondirective) play therapy. In C. E. Schaefer & K. J. O'Connor (Eds.), *Handbook of play therapy* (pp. 21-64). New York: John Wiley and Sons.

Gunsberg, A. (1989). Empowering young abused and neglected children through contingency play. *Childhood Education*, 66(1), 8-10.

Hahn, D. (Producer), Allers , R., & Minkoff, R. (Directors). (1994). *The Lion King* [Film]. (Available from Walt Disney Home Video)

Haley, J. (1973). *Uncommon therapy: The psychiatric techniques of Milton H. Erickson.* New York: W. W. Norton.

Harris, J. R., & Liebert, R. M. (1984). *The child.* Englewood Cliff, NJ: Prentice-Hall, Inc.

Health Care Financing Administration (HCFA), U. S. Department of Health and Human Services. (1984). Final rule. *Federal Register*, 49(1), 234-334.

Higgs, J. F., Goodyer, I. M., & Birch, J. (1989). Anorexia nervosa and food avoidance emotional disorder. *Archives of Disease in Childhood*, 64, 346-351.

Hodges, K., Kline, J., Stern, L., Cytryn, L. & McKnew, D. (1982). The development of a child assessment interview for research and clinical use. *Journal of Abnormal Child Psychology*, 10, 173-189.

Hoopes, M. M., & Harper, J. M. (1987). *Birth order roles and sibling patterns in individual and family therapy*. Rockville, MD: Aspen Publishers, Inc.

Irwin, E. C. (1983). The diagnostic and therapeutic use of pretend play. In C. E. Schaefer & K. J. O'Connor (Eds.), *Handbook of play therapy* (pp. 148-173). New York: John Wiley and Sons.

Joseph, R. (1992). *The right brain and the unconscious: Discovering the stranger within*. New York: Plenum Press.

Kazdin, A. E., Rodgers, A., & Colbus, D. (1986). The hopelessness scale for children: Psychometric characteristics and concurrent validity. *Journal of Consulting and Clinical Psychology, 54*, 241-245.

Keith, D. V., & Whitaker, C. A. (1981). Play therapy: A paradigm for work with families. *Journal of Marital and Family Therapy, 7*, 243-254.

Kempe, R., & Kempe, H. (1984). *The common secret: Sexual abuse of children and adolescents*. New York: W. H. Freeman.

Kernberg, P. (1989). Narcissistic personality disorder in children. *Psychiatric Clinics of North America, 12*(3), 671-694.

Kluft, R. (1985). The natural history of multiple personality disorder. In R. F. Kluft (Ed.), *Childhood antecedents of multiple personality* (pp. 197-238). Washington, DC: American Psychiatric Press.

Kovacs, M. (1981). Rating scales to assess depression in school-aged children. *Acta Paedopsychiatria, 46*, 305-315.

Landreth, G. L. (1987). Play therapy: Facilitative use of child's play in elementary school counseling. *Elementary School Guidance and Counseling, 21*, 253-261.

Landreth, G. L. (1990). *Keynote address*. Association for Play Therapy International Conference, Vancouver, British Columbia.

Landreth, G. L. (1991). *Play therapy: The art of the relationship*. Muncie, IN: Accelerated Development.

Landreth, G. L. (1993a). Child-centered play therapy. *Elementary School Guidance and Counseling, 28*(1), 17-29.

Landreth, G. L. (1993b). Self-expressive communication. In C. E. Schaefer (Ed.), *The therapeutic powers of play*. Northvale, NJ: Jason Aronson, Inc.

Lankton, C. H., & Lankton, S. R. (1986). *Enchantment and intervention in family therapy: Training in Ericksonian approaches*. New York: Brunner/Mazel.

Lankton, C. H., & Lankton, S. R. (1989). *Tales of enchantment: Goal-oriented metaphors for adults and children*. New York: Brunner/Mazel, Inc.

Lask, B., Britten, C., Kroll, L., Magagna, J., & Tranter, M. (1991). Children with pervasive refusal. *Archives of Disease in Childhood*, 66, 866-869.

Lask, B., & Bryant-Waugh, R. (1992). Early onset anorexia nervosa and related eating disorders. *Journal of Child Psychology and Psychiatry*, 33(1), 281-300.

Leland, H. (1983). Play therapy for mentally retarded and developmentally disabled children. In C. Schaefer & K. O'Conner (eds.) *Handbook of play therapy* (pp. 436-455). New York: John Wiley & Sons.

Levine, F., Olzey, F. F., & Lewis, M. (1969). *The California Preschool Social Competence Scale — Manual*. Palo Alto, CA: Consulting Psychologist Press.

Levinson, B. M. (1962). The dog as a "co-therapist". *Mental Hygiene*, 46, 59-65.

Levinson, B. M. (1964). Pets: A special technique in child psychotherapy. *Mental Hygiene*, 48, 243-248.

Levinson, B. M. (1965). Pet psychotherapy: Use of household pets in the treatment of behavior disorder in childhood. *Psychological Reports*, 17, 695-698.

Lewis, J. M. (1993). Childhood play in normality, pathology, and therapy. *American Journal of Orthopsychiatry*, 63(1), 6-15.

Lewis, M. (1974). Interpretation in child analysis: Developmental considerations. *Journal of the American Academy of Child Psychiatry*, 13, 32-53.

Livingston, R. (1987). Sexually and physically abused children. *Journal of the American Academy of Child and Adolescent Psychiatry*, 26(3), 413-415

Lofgren, D. P., Bemporad, J., King, J., Lindem, K., & O'Driscoll, G. O. (1991). A prospective follow-up study of so-called borderline children. *American Journal of Psychiatry*, 148(11), 1541-1547.

Looff, D. (1987). *Getting to know the troubled child.* Malabar, FL: Robert Krieger Publishers.

Lord, J. (1985). *A guide to individual psychotherapy with school-aged children and adolescents.* Springfield, IL: Charles C. Thomas.

Lowenfeld, M. (1939). The world pictures of children. *British Journal of Medical Psychology,* 18, 65-101.

Lowenfeld, M. (1979). The world technique. London: Allen & Unwin.

Lowery, E. F. (1985). Autistic aloofness reconsidered. *Bulletin of the Menninger Clinic,* 49(2), 135-150.

Maloney, M. J., McGuire, J., & Daniels, S. R. (1988). Reliability testing of a children's version of the eating attitudes test. *Journal of the American Academy of Child and Adolescent Psychiatry,* 27, 541-543.

Maloney, M. J., McGuire, J., Daniels, S. R., & Specker, B. (1989). Dieting behavior and eating attitudes in children. *Pediatrics,* 84(3), 482-487.

Martin, R. P. (1984). *The temperament assessment battery —interim manual.* Athens, GA: Developmental Metrics.

McCarney, S. B. (1989). *Attention deficit disorders evaluation scale (ADDES).* Columbia, MO: Hawthorne Education Services.

Miller, L. C. (1977). *School behavior checklist.* Los Angeles: Western Psychological Services.

Miller, L. C. (1984). *Louisville behavior checklist manual.* Los Angeles: Western Psychological Services.

Miller, C., & Boe, J. (1990). Tears into diamonds: Transformation of child psychic trauma through sandplay and storytelling. *Arts in Psychotherapy,* 17, 247-257.

Mills, J. C. (1993). *Gentle willow: A story for children about dying.* New York: Magination Press.

Mills, J. C., & Crowley, R. J. (1986). *Therapeutic metaphors for children and the child within.* New York: Brunner/Mazel, Inc.

Mills, J. C., & Crowley, R. J. (1988). *Sammy the elephant and Mr. Camel: A story to help children overcome enuresis while discovering self-appreciation.* New York: Magination Press.

Moustakas, C. E. (1953). *Children in play therapy.* New York: McGraw-Hill Book Co. Inc.

Moustakas, C. E. (1955). Emotional adjustment and the play therapy process. Journal of Genetic Psychology, 86, 79-99.

Moustakas, C. E. (1959). *Psychotherapy with children: The living relationship*. New York: Harper and Row.

Moustakas, C. E. (1973). *The child's discovery of himself.* New York: Jason Aronson, Inc.

Moustakas, C. E. (1992). *Psychotherapy with children: The living relationship*. Greeley, CO: Carron Publishers. (Original work published 1959.)

Murray, J. B. (1991). Psychophysiological aspects of nightmares, night terrors, and sleepwalking. *The Journal of General Psychology*, 118(2), 113-127.

Nemiroff, M. A. (1990). *A child's first book about play therapy.* Washington, DC: American Psychological Association.

Nickerson, E. T., & O'Laughlin, K. B. (1980). It's fun — but will it work? The use of games as a therapeutic medium for children and adolescents. *Journal of Clinical Child Psychology*, 9(1), 78-81.

Oaklander, V. (1978). *Windows to our children: A Gestalt therapy approach to children and adolescents.* Moab, UT: Real People Press.

O'Connor, K. J. (1991). *The play therapy primer: An integration of theories and techniques.* New York: John Wiley & Sons, Inc.

Perry L., & Landreth, G. (1990). Diagnostic assessment of children's play therapy behavior. In C. E. Schaefer, K. Gitlin, & A. Sandgrund (Eds.), *Play diagnosis and assessment* (pp. 643-662). New York: John Wiley and Sons Inc.

Petti, T. A. (1978). Depression in hospitalized child psychiatry patients: Approaches to measuring depression. *Journal of the American Academy of Child Psychiatry*, 17, 49-59.

Petti, T. A. & Vela, R. M. (1990). Borderline disorders of childhood: An overview. *Journal of the American Academy of Child and Adolescent Psychiatry*, 29(3), 327-337.

Pfeffer, C. R. (1979). Clinical observations of play of hospitalized suicidal children. *Suicide and Life-Threatening Behavior*, 9(4), 235-244.

Piaget, J. (1952). *The origin of intelligence in children.* New York: International Universities Press. (Original work published 1936)

Piaget, J. (1954). *The construction of reality in the child.* New York: Basic Books. (Original work published 1937)

Piaget, J. (1962). *Play, dreams, and imitation in childhood.* New York: Norton Publishers.

Piers, E., & Harris, D. (1969). *The Piers-Harris children's self-concept scale.* Nashville, TN: Counselor Recordings and Tests.

Plaut, E. A. (1979). Play and adaptation. *The Psychoanalytic Study of the Child,* 34, 217-232.

Poznanski, E. O., Grossman, J. A., Buchsbaum, Y., Banegas, M., Freeman, L., & Gibbons, R. (1984). Preliminary studies of the reliability and validity of the Children's Depression Rating Scale. *Journal of the American Academy of Child Psychology,* 23(2), 191-197.

Puig-Antich, J., Chambers, W. J., & Tambrizi, M. A. (1983). The clinical assessment of current depressive episodes in children and adolescents: Interviews with parents and children. In D. P. Cantwell & G. A. Carlson (Eds.) *Affective disorders in childhood and adolescents: An update* (pp. 157-179). New York: SP Medical and Scientific Books.

Putnam, F. W. (1991). Dissociative disorders in children and adolescents: A developmental perspective. *Psychiatric Clinics of North American,* 14(3), 519-531.

Quay, H. C., & Peterson, D. R. (1987). *Revised behavior problem checklist.* Coral Gables, FL: University of Miami.

Rapoport, J. L., & Ismond, D. R. (1990). *DSM III-R guide for diagnosis of childhood disorders.* New York, NY: Brunner/Mazel.

Reynolds, C. R., & Richmond, B. O. (1985). *The revised children's manifest anxiety scale.* Los Angeles: Western Psychological Services.

Robinson, E. A., Eyberg, S. M., & Ross, A. W. (1980). The standardization of an inventory of child conduct behavior problems. *Journal of Clinical Child Psychology,* 9, 22-28.

Rorschach, H. (1942). *Psychodiagnostic* (5th ed.). Bern, Germany: Hans Huber. (Original work published 1921)

Ross (1989). *Multiple personality disorder: diagnosis, clinical features, and treatment.* New York: John Wiley and Sons.

Schopler, E., Reichler, R. J., & Renner, B. R. (1986). *The childhood autism rating scale — CARS.* New York: Irvington Publications.

Shapiro, S. (1992). Trauma, ego defenses, and behavioral reenactment. In S. Shapiro & G. M. Dominiak (Eds.). *Sexual trauma and psychopathology: Clinical intervention with adult survivors.* New York: Lexington Books.

Sheldon, S., Spire, J. P., & Levey, H. B. (1992). *Pediatric sleep medicine*. Philadelphia: W. B. Aunders Company.

Sjolund, M. (1981). Play diagnosis and therapy in Sweden: The Erica method. *Journal of Clinical Psychology*, 37(2), 322-325.

Sjolund, M. (1983). A "new" Swedish technique for play diagnosis and therapy: The Erica method. *Association for Play Therapy Newsletter*, 2(1), 3-5.

Sjolund, M. (1993). *The Erica method: A technique for play therapy and diagnosis: A training guide*. Greeley, CO: Carron Publishers.

Sperry, R. W. (1968). Hemispheric deconnection and unity in conscious awareness. *American Psychologist*, 23, 723-733.

Sweeney, D. S., & Landreth, G. (1993). Healing a child's spirit through play therapy: A scriptural approach to treating children. *Journal of Psychology and Christianity*, 12(4), 351-356.

Terr, L. (1990). *Too scared to cry.* New York: Basic Books.

Thompson, C. L., & Rudolph, L. B. (1983). *Counseling children*. Monterey, CA: Brooks/Cole.

Treasure, J., & Thompson, P. (1988). Anorexia nervosa in childhood. *British Journal of Hospital Medicine*, 40, 362-369.

Ullman, R. K., Sleator, E. K., & Sprague, R. L. (1984). A new rating scale for diagnosis and monitoring of ADD children. *Psychopharmacological Bulletin*, 20(1), 160-164.

Wagner, E. E. (1983). *The hand test.* Los Angeles: Western Psychological Services.

Wallas, L. (1985). *Stories for the third ear.* New York: W. W. Norton & Co.

Wallas, L. (1991). *Stories that heal: Reparenting adult children of dysfunctional families using hypnotic stories in psychotherapy.* New York: W. W. Norton & Co.

Weiner, I. B. (1982). *Child and adolescent psychopathology.* New York: John Wiley and Sons Inc.

Wenning, K. (1990). Borderline children: A closer look at diagnosis and treatment. *American Journal of Orthopsychiatry*, 60(2), 225-232.

Whitaker, C. A., & Bumberry, W. M. (1988). *Dancing with the family: A symbolic-experiential approach.* New York: Brunner/Mazel, Inc.

Wirt, R. D., Lachar, D., Klinedinst, J. E., Seat, P. D., & Broen, W. E., Jr. (1984). *Personality inventory for children — Revised.* Los Angeles: Western Psychological Services.

Index

Authors

224

Murray, J. B., 33
Nemiroff, M. A., 111
Nickerson, E. T., 10, 194
O'Connor, K. J., 128, 223, 274
O'Driscoll, G.O., 44
O'Laughlin, K. B., 10, 194
Oaklander, V., 28
Olzey, F. F., 307
Perry, L., 4
Peterson, D. R., 308
Petti, T. A., 44, 307
Pfeffer, C. R., 151
Piaget, J., 3
Piers, E., 308
Plaut, E. A., 4
Popper, C., 41, 42, 148
Poznanski, E. O., 307
Puig-Antich, J., 308
Putnam, F. W., 39, 136, 141
Quay, H. C., 308
Rapoport, J. L., 308
Reichler, R. J., 307
Renner, B. R., 307
Reynolds, C. R., 308
Richmond, B. O., 308
Robinson, E. A., 308
Rodgers, A., 308
Rorschach, H., 48, 118
Rosenbaum, P. L., 307
Ross, A. W., 308
Ross, C. A., 155

Rossi, E., 253
Rudolph, L. B., 230
Schopler, E., 307
Seat, P. D., 308
Shapiro, S., 140
Sheldon, S., 33
Sjolund, M., 117, 118, 119, 120
Sleator, E. K., 307
Smith, H. F., 44
Specker, B., 33
Spire, J. P., 33
Sprague, R. L., 307
Springfield, S., 308
Stearns, G. B., 307
Streiner, D. L., 307
Strother, J., 9
Sweeney, D. S., 235
Tambrizi, M. A., 308
Terr, L., 148
Thompson, C. L., 231
Thompson, P., 33
Tranter, M., 33
Treasure, J., 33
Ullman, R. K., 307
Ulrich R. F., 308
Vela, R. M., 44
Wagner, E. E., 308
Wallas, L., 269
Weiner, I. B., 41
Wenning, K., 44
Whitaker, C. A., 20
Wirt, R. D., 308

Index

Subject